To Simon Taylor

With my best
wishes

Sam Basch.

June 2000

hamlyn history

Boer

the War

David Smurthwaite

Original concept - ET Archive
Publishing Director - Laura Bamford
Executive Editor - Julian Brown
Senior Editor - Trevor Davies
Art Director - Keith Martin
Art Editor - Geoff Fennell
Designer - Birgit Eggers
Picture Research - Anne-Marie Ehrlich
Production Controller -
Clare Smedley and Julian Deeming

First published in
Great Britain in 1999
by Hamlyn, an imprint of
Octopus Publishing Group Limited
2-4 Heron Quays,
London E14 4JP

Copyright © 1999
Octopus Publishing Group Ltd

ISBN 0 600 59652 4

A catalogue record for this book is
available from the British Library

Produced by Toppan
Printed in China

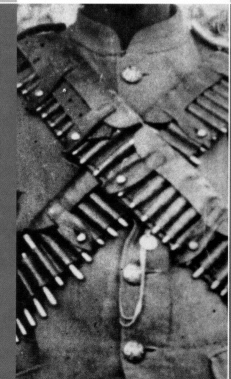

contents

1652	Dutch East India Company found shipping station at Cape
1795	Dutch lose Cape to British
1803	Dutch (Batavian Republic) resume control
1806	Second British occupation begins
1815	Slachter's Nek Rebellion by Afrikaans-speaking settlers. British rule at Cape confirmed
1820	4,000 British settlers arrive at Cape
1834	Slavery abolished at Cape, following decision of British Parliament
1835–7	The Great Trek. Frontier farmers (Boers) pour across Orange River, but majority of the Afrikaans-speaking settlers (Afrikaners) remain in the Cape
1838	(16 Dec) Pretorius beats Dingaan, Zulu king, at Battle of Blood River
1838–43	Boers concentrate in Natal
1843	British annex Natal as colony
1848	Transorangia annexed as Orange River Sovereignty. Smith defeats Pretorius at Battle of Boomplaatz
1852	Sand River Convention confirms independence of Transorangia as Orange Free State
1868–9	British annex Basutoland as Crown Colony at request of King Mosweshwe
1870–1	Diamond rush to Kimberley
1871	Annexation of Kimberley to Cape Colony, now self-governing. Cecil Rhodes, aged 18, joins diamond rush, followed by Alfred Beit (in 1875)
1877	Proclamation of Transvaal as British Crown Colony. Arrival of Frere
1879	British forces invade and (1887) annex Zululand, soon incorporated in Natal, now self-governing
1880–1	Kruger leads Transvaal rebellion against British rule: First Boer War (alias 'First War of Independence')
1881	Peace talks after Battle of Majuba (27 Feb). Pretoria Convention: Transvaal Republic obtains limited independence
1884	London Convention: Transvaal (South African Republic) obtains greater independence
1886	Gold rush to Witwatersrand begins
1888	Cecil Rhodes obtains British Royal Charter for his British South Africa Co. to exploit Lobengula's territory (Mashonaland and Matabeleland)
1889	Formation of Wernher, Beit & Co, soon to become the principal Rand mining-house
1890	Rhodes's BSA Co. (Chartere Company) sends pioneers to occupy Lobengula's country, renamed Rhodesia
1895	(29 Dec) Dr Jameson launches Raid into Transvaal with 500 Chartere Company police from Pitsani and Mafeking
1896	Battle of Doornkop. Jameson surrenders. Arrest and trial of Johannesburg Reform Committee. Rhodes resigns as Prime Minister of the Cape. Cape Enquiry into Raid
1897	London Enquiry into Raid. Sir Alfred Milner takes over as British High Commissioner at the Cape
1898	Kruger elected for fourth term as President of Transvaal
1898-9	Milner back in London for 'holiday'

1899

31 May–5 June	Bloemfontein Conference
8 Sep	British Cabinet decides to send 10,000 men to defend Natal
26 Sep	Penn Symons pushes up troops to Dundee
27 Sep	Kruger calls up Transvaal burghers, and persuades Steyn to follow suit in Free State
7 Oct	British mobilise 1st Army Corps etc. White lands at Durban
9 Oct	Kruger sends ultimatum
11 Oct	Expiry of ultimatum and outbreak of war
14–16 Oct	Boers begin siege of Kekewich at Kimberley and of Baden-Powell at Mafeking
20 Oct	Penn Symons gives battle at Talana. Möller surrenders
21 Oct	Battle of Elandslaagte
24 Oct	Battle of Rietfontein
30 Oct	'Mournful Monday': Joubert outmanoeuvres White at Battle of Ladysmith (Modderspruit) and Carleton is forced to surrender at Nicholson's Nek
31 Oct	Buller lands at Cape Town
2 Nov	White's 'field force' accepts siege at Ladysmith
15 Nov	Botha wrecks armoured train between Frere and Chieveley
22–3 Nov	Battle of Willow Grange
23 Nov	End of Botha's and Joubert's raid southwards into Natal. Methuen's first battle: Graspan
25 Nov	Methuen's second battle: Graspan
26 Nov	Holdsworth, with Linchwe's Africans, attacks Boer laager at Derdepoort
28 Nov	Methuen's third battle: Modder River
7 Dec	Hunter's night raid on Long Tom besieging Ladysmith
10 Dec	Gatacre's mishap at Stormberg
11 Dec	Methuen's repulse at Magersfontein
15 Dec	Buller's first reverse: Colenso
18 Dec	Robert appointed to succeed Buller as C-in-C in South Africa, with Kitchener as Chief of Staff
26 Dec	Baden-Powell's abortive attack on Game Tree Fort
29 Dec	German mail-steamer Bundesrath seized by Royal Navy

timeline

1900

6 Jan	Boers attack Caesar's Camp and Wagon Hill (Platrand) at Ladysmith
10 Jan	Roberts and Kitchener land at Cape Town
24 Jan	Battle of Spion Kop
5–7 Feb	Vaal Krantz captured, then evacuated
11 Feb	Roberts begins great flank march
14–27 Feb	Buller's fourth attempt to relieve Ladysmith
15 Feb	French relieves Kimberley
18 Feb	Battle of Paardeberg
27 Feb	Surrender of Cronje at Paardeberg
28 Feb	Buller relieves Ladysmith
7 Mar	Battle of Poplar Grove. Kruger escapes
10 Mar	Battle of Driefontein
13 Mar	Capture of Bloemfontein
15 Mar	Roberts' first proclamation: amnesty except for leaders
17 Mar	Boer Council of War at Kroonstad
27 Mar	Death of Joubert
31 Mar	De Wet ambushes Broadwood at Sannah's Post/British capture Johannesburg
24 May	British annex Orange Free State
5 Jun	Roberts captures Pretoria. Release of prisoners
7 Jun	Christiaan De Wet's success at Roodewal
11–12 Jun	Battle of Diamond Hill
12 Jun	Buller turns Drakensberg position and occupies Volksrust
11 Jul	Surrender of Scots Greys at Zilikat's Nek
15 Jul	Steyn and De Wet escape from Brandwater Basin
21 Jul	Roberts begins advance towards Komati Poort
30 Jul	Surrender of Prinsloo to Hunter in Brandwater Basin
14 Aug	Ian Hamilton fails to prevent De Wet's escape
27 Aug	Buller defeats Botha at Bergendal (Dalmanutha)
30 Aug	Release of last 2,000 British prisoners at Nooitgedacht
6 Sep	Buller captures Lydenburg
25 Sep	Pole-Carew reaches Komati Poort
19 Oct	Kruger sails for France on board the Gelderland
24 Oct	General Buller leaves South Africa for England
25 Oct	Formal proclamation at Pretoria of annexation of Transvaal
6 Nov	De Wet defeated at Bothville. Le Gallais killed
29 Nov	Kitchener succeeds Roberts as C-in-C in South Africa. Roberts to succeed Wolseley as C-in-C at home
11 Dec	Lord Roberts leaves South Africa
13 Dec	De la Rey and Smuts surprise Clements at Nooitgedacht
16 Dec	Kritzinger enters Cape Colony
29 Dec	Helvetia post captured

1901

22 Jan	Death of Queen Victoria
27 Jan–26 Mar	French's drive in E. Transvaal
31 Jan	Smuts captures Modderfontein. Massacre of Africans
10 Feb	De Wet crosses into Cape Colony
28 Feb	Abortive Middelburg peace talks between Kitchener and Botha
10 Apr	First drive in N. Free State begins
8 May	Milner sails for leave in England
18 Jul	First drive in Cape Colony northwards
7 Aug	Kitchener's proclamation of banishment for Boer leaders captured armed after 15 Sept
12 Aug	Kritzinger driven out of Cape Colony
1 Sep	Britain annexes the Transvaal
3 Sep	Smuts invasion of Cape Colony via Kiba Drift
5 Sep	Scobell captures Lotter's commando
7 Sep	Smuts cuts up 17th Lancers at Elands River Poort
17 Sep	Botha cuts up Gough's force at Blood River Poort
26 Sep	Botha attacks Forts Itala and Prospect
6 Oct	Botha escapes northward
11 Oct	Execution of Commandmant Lotter. Capture of Scheepers
30 Oct	Benson Killed at Bakenlaagte
7 Nov	Iam Hamilton appointed Kitchener's Chief of Staff
7 Dec	National Scouts inaugarated
16 Dec	Kritzinger captured
23 Dec	Kroonstad-Lindley blockhouse line completed
25 Dec	De Wet captures Yeomanry at Tweefontein

1902

17 Jan	Scheepers executed
6–8 Feb	New drive in E. Orange River Colony. De Wet breaks out
13–26 Feb	Second drive in E. Orange River Colony. Rawlinson's success
7 Mar	Lord Methuen defeated at Tweebosch
24 Mar	First drive in W. Transvaal
26 Mar	Death of Cecil Rhodes
4 Apr–3 May	Smuts besieges Ookiep
11 Apr	Battle of Rooiwal
12–18 Apr	Boer peace delegates' first meeting at Pretoria
1–10 May	Last drives in N.E. Orange River Colony
6 May	Zulu attack on Holkrantz
11 May	End of Ian Hamilton's last drive W. Transvaal
15–18 May	Final meeting at Vereeniging
31 May	Surrender terms signed at Pretoria

▲
**Queen Victoria's
Diamond Jubilee
in 1897.**

introduction

1

the last of the little wars

The South African (or Boer) War of 1899–1902 has been described as the 'last of the little wars'. In fact it was nothing of the sort. Although, with the military strength of the British Empire weighed against that of the two Boer Republics, the struggle was clearly one-sided, it still took a British and Empire force numbering 450,000 men over two-and-a-half years to defeat a maximum of 75,000 Boers, foreign volunteers and Afrikaners from Natal and the Cape. In the process, troops serving under the Union Jack came from Britain, Australia, New Zealand, Canada, India, South Africa and the United States, and notably, on the Boer side, they came from the United States, Russia, Ireland, Belgium, Holland, France, Italy, Spain and Germany. During the War the British lost nearly 22,000 officers and men in battle, from disease and through accidents, and the Boers, including civilians, probably some 33,000. Black African casualties are almost impossible to estimate accurately but they possibly numbered in excess of 20,000.

The British had fought the Boers unsuccessfully in 1881 when the war had lasted for barely three months. The Anglo-Boer conflict which began in 1899 lasted for nearly three years. What had happened to alter the scale and duration of war against the same enemy? There were a number of reasons, not least Britain's determination that in the second struggle against the Boers victory must be achieved at almost any price. The clash of 1899–1902 was much closer in nature to the all-embracing total wars that occurred in the

twentieth century. Thus the second Boer war pulled the civilian population into the conflict through the employment of tactics such as scorched earth and concentration camps. Civilians also came under direct fire for months on end during the sieges of Ladysmith, Mafeking and Kimberley, and they fell prey to the same diseases and infections as the troops on active service. The technology of war in 1899 was more sophisticated and more deadly than that of 1881, and the Boers were able to offset some of the advantages of superior British resources by using two principal strategies: adopting the defensive on the battlefield and later, when British strength was simply too great, adopting the tactics of guerrilla warfare. For the British the size of the force employed during the War and the sheer scale of the campaign posed fundamental problems for the Army in South Africa. The use of 450,000 men to defeat the Boers made all previous British imperial conflicts look puny by comparison. There was no existing corpus of knowledge or existing system of planning that would have enabled the British to prepare in advance for warfare on this scale. Lessons had to be learnt as the War progressed and they were often costly lessons in terms of lives and time.

The progress of the War

The first phase of the war from early in October 1899 to the end of January 1900 saw the British reel from disaster to

▲
Solomon T. Plaatje was an interpreter in Mafeking.

▲▲
Horace Nicholls whose photographs are heavily featured in this book.

▲
War correspondent, Rudyard Kipling.

▲▲
Winston Churchill, after release from POW camp.

disaster. The Boers dictated the nature and development of the War during this phase due to their superior numbers, their greater strategic mobility, their tactical mastery of the terrain, and the skill with which they exploited the quality and range of their personal weapons to pulverise the close order ranks of the British. During the second phase of the War from February to the beginning of July 1900 the British, under the careful leadership of Lord Roberts, advanced on all fronts, relieving Ladysmith, Mafeking and Kimberley and occupying both the Orange Free State and the Transvaal. At this point the British regarded the War as won and the campaign as effectively over. They could not see that the Boer leadership, with Bloemfontein and Pretoria in British hands, had any alternative but surrender. In fact the longest and in many aspects the most difficult phase of the War, from September 1900 to May 1902, was about to begin. Although many Boers did in fact surrender at this point their more capable, younger leaders reached a different conclusion. Although men such as Louis Botha, De la Rey, De Wet, Jan Smuts and President Steyn (the 'bitter-enders') recognised the impossibility of remaining in the field as an army, they kept alive the hope of victory of a sort through the adoption of a guerrilla campaign. While the armed struggle continued they believed that two things were possible; the exhaustion of Britain's will to continue the fight or outside intervention in the War, either through diplomatic or military means, by one or more of the European Powers. While the Commandos retained their ability to beat the British in small scale encounters, the 'bitter-enders' cherished the belief that peace on favourable terms was still possible. Despite many reverses the Boer Commandos were able to apply their capacity for humiliating British arms until the end of the War. On 7 March 1902, almost two years after the British captured Pretoria, a column under Lord Methuen was crushed by De la Rey at Tweebosch and Methuen himself was wounded and taken prisoner.

The Witnesses

In the course of those two-and-a-half years the Boer War brought to the world's attention the heroes of Ladysmith (Sir George White) and Mafeking (Robert Baden-Powell),

cemented the fame of at least one war correspondent (Winston Churchill), startled nations with the power of 'Jingoism', and alerted the British to the perils of modern warfare against a European enemy. Today the War is remembered largely for what Sir Henry Campbell-Bannerman referred to as its 'methods of barbarism'. Indeed, for many Boer civilians the War brought the experience of concentration camps, of burnt-out farmsteads and slaughtered livestock, of a landscape disfigured by 8,000 blockhouses and 4,000 miles of barbed wire, and of families decimated by plague and enteric fever. The events of the War and the experiences of the people caught up in it are revealed in thousands of letters, journals, diaries, official reports, and newspaper columns written by eye-witnesses. The correspondents included soldiers and civilians, men and women from Britain and the Empire, white and native South Africans, Boers and foreign observers involved in the struggle.

John Lane was one of them. An English Uitlander who had settled in the Transvaal with his family, Lane was forced to serve with the Boers on Commando. While he managed to avoid actually firing on his countrymen in person, his position in charge of the ammunition supply for his Commando meant that he frequently came under fire until his capture at Paardeberg. In complete contrast, another observer of the War, Solomon T Plaatje, was a black native of South Africa, 23 years old and a staunch Lutheran who had been raised in the Orange Free State. Passionate for education and self-improvement, Plaatje had come top in the Cape Civil service examination and by 1899 he was working as the official interpreter at the Magistrate's Court in Mafeking. He was present throughout the siege and his experiences were influential in his progress to become a distinguished author, journalist, lay preacher and politician with the South African Native National Congress. Their experiences, and those of other witnesses, form the substance of this book.

This book aims to give as much of a feel for the times as possible. The first-person accounts appear as they were originally written and as a result place names may vary in spelling and derogatory terms such as 'kaffir' occur.

the road

to

▲
**Missionary house
and church at
Groenekloff, Cape
of Good Hope.
Engraving by C
Latrobe 1818.**

▲
**Cape Town and
Table Mountain as
seen from the troop-
ship SS Cephalonia
moored in Table Bay
in February 1900.**

The southern tip of Africa became important to the traders
and sailors of the maritime nations of Europe because of its
geographical position on the sea route to India and the East.
In 1488 the Portuguese navigator Bartholomeu Dias achieved
the first recorded voyage round the Cape of Good Hope, but
the Dutch were the first to consistently exploit its advantages
as a staging post to the exotic markets that lay across the
Indian Ocean. In the seventeenth century competition
between the trading companies of Britain, France, Holland
and Portugal for the textiles and spices of Asia was intense.
The Cape, some 6,000 nautical miles from Liverpool and
roughly 6,400 nautical miles from the west coast of India,
was to become an important port of call for both
merchant ships and men-of-war.

The Cape settlement

The first staging post at the Cape was established in 1652
by an expedition mounted by the Dutch East India Company
and led by Jan van Riebeeck. The original inhabitants of the
Cape encountered by the expedition were a semi-nomadic
people known to the Dutch as 'Bushmen', and the Khoi-Khoi
who would be described by European settlers as 'Hottentots'.
Although there had been no intention to found a permanent
or extensive white settlement at the Cape, conditions there
appeared to offer a haven to those for whom life in Europe

was blighted by religious or economic oppression. By the beginning of the eighteenth century the Cape had become home to Dutch, German and French Huguenot settlers who created a local economy based on viticulture, cattle and cereal farming. Under the pressure of such colonisation the Bushmen fled inland while the Hottentots became a menial labour force which, after interbreeding with the settlers and their slaves, became the ancestors of South Africa's coloured, or mixed-race, population.

Even at this early period the Dutch settlers were known as 'Boers', meaning farmers, and their interests soon began to diverge from the strategic and trading priorities of the mother country. The settlement continued to be administered by the Dutch East India Company until the arrival of the British in 1795, and Dutch was its official language. The colonists regarded the Company as an overbearing master and a number began to leave Cape Town and move into the hinterland to escape the regulation the Company imposed on their daily lives. As they spread inland they met black settlers who were gradually expanding their lands towards the Cape. In 1780 at the Great Fish River the Boers encountered tribesmen moving south from East Africa. These were the Xhosa of the Nguni tribes and it did not take long for confrontation between blacks and whites to develop. In 1779–81 the white settlers went to war with the Xhosa on the eastern frontier of their lands. After this

encounter a common boundary was recognised along the Great Fish River but this did not prevent a second round of hostilities in 1789–93.

The arrival of the British

With the blessing of the Dutch House of Orange, British troops landed in South Africa in the Summer of 1795 during the war against Revolutionary France. The strategic position of the Cape of Good Hope meant that Britain could not tolerate its occupation by a hostile power and in June a naval expedition dropped anchor off False Bay. Consolidating a position ashore was not easy as the original British expedition was opposed and it was only after the arrival of reinforcements from St Helena that Major General James Craig was able to leave Simon's Town and defeat the Dutch at Wynberg and occupy Cape Town. The British found a population of about 15,000 Europeans of whom the majority were Dutch. Britain assumed the administration of the Cape from the Dutch East India Company but withdrew its troops in 1803 at the Peace of Amiens. With the fall of the Batavian Republic in 1806 a British force under Sir David Baird re-occupied the Dutch possessions at the Cape, but once again only after significant opposition had been defeated. In 1814 the Netherlands formally ceded their territories in South Africa to Britain.

A Boer farmstead near Cape Town in 1804.
▼

In recognition of the importance of the position of its new colony on the sea route to India, Britain maintained a permanent garrison at the Cape after 1814. It was not without work to do. The policy of introducing a British way of life and British values to the Colony quickly roused the hostility of the Boers. English rather than Dutch became the official language, immigration from Britain was encouraged, and a number of what were seen by the Boers as anti-Dutch laws were introduced. Coming from an strong-willed and hardy stock, the Boers were loath to acknowledge British authority to impose legislation and they were particularly incensed by the abolition of slavery in 1834. To the fact that the compensation offered by the British for the freeing of slaves was felt to be inadequate was added the problem that such compensation could only be collected 6,000 miles away in London. The Boers also believed that the British were too sympathetic to the land claims of native tribes and that when conflict broke out between settlers and natives, as it often did with the Xhosa people on the eastern frontier, the British administration was lukewarm in its support. To this injury was added the insult of the return in 1836 of land captured from the Xhosa during the Sixth Cape Frontier War of 1834–35. This territory, known during its brief existence as Queen Adelaide Province, had been eagerly sought by the Boers as a place of settlement.

The Great Trek

In the face of what many Boers thus considered to be, at best, sustained indifference more and more families, and especially those living in the south-east of the Colony, took the decision to emigrate beyond the reach of Britain. Their aim was to travel towards the immense interior of Africa to find land where they could establish communities within an independent Boer state. Their leaders, men such as the Voortrekker Hendrik Potgieter and Piet Retief, collected together anyone who wished to be free of British interference and took them and their flocks of sheep and cattle across the high veld or over the Drakensberg mountains. During a period of four years something close to half (estimates vary from 6,000 to 10,000 men, women and children) of the non-British population of the Cape sold their land and 'trekked' north and north-east to find new places to settle.

The 'Great Trek', as it became known to the Boers, was undertaken in the face of hardship, danger and disease. As they moved slowly northwards in their ox-drawn, covered wagons the settlers clashed with indigenous tribes such as the Matabele and the Zulus. There were pitched battles, massacres and murders before the Trekboers had established themselves beyond the Orange and Vaal rivers in what became, respectively, the Orange Free State and the Transvaal. The settlers with Piet Retief trekked into Natal and on to land

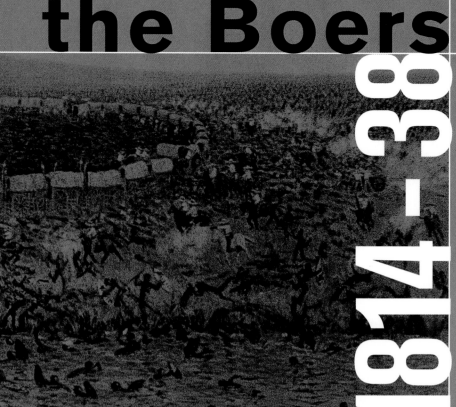

the Boers

controlled by the Zulu. In one of their first encounters with this warrior nation Retief and his immediate party were murdered, but a Boer force of less than 500 white men under Andries Pretorius exacted revenge when it defeated a Zulu army roughly 10,000 strong at the battle of Blood River in December 1838. Such engagements, often one-sided to the extent that the Boers, although heavily outnumbered, were armed with muskets or rifles and fought from within the protection of laagers constructed from wagons and thorn branches, did much to create the heroic image of Boer society.

For the settlers, with their Biblical attitude to life, the Great Trek was a unifying influence of considerable significance. It brought home to them the belief that they were a chosen people who had an opportunity to create an embracing Boer identity based upon an independent state governed by God's will. That was if the British, and the innate Boer talent for squabbling, would let them. The Dutch who chose to remain under British jurisdiction in the Cape became known as 'Afrikanders'; the term 'Afrikaners', used to describe all white settlers in South Africa who spoke 'Afrikaans', only came into general use in the twentieth century.

The great test for Boer nationalism was to come during the Anglo-Boer War of 1899–1902 when tensions between those who wished to make peace with the British in 1900 and those who wanted to fight to the 'bitter end' created dramatic rifts in Boer society.

▲
Zulu warriors recoil from Boer musketry at the Battle of Blood River. The Boers saw their decisive victory over the Zulus and their chief Dingane as an expression of God's will and divine support for their cause.

◄
A Moravian missionary settlement founded in Cape Province in 1737.

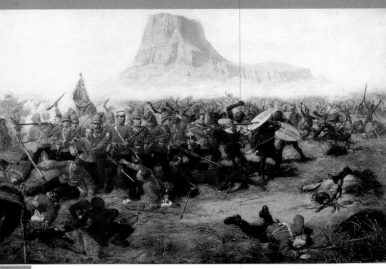

▼ The Battle of Isandhlwana on 22 January 1879. A force of nearly 1,300 British and African troops were overwhelmed and destroyed almost to a man when 20,000 Zulus attacked their camp. Oil on canvas by Charles Fripp 1885.

The settlers who took part in the Great Trek had sought a 'promised land' where they might establish independent republics dedicated to Calvinism and an essentially Dutch style of life. The realisation of this ideal was to prove difficult. In some instances the British followed them inland, or along the coast, and new Boer enclaves, such as Natal, were taken back into colonial rule. To the British administration the settlers who participated in the Great Trek, no matter how hard they might try to escape civilisation, were still British subjects. For some Boers their dream, based on the ideals of republicanism, was to found a united South African Republic embracing the land beyond the Orange and Vaal Rivers. Their hopes seemed closer to realisation when the government in London became increasingly annoyed with the tendency of the Cape Governor, Sir Harry Smith, to annex vast tracts of land seemingly at the drop of a hat. In 1852 Smith was forced to make concessions to the Boers. At the Sand River in January his emissaries signed a Convention with the Boer leader, General Andries Pretorius, which granted self-government to those who had settled beyond the Vaal. In 1854 the British recognised the same rights with regard to the 'Orange River Sovereignty'. There were now four states in South Africa: two independent Boer republics – the Transvaal and the Orange Free State – and the two British colonies of Natal and the Cape. Even though the Boers had their independence they could not sever their ties with the British

completely. The republics, and especially the Transvaal, were in a parlous state financially and needed British help from time to time. Equally, Britain continued to keep a close eye on the Boer republics, particularly where the interests of Imperial defence and foreign policy were involved.

Anglo-Boer friction

The British did have grounds for concern. The Boers were by nature quarrelsome and the new republics gave every sign of instability even, in 1857, coming close to 'civil war'. On top of this the Boers, driven by their well developed sense of nationalism, aggressively set about the task of expanding their territories at the expense of their African neighbours. When diamonds were discovered on land within the Orange Free State the British needed little urging to annex the diamond territory of the Griquas in 1871. Six years later the Transvaal, almost bankrupt and beset by native enemies, was also annexed despite the protests of Dutch- speaking settlers throughout southern Africa. Boer counter-action was delayed while British troops first crushed the power of the Zulu king, Cetewayo, and then suppressed an uprising of the Basuto tribe. Once these dangers had passed, and in the absence of a positive British response to their demands for the return of the Transvaal's independence, the Boers rose in rebellion in December 1880.

Anglo-Boer conflict

The First Boer War

At the start of what was later known as the First Boer War it quickly became apparent that the British had seriously underestimated the military effectiveness of the Boers. The rate of fire and accuracy of the Boers' musketry devastated British columns that were unlucky enough to come under attack in the first weeks of the War. On 20 December 1880 a party of 160 Boers attacked a detachment of the 94th Regiment near Bronkhorstspruit and inflicted nearly 200 casualties on the British column in an action that lasted barely 15 minutes. In the last battle of the War on 27 February 1881 a British force was overwhelmed, and their commanding officer Sir George Pomeroy-Colley killed, at Majuba. In this one-sided affair the British lost 280 men while the Boers are reputed to have suffered only a single casualty. Gladstone, who had ousted Disraeli as Prime Minister in Britain before the start of the War, had an intense dislike for unnecessary or expensive overseas military commitments and he initiated a compromise peace with the Boers. Although the Transvaal was granted full self-government in its internal affairs it remained a British Colony and this dichotomy, no less than the humiliation heaped on British arms at Majuba, would be the cause of intense friction between Britain and the Boers.

▲ The burial of the British flag by loyalists in Pretoria on 3 August 1881. With the granting of self-government to the Transvaal, members of the British community interred the Union Jack under a cross which carried the legend: 'In memory of the British Flag in the Transvaal which departed this life August 3rd. 1881, aged 4 years... "RESURGAM"'.

▼ On the same day as the disaster at Isandhlwana 4,500 Zulus attacked a company of the 2/24th Regiment, together with a number of auxiliary troops, at Rorke's Drift on the Buffalo River. During an epic defence which lasted through the night eleven Victoria Crosses were won by the garrison. Oil on canvas by Alphonse de Neuville.

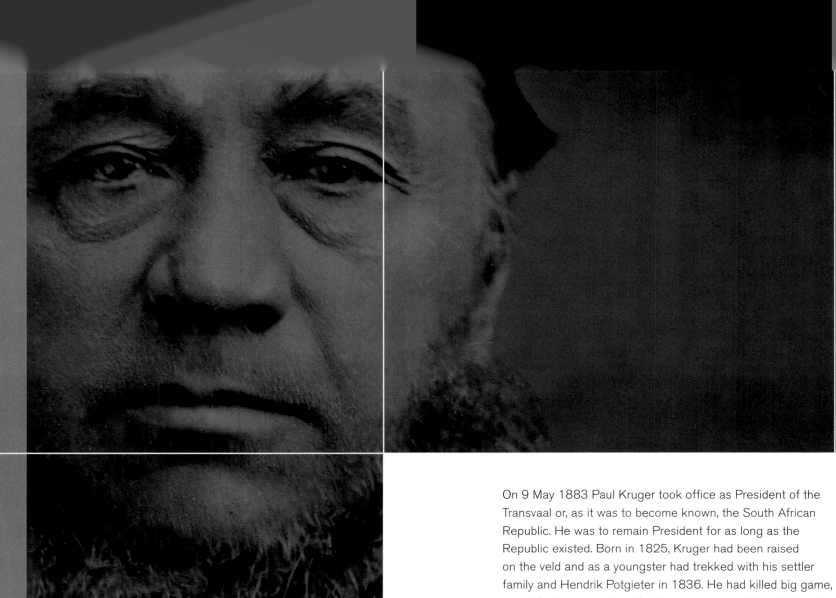

On 9 May 1883 Paul Kruger took office as President of the
Transvaal or, as it was to become known, the South African
Republic. He was to remain President for as long as the
Republic existed. Born in 1825, Kruger had been raised
on the veld and as a youngster had trekked with his settler
family and Hendrik Potgieter in 1836. He had killed big game,
joined battle against hostile tribes and married his childhood
sweetheart by the time he was seventeen. In his physical
attributes Kruger had been well equipped for the life that he
was to lead. He had a considerable personal presence, great
strength and was apparently impervious to pain. Indeed his
enemies would allege that he was often without feeling at
all when it came to dealing with his fellow human beings,
particularly those of opposing views. His solemn image in later
life, centring on a full beard and dark clothing, was very much
the facade expected of a Boer leader of the period. Yet there
was much more to the man than the image might suggest. It
was true that Kruger was self-assured, and as a strict Calvinist
he played a full role in a branch of the Dutch Reformed
Church whose beliefs were not unlike those of the Quakers.
Equally, he had an impish sense of humour, relished practical
jokes and enjoyed telling anecdotes in his deep, double-bass
voice. A largely self-taught man of considerable intellect and
prodigious powers of memory, and with a talent for acting
when it was required on the political stage, Kruger was an
excellent mediator. Before the presidential election he had set

As President of the Transvaal Kruger was at once typical and extraordinary. He exemplified the Boer passion for independence and brought the talents of soldier and politician to his country's cause.
◄

Kruger at the dedication of a new Synagogue in Johannesburg, September 1892.
►

out his essential philosophy for government: 'God's Word should be my rule of conduct in politics and the foundation upon which the State must be established.' He was to need both the strength of his religious belief and all his personal skills as he embarked upon the task of governing the Republic.

The South African Republic

Kruger's overriding political desire was that the Republic should be fully independent. As a result of the Pretoria Convention of 1881, which had concluded the First Boer War, the Republic now controlled its internal affairs, but it was still subject to British suzerainty and Britain still governed its foreign relations. In 1883 Kruger travelled to London seeking a modification of the terms of the Convention, particularly as it affected the Republic's definition of its own borders and the disputes with tribal rulers which frequently arose there. As Kruger remarked, the Transvaal Delegation would 'endeavour to have the Convention of 1881 replaced by one more in harmony with the people.' With what may appear careless timing, the Convention of London was signed on Majuba Day, 27 February 1884. It gave the Boers much, but by no means all, of what they were seeking. Under the Convention British control over treaties remained (except in the case of agreements with the Orange Free State) but the imposition of British sovereignty was dropped and the Transvaal was able to adopt

its original name of the South African Republic. The social and political integrity of this republic, however, would soon be put to the test.

When President Kruger assumed office the economy of the Transvaal was essentially agrarian with the majority of its citizens surviving as relatively poor farmers. In consequence the State could call upon only a small tax revenue together with an equally inadequate level of customs duties from the import and export of goods. It was therefore difficult to support any development of the Republic's administration or to provide the necessary investment for the modernisation of the country. But in 1886 a discovery was made in the Witwatersrand that would transform the economic life of the Transvaal while at the same time complicating its political development even further. A number of gold deposits had been opened up in the 1870s and early 1880s throughout the Transvaal, but production levels had remained comparatively low. In 1886 the industry's potential was transformed with the declaration of some 17,000 square miles of the Witwatersrand as a gold field for public digging. This bleak highland in the south of the Republic was to fuel an economic revolution. It was also to ignite a period of political ferment that would centre upon the influx of workers and experts from outside South Africa. These men, used to life in societies that were on the whole politically and economically 'liberal', were to find the defensiveness of the Boer administration continually frustrating.

British troops on parade in Pretoria in 1877.
▶

As the nineteenth century drew to a close Britain's imperial achievement – an Empire on which the sun never set – was the envy of the major European powers, France, Germany and Russia, and even of the lesser ones such as Belgium, Italy and Portugal. Yet it was a peculiarly vulnerable achievement. The Empire might have been the greatest that the world had seen in terms of its size and the number of people who lived under its rule, but its military strength was thinly spread and its economic primacy already fading under the challenge of newly industrialised nations such as the United States and Germany. The traditional leaning of British politicians towards the avoidance of unnecessary entanglements and commitments overseas became increasingly difficult to maintain in the face of the imperial aspirations of the European powers. Nowhere was this to be seen to greater effect than in Africa.

The scramble for Africa

For much of the nineteenth century Britain, fascinated and re-assured by the expeditions conducted by Sir Richard Burton, John Speke, David Livingstone, Sir H M Stanley and other explorers, regarded Africa as an area where her influence was paramount. From the 1870s, however, this assumption was challenged as France, Germany and King Leopold of the Belgians, in particular, sought to claim a share in the partition of Africa. It was logical, given this pressure, that

Britain should scramble to maintain its territorial position, even if defence meant in reality expansion. This was no easy task since Britain was essentially on her own when it came to defending her imperial interests, and the benefits of what was no longer such a 'splendid isolation' appeared increasingly fragile. Britain's volunteer army was small in European terms and the Royal Navy's maritime supremacy was under growing pressure from the United States and other powers. The liberal democracy established by Britain in the nineteenth century was also widely believed to work against the speed of reaction and decisiveness of purpose that was necessary for the successful defence of her interests overseas. This feeling of vulnerability and isolation focused British attention on ensuring that the countries of the Empire subscribed to a shared vision and common sense of purpose. It was felt that in this way a strong natural cohesion might provide a barrier against outside encroachment whether it be by native or European rivals.

A resurgent Transvaal

In this climate of imperial foreboding an English-speaking South Africa that was independent of Britain was seen as completely unacceptable. It would inevitably, it was thought, lead to openings within the area for the Germans, the French and possibly the Portuguese, who already held adjacent territories in German South-West Africa, Madagascar

Africa and the British

and Mozambique. Such weakness might then lead to repercussions in other areas of the Empire where Britain was also under pressure. From Kruger's point of view, British isolation and the rise of other powers as direct rivals to the Empire could not be more welcome. The Transvaal was ready to accept foreign support and investment as a means of strengthening its ability to progress towards full independence. The opening-up of the Witwatersrand for large-scale gold mining created an immediate demand for such investment and also provided a level of return which ensured that financial commitments would not be merely temporary. Britain was keenly aware that much of the investment sought by President Kruger could come from Europe and that where economic assistance went diplomatic support was likely to follow. Driven by gold mining, the financial growth that occurred in the Transvaal after 1886 led to a dramatic shift in the balance of economic power in southern Africa. From the brink of bankruptcy in 1885 the Transvaal had progressed by 1896 to a position where its revenue income from gold alone totalled £4,000,000 a year. As a result the Republic now assumed the economic supremacy which had previously belonged to Cape Colony. From Britain's point of view this change made it more desirable than ever that the Transvaal should become a full and loyal member of the Empire. At the same time, the growth in gold revenues meant that it would be more difficult to achieve this end by purely political means.

The gold of the Witwatersrand required not only financial investment and expensive technology to ensure that it could be successfully mined, but also a ready supply of both skilled and unskilled labour. Manpower on the scale and with the necessary expertise was not available from the scattered farming communities of the Transvaal. It had to be provided from outside. To the Boers the men who came to mine gold from Britain, Germany, America, Australia and the indigenous native populations were literally 'outsiders', or 'Uitlanders' in Afrikaans. In the face of the Uitlander invasion the Boer farmers and their government closed ranks. The defence of their national identity seemed more urgent than ever and the revenue derived from the gold of the Rand stiffened Boer resistance to Britain's wishes, both economically and politically.

Uitlanders

The presence of the Uitlanders within the Republic presented Kruger with a raft of problems. To the Boers, the white settlers who were mining and delivering the gold of the Rand were representatives of an alien culture and of political traditions that were often unwelcome. The most striking expression of everything that was anathema to the Boer was to be found in Johannesburg. A mere tented camp in the early days of the gold rush, by the Autumn of 1887 it had grown into the largest town in South Africa. Kruger admitted

that when he was in Johannesburg he felt like a stranger in his own country. It seemed that it would only be a question of time before the Uitlanders outnumbered the Boer population of the Republic. In an attempt to keep the Transvaal Dutch, Kruger and his government embarked on a programme of legislation designed to protect Boer control of the administration of the country and the essentials of its culture. These measures included an Education law, a Press law, an Aliens Immigration law, an Aliens Expulsion law, a law making the Dutch language compulsory in some areas of commerce, a 'Hollander Policy' which favoured Dutch companies and administrators and a closer alliance with the Orange Free State. All were aimed at protecting Boer primacy at the expense of the Uitlanders' civil rights. An additional cause of antagonism between Boer and Uitlander was the difficulty experienced by the latter in gaining the full franchise. Only after an Uitlander had been resident in the Transvaal for fourteen years could he gain the right to vote in presidential and Volksraad (the all-white parliament of the Republic) elections. Coupled with this was the Uitlander's resentment at the fact that he was heavily taxed for the work he did in mining the gold of the Transvaal, for him a straightforward case of taxation without representation. In order to seek redress for the grievances professed by many Uitlanders, and by now there were some 76,000 aliens out of the Transvaal's total population of 150,000, a Reform Committee

the Jameson raid

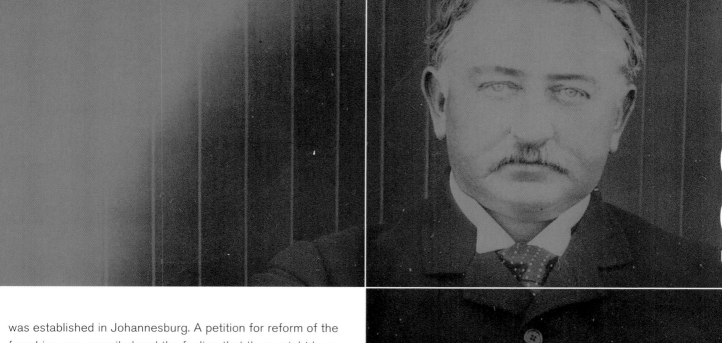

1887-9-05

was established in Johannesburg. A petition for reform of the franchise was compiled and the feeling that there might be a revolution in Johannesburg grew.

Rhodes and Jameson

Cecil Rhodes was pre-eminent among those who sought to exploit unrest in Johannesburg as a means of establishing British control over the Transvaal. Born the son of a clergyman in Hertfordshire, Rhodes made his fortune in the Kimberley diamond fields and by the age of 30 was among the richest men in the world. In 1895 his position as managing director of the British South Africa Company and Prime Minister of the Cape gave him immense power. Rhodes made plans to intervene with armed force on the side of the Uitlanders should a rising in Johannesburg occur, and he entrusted the 'invasion force' of 500 Rhodesian mounted police to his agent Dr Jameson. The intention was that when the uprising of Uitlander activists took place, Jameson's force would cross into the Transvaal from Bechuanaland to support the rebels. On the last day of 1895 Jameson, prematurely and without Rhodes's express order, launched his armed incursion. There was no uprising and Jameson and his force of 470 men were rounded-up by armed Boers within days. The 'invasion' ended in near farce, but the consequences for Rhodes and southern Africa were to be far-reaching.

Rhodes,

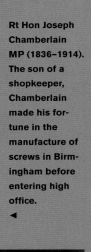

Cecil Rhodes was by turn a man of dreams and a practical realist. His overriding ambitions were to see a federated South Africa under British sovereignty and to push British influence ever further northwards. By the end of 1895 Rhodes and his circle had done much to ensure that the Transvaal was locked within a boundary of British territory. The Bechuanaland Protectorate ran along the Transvaal border to the west while the acquisition of Rhodesia had covered the northern border of the Republic. Rhodes hoped that this encirclement would persuade President Kruger to co-operate on economic matters, but Kruger had exploited Portugal's unwillingness to side with the British and had pushed a railway through Portuguese East Africa to the sea at Delagoa Bay. This provided the Transvaal with access to a port through which it could trade with the world independently of Britain. A laissez-faire attitude to imperial interests by the British government meant that policy had largely followed in Rhodes's footsteps, but the disastrous incursion into the Transvaal by Jameson irrevocably changed the political map. Rhodes lost the support of the Cape Dutch, resigned his office of Prime Minister and effectively relinquished his imperial role in South Africa. Kruger's position in contrast was considerable strengthened by the outrage felt by Afrikaners throughout southern Africa and by the telegram of congratulations he received from the German Kaiser after the Jameson raid.

Chamberlain, Milner

Chamberlain and Milner

With Rhodes's departure Joseph Chamberlain, appointed Secretary of State for the Colonies in Lord Salisbury's cabinet following the general election of 1895, found himself with something of a vacuum in the direction of imperial affairs in South Africa. It was one which he was not reluctant to fill in the interests of asserting Britain's claims. Chamberlain was dedicated to increasing the unity of the Empire, both politically and economically, in the face of a hostile world. He also wished to see its peoples brought to an understanding of the immense value of the Empire as a force for stability, prosperity and justice. Chamberlain's views on South Africa had been forming over 20 years and during that period he had become increasingly critical of the intransigence of both Kruger and Rhodes. Chamberlain had attempted to control Rhodes's activities while maintaining a balancing act between outright complicity in Rhodes' schemes and provoking confrontation with Kruger. After the Jameson raid, and Chamberlain's subsequent attempts to defend Rhodes and support the British South Africa Company, many observers, both in Britain and in South Africa, felt that the Colonial Secretary was no longer to be trusted. Moreover, Kruger's fears regarding imperial policy and its intentions towards the Transvaal appeared to be more than justified by events. In turn, British politicians viewed with extreme suspicion Kruger's search for

overseas allies, his attempts to exert control over the port at Delagoa Bay and his steadfastness in the face of Britain's requests for justice for the Uitlanders. The basis for successful diplomacy between Britain and the Transvaal was surely but steadily eroding.

Into this climate of distrust and latent hostility stepped Sir Alfred Milner, a senior civil servant, who landed in South Africa early in May 1897 to assume the position of High Commissioner and Governor of the Cape Colony. Milner, who had trained as a lawyer but had been diverted by journalism, politics and financial administration in Egypt and at home, was a committed imperialist who believed passionately in the capacity of Britain to deliver 'honesty, humanity and justice' to the peoples she ruled. Given his background, and the prevailing political situation in South Africa, it was inevitable that Milner should focus on the question of 'civil liberties' for the Uitlanders as a means of drawing the Transvaal fully into the Empire. Initially, however, he urged patience with the Boers, hoping that progressive opinion within the Transvaal might secure reform in the Republic without the need for external interference. By Spring 1898, disillusioned by Kruger's re-election for a fourth term as President with an overwhelming majority, Milner had concluded that without reform there could only be war. Increasingly Milner, despite Chamberlain's attempts to hold him in check, worked to bring about a final showdown with the Boers.

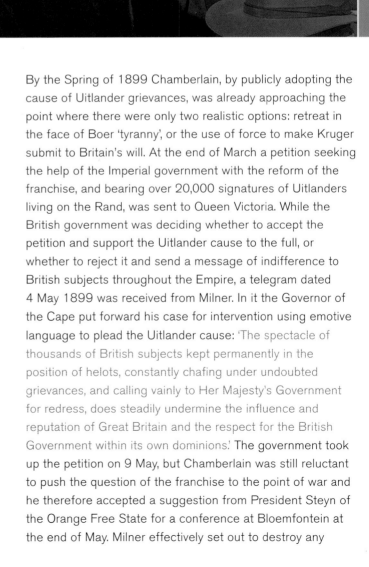

By the Spring of 1899 Chamberlain, by publicly adopting the cause of Uitlander grievances, was already approaching the point where there were only two realistic options: retreat in the face of Boer 'tyranny', or the use of force to make Kruger submit to Britain's will. At the end of March a petition seeking the help of the Imperial government with the reform of the franchise, and bearing over 20,000 signatures of Uitlanders living on the Rand, was sent to Queen Victoria. While the British government was deciding whether to accept the petition and support the Uitlander cause to the full, or whether to reject it and send a message of indifference to British subjects throughout the Empire, a telegram dated 4 May 1899 was received from Milner. In it the Governor of the Cape put forward his case for intervention using emotive language to plead the Uitlander cause: 'The spectacle of thousands of British subjects kept permanently in the position of helots, constantly chafing under undoubted grievances, and calling vainly to Her Majesty's Government for redress, does steadily undermine the influence and reputation of Great Britain and the respect for the British Government within its own dominions.' The government took up the petition on 9 May, but Chamberlain was still reluctant to push the question of the franchise to the point of war and he therefore accepted a suggestion from President Steyn of the Orange Free State for a conference at Bloemfontein at the end of May. Milner effectively set out to destroy any

Coal trucks packed
with British Uit-
lander refugees
leaving Johannes-
burg as the crisis
between Britain and
the Boer republics
worsened in July
and August 1899.
◀

The Dogs of War are
excercised in front
of Kruger. A satirical
look at the mount-
ing crisis from the
pages of *Punch* – 21
June 1899.
▶

"DOGS OF WAR."

chance that the meeting with Kruger would reach a mutually acceptable solution and on 5 June the High Commissioner withdrew from the conference. Milner's attitude extinguished the last traces of Boer confidence in the sincerity of Britain's wish for compromise. Equally, offers to reduce the qualification for the franchise were met with suspicion by British politicians and the concessions on suzerainty required by Kruger were not forthcoming. By September 1899 the Boers had had enough and they withdrew their offer to negotiate and advanced their preparations for war. On 27 September the Orange Free State linked its fate to that of the Transvaal.

The outbreak of War

On 9th October 1899 the British Agent in Pretoria, Sir William Conyngham Greene, set out in a telegram to Sir Alfred Milner the assurances required by the government of the Republic: 'First - That all points of difference be settled by Arbitration or by peaceful means to be agreed upon. Second - That the troops on the borders of the Republic be instantly withdrawn. Third - That all increase of troops arrived since June 1st in South Africa be sent back to the sea coast, with an assurance that they will be removed from South Africa within a time to be agreed upon with the Government of the S.A.R., ... and that the government of the S.A.R. shall, on fulfilment of the above, be ready to withdraw its armed burghers from the border. Fourth - That H.M. troops which are now on the sea shall not be landed in any part of South Africa. Government S.A.R. urges an affirmative answer to these four questions not later than 5pm. on Wednesday, October 11th. Should no favourable answer be received within that interval, Government S.A.R. will regard action of H.M. Government as a formal declaration of war.' The British government replied on 11 October that it deemed it impossible to discuss this ultimatum. Britain was at war with the Transvaal and the Orange Free State, and by evening Boer forces were already crossing into Natal and Cape Province.

In a letter dated 11 October 1899 to Lord Selborne, Milner wrote: 'War dates from to-day, I suppose. In any case it is a day of such inconceivable rush that I cannot say more than just this: We have a bad time before us, and the Empire is about to support the greatest strain put upon it since the Mutiny. Who can say what may befall us before that Army Corps arrives?'

Milner's gloomy prognosis was about to be fulfilled more accurately than he could have expected. The opening months of the conflict were to prove a severe test for the small British garrison in South Africa, and even when the military strength of the Empire had been brought to bear on the Boer republics the struggle would be both difficult and protracted. A war that both sides had ultimately wished to avoid was about to irrevocably alter the lives of thousands of people.

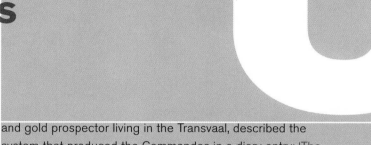

the Boer offensive

the Boers' forces

Roaming large distances across the veld in pursuit of game or a native enemy most Boers became expert horsemen and formidable scouts and trackers. Many were excellent shots who were trained in the family or settlement in the standards of marksmanship required to bring down a charging lion or a fleeing gazelle. Paul Kruger began to shoot big game at the age of seven and within a few years had killed a lion that was preying on settlers' herds. By the age of seventeen he had experienced the command of men in battle having become a Veldcornet (Field-Cornet) in 1842. Thus conditioned by life in what was always a potentially hostile environment, individual Boers were resilient fighters able to live in the saddle and move rapidly when danger threatened. These qualities were reflected in the principal Boer fighting unit, the Commando.

'Going on Commando'

Despite each Boer Republic having a small well-equiped artillery corps trained by German artillerists, neither republic had a standing army or a General Staff composed of professional soldiers. Instead they relied upon a militia system designed to suit campaigns against native enemies on the South African veld. This system of military service, built around the 'call-up' of able-bodied burghers and known generally as 'going on Commando', dated from at least 1715 and had served the Boers well in the Cape Frontier wars and against the British. John Moody Lane, an English storekeeper and gold prospector living in the Transvaal, described the system that produced the Commandos in a diary entry: 'The Country is divided into Landdrostships. These Districts have so many wards, each ward has its Field Cornet, Assist-ant Field Cornet etc. These are elected by popular vote, for five years, and get a salary. Each Field Cornet has to keep a register of all Burghers in his District. A yearly list is made up and published in Govt. Gazette, every name so published is a Burgher of the Country. Each District has its Commandant, also elected by popular vote, and lately paid a yearly salary. These are all under control of the Commandant General, also elected by the Burghers. In him rests the sole control of all the Boer Army and he resides in the Capital of the republic. The Generals are appointed by the Commandant General, who in this war appoint different officers under them.'

Every able-bodied male Burgher between the ages of 16 and 60 was liable for enlistment in a Commando or for assessment for a contribution to the war effort in money or kind. The majority of the men raised for a particular Commando were mounted and came from the same district. This explained the speed with which the Boers could raise and deploy a Commando. Each man came ready with his rifle, a supply of ammunition and food for a limited period. Further supplies were assembled in carts which could, as of old, be used as an impromptu fortification when chained together in a laager. Once mobilised, individual Commandos, which usually ranged in strength from approximately 200 to 1,000

▲

The Burghers of a typical small Boer Commando ready for action in their civilian clothes and equipped with rifles and ammunition bandoleers.

►

Boers at target practice on the perimeter of their camp.

men, could operate independently or be merged to form a larger force. The Burgher was the equivalent of a private soldier with above him in the immediate chain of command a Korporaal or Assistent-Veldkornet responsible for roughly 25–35 Burghers. The senior officer of a Commando was a Kommandant and he was supported by a deputy and a Hoof- Veldkornet (senior Field-Cornet). Each company or squadron of Burghers was commanded by a Veldkornet. The members of a Commando elected their own officers and could participate as equals in a general council of war. They had their own ideas not only on tactics but also upon their conditions of service while on Commando and they did not usually hesitate to make them known. As a result, discipline within a Commando depended largely upon the personality and strength of character of its senior officer. The Burgher went to war dressed in his civilian clothes and with his preferred weapon, the German Mauser rifle.

The International army

One of the strengths of the Boer military system had always been that it produced a citizen army in which the ties of society and family helped to bind units together to produce a formidable esprit de corps. This still held good to a large extent in 1899 and from President Kruger's own family, for example, four sons, 33 grandsons and six sons-in-law served at the front during the Boer War. But the recruiting position was not as clear cut as it had been in the past. In 1899 the Boer Army drew upon a male population that was no longer composed solely of settler farmers of Dutch or German origin. The populations of the Transvaal and Orange Free State were now more cosmopolitan and many nationalities, including Englishmen, were eligible for conscription into the Commandos. Enfranchised Uitlanders were considered Burghers and thus obliged to seve under the terms of the constitution, whether they were willing to do so or not.

To the problem of Uitlander recruitment was added that of the hundreds of foreign volunteers who came to South Africa to fight with the Boers.

From 1897 the Transvaal government had begun the serious purchase of armaments against the possibility of war, using the revenue from the Witwatersrand gold fields. Among these munitions were Creusot and Krupp artillery pieces and Vickers-Maxim pom-poms that were destined for the uniformed regulars of the Transvaal Staatsartillerie. The other main permanent uniformed unit was the Transvaal police which served in the field as mounted infantry. Similarly, the Free State maintained a permanent artillery unit and a small mounted police force. At the start of the War Boer military strength was estimated at 54,500 men comprising 21,000 from the Free State, 33,000 from the Transvaal and 500 foreign volunteers, though not all were necessarily mobilised.

Monday, November 16

THE FATE OF BOER PRESS-GANGING BEFELL **JOHN LANE** WHO GAVE VENT TO HIS ANGER IN DESCRIBING THE CIRCUMSTANCES OF HIS ENLISTMENT IN A DIARY ENTRY DATED 16 NOVEMBER:

'After an anxious time, since the 25th Sep., hoping I would escape being commandeered, having previously been informed by the authorities I would be overlooked, the climax came this morning. About 8 o'clock, the Lieutenant of Police, a man I know well, came into my store. After a lot of talk, it was not his fault, and a lot more, I asked him sharply what the 'devil' he wanted, this brought him to attention. Producing from the vest pocket of his uniform an ominous blue envelope, (I knew now what it all meant) from it took an official sheet of paper, clearing his throat, he commenced to read out in a loud voice. "In the name of S.J.P. Kruger, President of the South African Republic, I commandeer you, a Burgher of the State, with Rifle, ammunition, Horse, saddle and bridle, food for 8 days. To appear tomorrow morning the 17th inst at ... and there to await further orders and on failure of non-compliance to be treated under Martial Law. 'God save Land and people'"...It is dammed hard lines to be in the position I find myself today. To go and fight against my countrymen...To put it in other words to go, and be shot at, as I am determined not to fire a shot, come what may.'

the British forces

The colonial experience

With the exception of a mismanaged war against the Russians in the Crimea and the short disastrous campaign against the Boers in 1881, the British Army spent the majority of the nineteenth century fighting campaigns against 'native' enemies across the world. While these enemies were often supremely courageous, hardened by their own local battles, and adept at using terrain to their advantage, they were not usually armed with modern weapons. The British soldier often found that his use of long range weapons such as artillery, machine guns and rifles was matched by short range weapons such as clubs, swords, spears and animal skin shields. This is not to say that British arms could not be worsted by these enemies; the destruction of British columns in Afghanistan, India and southern Africa showed only too clearly what could happen if care was not taken in the conduct of a campaign or engagement. But on the whole a British soldier could count upon enjoying a marked technological superiority over his colonial opponent. Providing that his nerve held, that the integrity of his battle line was maintained and that the ammunition supply did not fail, Tommy Atkins was unlikely to be vanquished by native armies, no matter how courageous. This created both a confidence in arms and also, in some quarters, an overweening disdain for 'colonial' enemies. As British troops prepared to sail from around the Empire to take the field against the Boers, their approach to battle was conditioned more by their experience of campaigns against native armies than by the reality of war against a tactically sophisticated enemy of European stock armed with the latest magazine rifles and long range artillery.

The modern battlefield

The humiliation of Majuba in 1881 was still deeply felt in the British Army and most of its officers and men would accept nothing short of outright victory in this war. Many observers believed that victory would be achieved, and quickly. This confidence did not mean that the British Army was ignorant of the realities of modern 'European style' warfare. Britain's growing imperial and commercial rivalry with other great powers focused attention on how the Army would deal with enemies who might not always be poorly-armed irregulars. Reform, often pushed forward against considerable opposition, was set in train in both the British and Indian armies. As early as the 1870s Edward Cardwell, Secretary of State for Defence, had addressed many of the fundamental problems affecting the Army, notably recruiting, the purchase of commissions, the re-organisation of the War Office and the supply of reinforcements to battalions overseas. Much of what Cardwell hoped to achieve was frustrated by government parsimony, but a number of his successors as Secretary of

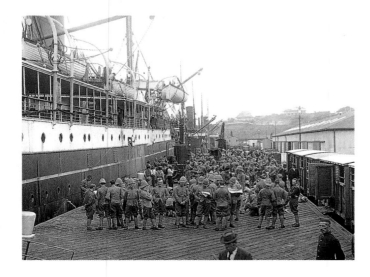

◀
British troops disembarking in South Africa before boarding a train for the journey inland.

◀
British troops receive a rousing send-off as they leave Southampton on the voyage to South Africa. Oil on canvas by Charles deLacy.

▲
A British 12-pounder gun in action near Waterval Drift on the Riet River.

State upheld the cause of reform. As a result conditions of service did slowly improve, mobilisation for war was put on a realistic footing, and new weapons were procured. Tactics too had to be subjected to rigorous examination. Shoulder-to-shoulder volley firing and close-order advances by soldiers en masse were dealt a death blow by the introduction of the machine gun and quick-firing artillery. The British witnessed a startling demonstration of the effectiveness of these weapons in their victory in the Sudan at Omdurman in September 1898. In this battle the British artillery, together with machine gun and rifle fire, accounted for 11,000 Dervish dead against 48 British and Egyptian casualties.

One problem for the Army as it began to take the field against the Boers was the gap that had arisen between the examination of the problems of the modern battlefield and the implementation of solutions. Reformers had to struggle not only with the indifference of the government and the public, but also with the opposition of the Duke of Cambridge, who had been the Army's Commander-in-Chief for almost 40 years. Organisational improvements through the formation of supporting services such as the Ordnance, Medical, Pay and Service Corps, and the introduction of a mobilisation scheme alongside tactical developments such as the use of mounted infantry and modern breech-loading weapons using a smokeless propellant had been introduced in time. Even so the British Army could not be described as an up-to-date military machine. For example there wasn't a General Staff and thus there was no plan for dealing with the Boers. In large measure the Army which fought in South Africa still depended not only upon the undoubted tenacity of its soldiers, but also upon their individual powers of foresight, innovation, and flexibility and at times these qualities were found wanting.

The British Army in South Africa

Of Britain's 222,373 Regular soldiers at the start of the War the Commanding officer in South Africa had at his disposal only 14,750 (22,104 including troops still on passage from India and elsewhere). A substantial reinforcement of 41,000 fighting men was on its way from the United Kingdom, but as mobilisation had only commenced on 9 October 1899 an expanded field force would not be able to join action with the Boers before December. As it was, mobilisation proceeded swiftly and by 17 November eight regiments of cavalry, 32 battalions of infantry, 19 batteries of artillery, and eight companies of mounted infantry had embarked for South Africa. By 1 December, Buller could deploy 84,016 Regulars of whom 58,574 were infantry, 7,513 cavalry, 7,756 horse, field and garrison artillery and 3,430 Royal Engineers. An important part of the British forces were units raised locally in the Cape and Natal. Prominent among these were the Cape Mounted Rifles, the South African Light Horse, Rimington's Guides, and Thorneycroft's Mounted Infantry. Such units were often cosmopolitan in composition and included Uitlanders, loyal Afrikaners, a group of Texans and even former Boer prisoners of war. Together with the formation of the Imperial Yeomanry many of these local units reflected the British need for mounted troops which could meet the Boers on level terms. This was also true of a significant proportion of the 30,000 troops which were raised in the Dominions for service in South Africa. The size of the force employed during the War and the sheer scale of the campaign was the fundamental problem facing the British Army. The use of 450,000 men to defeat the Boers made all previous British imperial conflicts look puny by comparison. Such a force presented organisational and logistical problems of an order which had

Troops bid goodbye to their loved ones as they leave London for South Africa.
▶

Despite the public's initial indifference to the conflict, this soap advertisement reflects the growing sense of Nationalism that developed as the war dragged on.
◀

Men of the City Imperial Volunteers marching through Pretoria in the Summer of 1900. Raised and paid for in the City of London in the wake of 'Black Week' (see page 52) the CIV served in South Africa until October 1900.
▶

simply not been encountered by the Army before. The tactical use of large bodies of troops in combination was beyond the experience of most British officers since large scale manoeuvres had been held on only four occasions in the previous 28 years.

Weapons and training

The British infantry were generally equipped with the .303 inch Magazine Lee-Enfield Mark 1 rifle introduced in 1895 or the earlier Lee-Metford, although the Lee-Enfield was more widely used particularly as the War progressed. While not quite in the same class as the Boers' Mauser Model 1896, both rifles were more than adequate as infantry weapons once sighting problems (a deflection of between 6 to 20 inches to the right at 200 yards) had been solved on the Lee-Enfield. The cavalry was armed with a combination of carbine, sword or lance depending upon the type of unit. The artillery employed mainly 12- and 15-pounder breech-loading

guns together with a comparatively small number of heavy ordnance and light, quick-firing weapons. Musketry training was generally inadequate and was practised using large inanimate targets placed in conspicuous positions. More attention was paid in the soldier's training to complex drills and to route marching than to fire and movement or concealment on the battlefield. The Army had, thanks to Wolseley, adopted a khaki uniform for active service, but a parade ground mentality still conditioned much of the thinking within regiments. Reserves of ammunition, transport, equipment and clothing for the Army were totally inadequate for the task of fighting a full-scale war in South Africa. There were not even any maps available that were suitable for military use. Yet at the outbreak of hostilities the Nation as a whole, together with the majority of officers charged with fighting the War, were sublimely confident of the outcome. The Army knew South Africa. Its senior men had fought there before or had administered vast tracts of its territory. What they did not appreciate was that they were about to undertake not a minor war, but a major one.

the rival commanders

The Boer leaders

As President of the Transvaal, Kruger was nominally commander of the Boer forces but he took no active part in the fighting itself, though his appearance on the battlefield after Boer defeats did much to stabilise morale. Even if the President's advancing years – he was 74 in October 1899 – and his poor health had not argued against actual participation in the Boer offensive the possibility of Kruger being captured by the British could not be countenanced. The President's daily contribution to the conduct of the war came through the transmission of advice on military matters from his office in Pretoria by telegraph. Commandant-General Petrus Jacobus Joubert served as Commander-in-Chief of the Boer army until his replacement by Louis Botha, a born soldier, in December 1899. President Steyn, whose military experience was exactly nil, but whose determination to see things through to the bitter end once hostilities had begun was unquestioned, was head of the forces of the Orange Free State.

Many of the Boer commanders were politicians rather than professional soldiers and a number were far from being in the first flush of youth. Once the dross of the existing command structure had been removed the Boers were fortunate in the quality of men who took charge on the battlefield. In Christian de Wet the Orange Free State possessed the outstanding Boer commander of the guerrilla campaign, while from the

An election poster for General Joubert. ◄

Commandant-General Louis Botha (1862–1919). Botha, originally a supporter of General Joubert, became adept at co-ordinating the activities of the Boer Commandos during the guerrilla phase of the War. ◄◄

Transvaal came a number of first class leaders, among them Louis Botha and Jacobus Herculaas ('Koos') de la Rey who proved to be an excellent tactician.

Britain's commanders

A number of Britain's senior army officers were under no illusions that war against the Boers would be a deadly business and that victory would have to be bought dearly after the deployment of a substantial Imperial force. Sir William Butler, commanding British troops in South Africa until August 1899, argued that 200,000 men would be required to win a war against the Boer republics. Rebuked by the War Office for his views he resigned his command. Sir Garnet Wolseley, Commander-in-Chief of the Army from 1895 to 1899, repeatedly warned the government of the seriousness of any military undertaking against the Boers and urged the creation of an efficient and fully-equipped expeditionary force in good time. Appropriate action was delayed by the politicians on grounds of expense and the possibility that effective preparation might provoke the Boers. As a result Sir Redvers Buller, commanding the main British field army in South Africa, found himself about to embark on a difficult campaign in December 1899 with a force that was barely equal to that of the Boers.

A protégé of Wolseley, Buller, at 60 years of age, had a long and impressive record as a fighting soldier, serving in China (1859–69), Canada (1869–70), Ashanti (1873–74) South Africa (1878–79 and 1881), and Egypt and the Sudan (1882–83 and 1884–85). He was awarded the Victoria Cross for his action in saving the lives of three men at Inhlobana in March 1879 during the Zulu War. Buller's battlefield credentials were impeccable and his ten years at the War office showed him to be an efficient and economic administrator. The experience which he fatally lacked was that of large-scale independent command and the talents of decisiveness and confidence which go with it. In short Buller was a brave, energetic, thorough and much admired subordinate who proved to be a cautious and uncertain commander. Buller's loyalty to, and concern for, his troops was reciprocated in full measure and the men under him rejected the criticism that was heard as the Army in South Africa staggered from defeat to defeat. While attempting to carry out Buller's strategy General Lord Methuen and General Sir William Gatacre were repeatedly worsted by the Boers. Only General French emerged from the opening campaign of the war with his reputation enhanced. Of the Officers commanding in towns under siege Sir George White, the defender of Ladysmith, was criticised for his initial dispositions, but emerged as a popular hero, as did Colonel Robert Baden-Powell in Mafeking. Faced with abject failure on the battlefield the Army sent for two of its Imperial heroes: Field Marshal Lord Roberts of Kandahar and, as his Chief-of-Staff, Lord Kitchener of Khartoum.

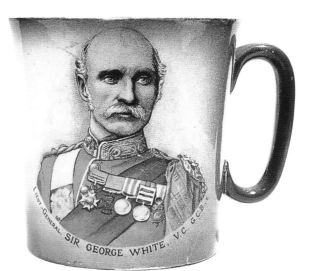

British heroes of the War such as Sir George White (1835–1912), the defender of Lady-smith, were immortalised in mass-produced commemorative wares such as this mug.
◄

the Boer strategy

The opening offensive

The essentials of the Boers' strategy had to be boldness, speed and decisiveness if there was to be any hope of forcing the British to the peace-table on terms acceptable to the Transvaal and Orange Free State. The best chance of success against the might of the British Empire was to bypass enemy garrisons and sweep through Cape Colony to the coast before British reinforcements could arrive in strength. Many Boers, including Kruger, failed to grasp this initiative at the start of the war, expecting instead that an early success for Boer arms – another Majuba – would swiftly be followed by negotiations and peace with honour. Others saw the need for a rapid and deep incursion into British territory if only in the hope of sparking rebellion in Cape Colony. In the event the Boer offensive began in this vein and they assembled 30,000 spare rifles for use by allies in the Cape.

With their superior mobility and initial advantage in numbers the Boers could largely choose the time and the place of

▲
A Boer Commando rides out of Johannesburg on 26 October 1899.

▲
▲
General Sir John French (1852–1925) painted in 1903. Oil on canvas by Edmund Van Someren. French was one of the British successes and his exploits did much to perpetuate the myth that the role of cavalry was still relevant on the modern battlefield.

►
Sir Ian Hamilton (1853–1947). Oil on canvas by John Singer Sargent. Hamilton gave much distinguished service during the War both in staff positions and field commands.

action against the British and they decided to strike in four directions. All their thrusts were initially aimed at railway routes which in the vast spaces of South Africa were critical to the success of military operations. The main invasion force from the Transvaal and the Free State, a total of 24,000 men under Commandant-General Joubert, advanced into northern Natal in two elements. Its first target was Dundee (Talana) Ladysmith, which was the principal town on the railway running through Natal to Durban. The prime objective, however, was the capture of Natal and of Durban itself. From the Orange Free State, Commandos pressed southwards into Cape Colony in the direction of the railway linking Port Elizabeth with Mafeking and Cape Town, thereby also sealing the rail route into the Boer republics. Other forces from the Transvaal and the Free State moved west to cut the railway to Bulawayo in Rhodesia at Mafeking and Kimberley.

The first serious clash of the War occurred when a British armoured train en route from Cape Town to Mafeking was attacked and derailed by Boers 40 miles south of Mafeking at Kraaipan on 13 October 1899. After bombarding the train with artillery for 30 minutes the Boers captured the train and its occupants, including the detachment commander Lieutenant Nesbitt VC who was wounded in the action. On the same day the Portuguese Government signed an agreement with the British declaring that it would not proclaim neutrality and that it would prevent the passage of war materials through its territory to the Transvaal or Orange Free State.

In the open space of the veld, intelligence of the enemy's intentions together with effective scouting was of the greatest importance. Boer reconnaissance was usually a lot more efficient than that of the British, especially in the early stages of the War. For British troops this often meant that aggressive patrolling resulted in little but the expenditure of a great deal of energy. On 13 October 1899 Sir George White and a strong flying column of The Natal Field Force left Ladysmith in the hope of intercepting a Boer Commando at Dewdrop.

Friday, October 13

BREVET-LIEUTENANT COLONEL S H RAWLINSON SERVING ON SIR GEORGE WHITE'S STAFF:

'We marched off with the five Lancers, Roystons [Natal Mounted Volunteers] men, two Batteries of A. and the Devons, Liverpools and Gordons to Dewdrop expecting to meet a force of Free Staters somewhere there. It had rained in the night but the day turned out fine. The Manchesters were to arrive by train [from Dundee] and follow us out. We got to Dewdrop an excellent junction and there bivouacked but could not gain touch with the enemy. At about one we marched back to Ladysmith. The Column had taken the wrong route out in the first instance and our march was increased by two miles in consequence. We all expected a fight and were in high spirits but no sign of Boers. The transport worked well on the whole, but straggled much and Sir George allowed the troops to march home independently which was not good for discipline I think.'

the British are contained

Although the British had decided that in the event of war they would advance through the Orange Free State to Pretoria they were in reality obliged to act defensively until the field force arrived at the Cape. Some temporary loss of territory was expected, but the speed with which the Boers accomplished their initial advance caused alarm. Fighting three engagements in five days (Talana Hill 20 October, Elandslaagte 21 October, and Rietfontein 24 October) the British gained time to fall back on Ladysmith and blunt the Boer advance on Durban. By November 1899, however, the three critical railway towns singled out by the Boers – Mafeking, Kimberley and Ladysmith – were all effectively under siege.

HMS Powerful arrived at Durban and disembarked a Naval contingent of 282 sailors under Captain Lambton. The contingent, with four Maxim machine guns, four 12-pounder guns and two 4.7 inch guns, marched for Ladysmith.

At Orange River Station, close to the border between Cape Colony and the Orange Free State, 2,000 British troops were deployed to keep open the route north that would have to be taken by any force advancing to the relief of Kimberley and Mafeking. To this end the 9th Lancers together with mounted Infantry carried out daily reconnaissance patrols. Usually such work was uneventful, but there were some brushes with the enemy, both real and imagined.

NAVAL 10-POUNDER. ON TALANA HILL.

HORWICH. BROS.
BOER WAR. 1899–1900. CoPT 281.

A 10-pounder field gun on Talana Hill near Dundee where one of the first major actions of the war was fought on 20 October 1899.
◄

General Sir Redvers H Buller VC was to find a great number of his troops trapped in Ladysmith.
▼

Boer prisoners of war and walking wounded under escort at Eland-slaagte after the town's recapture by British troops under General French on 21 October 1899. In the background ambulance wagons bring casualties into the town.

►

British infantry crossing the Drift at Talana Hill. The British drove the Boers from their positions around Dundee but only at a heavy cost in casualties which included their commanding officer, General Penn Symons.

►►

Sunday, October 29

LIEUTENANT EUSTACE ABADIE OF THE 9TH LANCERS:

'We have had nothing to do here yet, but managed to catch eight Boers the other day. They sent five of them and kept three who are now cooling their heels in prison here. On Friday night we had a taste of a South African thunderstorm and I can't say I enjoyed it. About half the tents were blown down and the remainder flooded and then to crown everything a night alarm – shots whizzing all over the place, and then silence and a long wait in the rain trying to make people believe you were enjoying yourselves immensely. The Northumberland Fusiliers started the show by shooting at a donkey which came up to one of their outlying pickets and then of course every sentry in the place saw something and blazed at it. We were strengthened by a battery and a half of field gunners yesterday and very pleased we were to get them.

The remainder of the Brigade Division of artillery, another one and a half batteries arrive tomorrow. We shall then have 22 guns and four Maxims; beside ourselves about 2,200 infantry so ought to be able to look after ourselves a bit. The horses are much fitter now, but will be all the better for a fortnight's rest here before beginning any hard work. The gunners' horses looked awful when they arrived and a very poor lot too. They don't seem to be a patch on the Walers they are getting from the Indian batteries; they are too fleshy and flatfooted for this ground. My new mare is very seedy still; she has had a bad go of congestion of the lungs and pleuro-pneumonia which she must have caught on board; her temperature is still 104°F but she is feeding better and we have at last got a vet here, so she will be looked after properly I

suppose now...Tell Dick to get either a Wolseley or a Roberts sleeping valise and not a rug roll. The valise is rather more expensive but twice as useful and absolutely necessary if on service in this country. Give him a good telescope and a good pair of glasses, as a telescope is the only thing we are using on patrols out here, the best glasses not being half as useful. The glasses do as finders, but the telescope is wanted to bring up anything at a great distance. Perhaps we notice this more here than we should elsewhere, as the country is so open. At one point where we have a vedette, we command about thirty miles of country in every direction, so a good telescope is of the greatest use.'

war on the lines

A British armoured train that was moving north from Estcourt towards Colenso was attacked near Chieveley by a Boer force estimated at 1,000 men with three guns. The Boers blocked the railway line with boulders at the bottom of a sharp incline and the leading three wagons of the train were derailed. The train was carrying nearly 150 men, under the command of Captain A Haldane, Gordon Highlanders, drawn from the 2nd Battalion Royal Dublin Fusiliers, the Durban Light Infantry and a nine-pounder naval gun detachment from HMS Tartar. Among those who were on board was the then war correspondent of the *Morning Post*, Winston S Churchill (*see* opposite).

The Boers opened fire on the train with rifles, a Maxim gun, and three 15-pounder Creusot guns. Churchill led a party of men that attempted to clear the line and after an hour's hard and dangerous work the engine was finally able to move past the obstruction. The coupling between the engine and the rear trucks had been completely destroyed by a Boer shell and only the engine, now crammed with wounded, was able to retreat towards Frere. The troops left behind continued to return the Boer fire but the odds were too great and eventually they, and Churchill, were forced to surrender. The British lost five killed, 45 wounded and 52 taken prisoner.

British troops boarding an armoured train. The railways were vital for the rapid movement of troops and supplies in South Africa.
▼

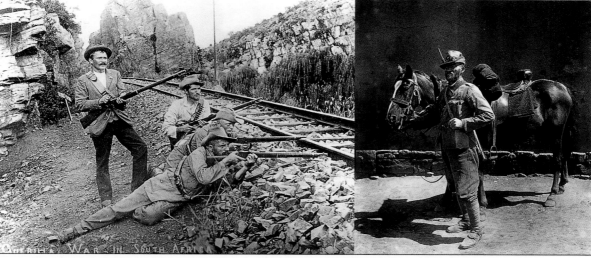

Boer Commandos posing beside the railway in a typical ambush area.

▶

Corporal Noble of Rimington's Guides, a locally raised unit serving with the British.

▶▶

Wednesday, November 15

AMID THE WRECKAGE OF THE ARMOURED TRAIN AND UNDER CONSTANT FIRE,
WINSTON CHURCHILL ATTEMPTED TO FIND A WAY OUT OF A BOER TRAP:

'I nipped out of the truck accordingly and ran along the line to the head of the train... As I passed the engine another shrapnel burst immediately as it seemed overhead, hurling its contents with a rasping rush through the air. The driver at once sprang out of the cab and ran to the shelter of the overturned trucks, his face cut open by a splinter streamed with blood, and he complained in bitter, futile indignation. "He was a civilian. What did they think he was paid for? To be killed by a bombshell – not he! He would not stand another minute" It looked as if his excitement and misery – he was dazed by the blow on his head – would prevent him from working the engine further, and as only he understood the machinery, the hope off escape would thus be cut of. So I told him that no man was hit twice on the same day:

that a wounded man who continued to do his duty was always rewarded for distinguished gallantry, and that he might never have this chance again. On this he pulled himself together, wiped the blood off his face, climbed back in to the cab of his engine and thereafter obeyed every order which I gave him. I formed the opinion that it would be possible, using the engine as a ram, to pull and push the two wrecked trucks clear of the line, and consequently that escape for the whole force was possible. The line appeared to be uninjured, no rail had been removed... I was very lucky in the hour that followed not to be hit. It was necessary for me to be almost continuously moving up and down the train or standing in the open, telling the engine-driver what to do. The first thing was to detach the truck which was half off the rails from the

one completely so. To do this the engine had to be moved so as to tug the partly-derailed truck backwards along the line until it was clear of the wreckage, and then to throw it completely off the rails. The dead weight of the iron truck half on the sleepers was enormous, and the engine wheels skidded vainly several times before any hauling power was obtained. At last the truck was drawn sufficiently afar back, and I called for volunteers to overturn it from the side, while the engine pushed it from the end... It was very evident that these men would be exposed to considerable danger. Twenty were called for and there was an immediate response, but only nine men, including the Major of the Durban Light Infantry and four or five of the Dublin Fusiliers, actually stepped out into the open. The attempt was nevertheless successful.'

the battle of Modder River

'Mournful Monday'

On his arrival at Cape Town on 31 October 1899 to assume command in South Africa, General Sir Redvers Buller found a military situation which he regarded as of 'extreme gravity'. The day before Buller disembarked Sir George White's tactically inept attempt to break the closing enemy grip at Lombard's Kop had failed with the loss of over 300 officers and men. This was not the sum of disaster on 'Mournful Monday' for another defeat occurred at Nicholson's Nek when the flank guard sent out by White surrendered to the Boers with the loss of nearly 1,000 men. The main strength of Buller's command was trapped in Ladysmith. He was thus unable to implement decisive action until the arrival from Britain of the army corps of one cavalry and three infantry divisions.

Buller had been given orders in London to launch all his strength in an attack up the railway to Bloemfontein and then on to Pretoria. As he surveyed the strategic picture before him, and as more troops arrived daily at the Cape Buller, now out of his depth, abandoned his orders and decided that his main priority must be to advance from Durban to the immediate relief of Ladysmith. He then split his forces. Buller was also under pressure to relieve Kimberley from where Cecil Rhodes maintained a constant clamour for military assistance. Tasking Lord Methuen with an advance along the western railway to Kimberley, Buller ordered

Generals French and Gatacre to prevent any further Boer incursion into Cape Colony and to reinforce Natal. On 22 November Buller with a few of his staff left Cape Town quietly for Natal. The Commander-in-Chief had now removed himself some hundreds of miles from his administrative and command centre at the Cape.

The troops of Lord Methuen were the first into action as they advanced along the western railway. On 23 November the British drove the Boers from three ridges they had occupied at Belmont at a cost of 300 casualties and the expenditure of 126,000 rounds of small-arm ammunition. Two days later Methuen forced 2,500 Boers out of their position at Enslin. Once again the Boers fought from an excellent position, inflicted heavy casualties for little loss to themselves and then withdrew in good order to a further line of defence. As at Belmont, where the majority of the British casualties had been suffered in only a few minutes by the Grenadier Guards, half the British losses occurred in one unit. Of Methuen's 195 casualties at Enslin the Naval Brigade lost 98. Such were the consequences of frontal attacks across open ground. Emboldened by these minor and limited successes Methuen pressed on straight into the middle of the next and rather more formidable Boer position at the Modder River.

The Boer force of approximately 8,000 men at the Modder River was commanded by General Cronje but its tactical

◄
British troops slaughtering cattle at the Modder River.

▶
A room in a Boer house at the Modder. Its walls have been inscribed with graffiti: 'Don't forget Majuba Boys. Boers no fear.'

deployment was controlled by General de la Rey. Instead of placing his main defence position on the top of kopjes, which could be easily identified and shelled by the British, de la Rey deployed his men in trenches in advance of the Modder along the banks of the Riet River. They could thus deliver grazing fire at ground level across an area that had been carefully marked with painted mounds and stones as ranging aids. Obligingly, and with little preparation except for some exploratory artillery fire, Methuen launched his force of 10,000 men into this killing ground. Fortunately for the British the Boers

sprang their ambush slightly too soon and the leading battalions went to ground and attempted to return the Boer fire. For nearly ten hours in blistering heat the British troops lay on the veld unable to move without drawing withering Mauser fire. Stretcher bearers could not reach the wounded and fresh supplies of ammunition and water could not be distributed. Tortured by sunburn, ants and thirst the exposed troops, and in particular the highlanders in kilts which left the backs of their legs bare, could do little but suffer stoically and wait for nightfall and the opportunity to fall back.

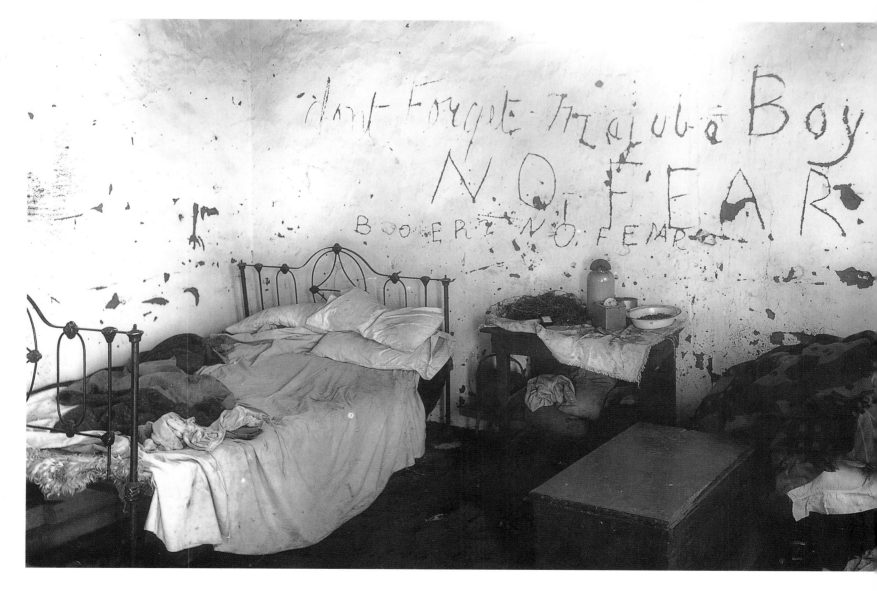

Tuesday, November 28

JOHN LANE THE BRITISH UITLANDER SERVING WITH THE BOERS WAS PRESENT WITH HIS COMMANDO TOWARDS THE RIGHT OF CRONJE'S POSITION AS THE BRITISH ARTILLERY ATTEMPTED TO ASSIST THE INFANTRY:

'I look about me, and take as safe a position, at least what I think safe, and work up a bit of a sand mound in front of me with the butt of my rifle; got it about a foot high and two feet thick, settled myself down to await events. I asked a fellow, who was lying about five yards from me, where the British were, as devil a sign I could see, he pointed in a certain direction to our right, with my glasses I could then see them, looked like a swarm of locusts, all over the veldt. I can now see the Artillery, or what I imagine is. We are without Artillery, all ours being down at our extreme right. About two thousand yards below us, on our left, is a farm house and kraal, this the British must think occupied by us, as now seven o'clock, they have commenced sending shell after shell into it. It is a grand sight to see the house being knocked to pieces....The cavalry swung round as if they were coming for us, or at all events in our direction, but the body of men that were sent up the river opened up on them, and they changed their movement. The two Maxims kept us here, that we cannot move, and all along the river, down to the Station, the fire is incessant, Artillery and small arms, from both sides, it is simply "hell let loose". I could never have realised, or can one who is not here, what it is like... Now a battery of Artillery are shelling us properly, the shrapnel are falling here, there and everywhere. For two hours I laid in one position on my stomach making myself as small as possible, Maxim shrapnel bullets hitting to within two inches of me, once got a charge of partridge shot, No. 6, over my body, this must have come out of some shell, was just like a shower of hail, did no harm, I picked up about ten shots, it did not go even into the sand.'

LATER **LANE** WITNESSED THE BOERS REPULSE A BRITISH ATTACK:

'The artillery fire eases off, and I can see the cavalry and infantry coming in a half circle towards us, now I think it is all up, we are only about 300 in this special position. I don't feel particular happy, I hear, word being passed along, to keep quiet till they come within 700 yards. The troops are now in a hollow, more or less out of sight, when they come a little on the rise, the order is to give it "hot". Not a word is spoken, everyone seems, so to say, holding his breath, we are lying about ten yards apart, about three deep. I am in second row, and feel more afraid of the man behind me than of the British. Just expecting the Cavalry to appear, when from behind us goes the boom, boom, of shells, going over our heads, into the advancing cavalry and infantry, our artillery had just come in time. For a moment the British seemed to stand still, made a turn to the right and left us. The Boers then sprang open their Mausers and poured a heavy fire. I quickly, having a good look, with my glasses to see the effect, from the Mauser fire. I only saw a stray one here and there fall, from the Artillery I could not say, as it was unexpected, and did not know on the moment whether it was meant for us or them. Of course, the Boers swear with the Mausers they killed hundreds, but I saw different. When it was all over, there was a general sigh of relief, we, I mean this commando I am with, had not a single man hurt. I fully expected, at least half of us would have been knocked over, had we been lying closer together, then I think, we would have suffered.'

British troops and supplies crossing the Modder River near Paardeburg in February 1900.
▼

Wounded British soldiers receiving medical attention at a field dressing station in Waggon House, Klip Drift. Providing the patient survived the initial shock of his wound and the subsequent loss of blood he stood a good chance of recovery. British surgical techniques were of a high standard and general anaesthesia was used for all operations. The British Army took a number of X-ray machines to South Africa.
►

Stormberg and Magersfontein

Buller had expected Methuen to relieve Kimberley by 28 November, the day he fought the Boers at the Modder River. The Commander-in-Chief had been supremely optimistic for on 1 December Methuen advised the authorities in Kimberley by signal that they should plan to make their supplies last for three months; but although he had been repulsed Methuen found that he was free to advance again. The Modder position was not of great importance to the Boers and having inflicted 475 casualties on the British they retired to a new defence line at Magersfontein where they were significantly reinforced before Methuen's arrival.

As Methuen followed Cronje, General Gatacre, advancing north from his headquarters at East London, launched an attack upon a Free State Commando at Stormberg. This important railway junction on the line to Bloemfontein had been taken by 1,700 Boers on 22 November. Alive to the danger that this Boer garrison might succeed in raising the countryside, Gatacre planned a surprise attack for dawn of 10 December. Once the British had de-trained the previous evening they still had to complete a night march of eight miles. The force lost its direction in the dark and far from being in position at dawn Gatacre's exhausted troops were still marching, unbeknown to them, as there were no scouts deployed, into the centre of the Boer defence. The enemy unleashed a deadly storm of rifle fire and although the 2nd Battalion Northumberland Fusiliers and the 2nd Battalion

Irish Rifles attempted to fight their way forward, the British were soon in full retreat. They suffered 135 casualties and left 561 officers and men behind to become prisoners. So began the series of three humiliating defeats (Stormberg, Magersfontein and Colenso) that were to be known by the British as 'Black Week' (10–15 December).

Monday 11 December 1899

In his first attack since 28 November Methuen struck against Cronje's position at Magersfontein on 11 December. His artillery had been attempting to search out the main Boer position during the previous 48 hours but without, as John Lane reported in his diary, much success: 'Hear this afternoon (9 December) for the first time cannon firing in direction of "positions", not a continual fire, every now and then, I fancy the British are trying to "locate" where our "positions" are, also to find out where our cannon are. I hear the General has given artillery orders not to fire a shot until he sends orders, he evidently won't have the position of his artillery found out, "Oh slim Piet".'

Cronje's forces were cleverly deployed. His men occupied a string of low kopjes, but instead of placing his riflemen on top of the hills they were entrenched at their base. John Lane was pessimistic concerning the success of another frontal assault by Methuen:

◄
Roaming large distances across the veld in pursuit of game meant the Boers were expert horsemen.

'If we are tackled by a flanking movement it will be all up with the Boers. But a frontal attack will be fatal to the British as the Boers are all too well entrenched...During the 10 days [since 28 November] Cronje has not let the grass grow under his feet. Realising the importance of the place he has got his "positions" at he has had a large reinforcement and has been able to entrench his forces in a most elaborate manner, without let or hindrance from the British.'

No wiser as to the Boer "positions", Methuen, like Gatacre at Stormberg, decided upon a night march to contact followed by a dawn attack. As at Stormberg the assault, the burden of which fell upon the Highland Brigade, misfired badly as any hope of co-ordinated pressure was rendered impossible when the highlanders were caught in deadly rifle-fire while they attempted to deploy for battle. Thereafter, the assaulting British troops could only hope to go forward or to retire in isolated groups, according to conditions in their immediate vicinity. Again whole regiments were reduced to spending the daylight hours seeking whatever cover they could find on the battlefield. Those troops that were able to go forward and ascend parts of Magersfontein were sprayed with shrapnel by their own artillery who believed that the assault units were all halted at the bottom of the hill. Methuen, having lost 970 men, retreated to the Modder River and made no further attempt to turn the Boers out of a position which they occupied until March 1900.

▶

Major-General Andrew Wauchope (1846–1899) was the commanding officer of the Highland Brigade. A soldier of great courage he was widely respected by his officers and men. It was said that he had been wounded in every action in which he had taken part. He was killed at the Battle of Magersfontein.

◄
A Boer picket at
Magersfontein. The
Boers were much
admired by the
British for the qual-
ity of their scouting
and reconnaissance.

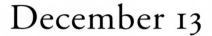

COLONEL J W HUGHES HALLETT OF THE SEAFORTH HIGHLANDERS WROTE IN A LETTER DATED 13 DECEMBER 1899 OF THE FUTILITY AND SACRIFICE OF THE BRITISH FRONTAL ATTACK:

'I am just broken hearted at our awful loss on the 11th. Five Officers killed and 7 wounded and over 200 men killed and wounded. The loss in the Highland Brigade alone was 54 Officers, 20 killed, 34 wounded, and 813 men killed and wounded, including our General killed and his A.D.C. severely wounded. Simply terrible and all absolutely quite unnecessary. Our Divisional General, Lord Methuen, still sticks to his suicidal idea of a frontal attack, you will have seen all the accounts in the papers by now. I am afraid they will lay all the blame on poor Wauchope. It was not his doing but Lord Methuen himself. Wauchope was dead against the night march and the whole plan, and was merely carrying out orders. We left here in the afternoon of the 10th and marched about four miles where we stayed till 12.30 a.m. We then started in pouring rain, inky darkness, and awful ground to the position. The Black Watch leading, then we came, then the Argyll and Sutherland and the Highland Light Infantry in rear. We got quite close to the position just before daybreak and were just extending to attack when a perfect storm of bullets came into us from close quarters. The enemy were evidently quite prepared for us, and had waited till we were within a very

short distance of them. I don't understand how not more of us were killed at this minute. Naturally in the dark and not being able to see the enemy the men were a little unsteady, and some of the Black Watch turned and rushed through our ranks, but I was able to steady our men and make them lay down at once. The Argyll and Sutherland's and H.L.I. could not be stopped till they had retired some way. All this happened at 4 a.m. From then till 2 p.m. – 10 mortal hours – about 400 of my men had to lie flat on their faces in the sun, being fired at all the time, and unable to fire back or to move. Whenever one had to rise or move he was instantly shot down. I tried two rushes with the men but nearly every man fell. Meantime the remainder of the Brigade tried to work round to our right, but were driven back, also the Brigade of Guards, who also attempted to help us. At about 2 p.m. I found the enemy were surrounding us, so we were obliged to make a rush for it, and it was then we suffered very badly. I personally had some wonderful escapes, but did not get touched...The colonels of the Gordons, the Argyll and Sutherlands and the Black Watch were all killed during the day, and the poor General was killed at the first volley. Altogether as you may imagine it was a

most terrible day. We buried most of the poor fellows yesterday, and the worst of it is that all this has been for nothing, and I consider we are in a very tight place now. The enemy numbered 20,000 [8,200 would be a more realistic estimate] and we were 8,000 [Mehtuen's fighting troops actually numbered 12,000] and their position was absolutely impregnable. I don't know what the General intends to do now. One thing is I don't see how he can possibly attempt to go on and attempt the relief of Kimberley with the troops here. All are absolutely demoralised. At present I am in command of the Highland Brigade. Poor old Mc'Cone was killed. Poor Waterhouse is very badly wounded. I fear he will not get over it. Anyway he will lose one eye if not both. Young Hall was hit four times, he had a very lucky escape. I fear he will be lame for life. All the Officers killed were I am thankful to say killed dead at once. Clarke, Brodie, and Cowie shot through the head. Cox simply riddled with bullets. I have no heart to write more of this awful business.'

Colenso and Black Week

When Buller finally advanced in Natal he did so with an exemplary care for supply and transport arrangements and for the well-being of his troops. Consequently his force moved extremely slowly. Fortunately Joubert had limited his offensive actions outside the siege of Ladysmith to persuading the 2,000 British troops at Colenso to fall back to Estcourt. Here Buller's force assembled ready to advance but further delay was occasioned by the lack of adequate maps and the scarcity of intelligence of the Boers' positions. Realising at last that the growing British force at Estcourt was a significant threat Joubert made a brief, unsuccessful thrust against its line of communication. He then fell back across the Tugela to await Buller's advance. Before battle was joined Joubert, who had been injured in a riding accident, had been replaced by the youthful and energetic Louis Botha.

After a reconnaissance of the Boer position at Colenso Buller had formed the opinion that a frontal assault on the enemy defences would prove extremely costly. He had therefore decided upon a turning movement of the Boer position by a 45-mile flanking march via Springfield and Potgieter's Drift and on to Ladysmith from the west via the Acton Homes road. With the defeat of Methuen at Magersfontein he concluded that such a manoeuvre would now place his communications at extreme risk and he chose instead to make a direct assault on Colenso. In such an attack his troops would face almost insuperable problems. The Boers

occupied high ground which commanded the clearly predictable points at which the British would attempt to ford the Tugela. Early in the morning of 15 December Buller's troops advanced from Chieveley upon a Boer force that knew exactly what to expect. In contrast the British had little idea of either the enemy's strength or his dispositions. It was not long before they ran into trouble.

By 8 am Buller had called a halt to the attack and ordered a retirement to Chieveley. He had suffered casualties totalling 1,100 men, a loss which Buller did not consider to be 'very heavy'. Indeed the troops probably came out of the battle better than their Commander-in Chief whose remaining confidence drained away with every hour that passed. In his report Buller concluded that 'I ought to let Ladysmith go and to occupy a good position for the defence of South Natal'. On 16 December he advised Sir George White in Ladysmith to seek terms for the surrender of the town. White refused and Buller received a stinging telegram from London: 'The abandonment of White's force and its consequent surrender is regarded by the Government as a national disaster of the greatest magnitude. We would urge you to devise another attempt to carry out its relief...'

Buller's loss of confidence and the Nation's fury at the events of Black Week persuaded the government that a new Commander-in-Chief had to be found. On 17 December 1899 Lord Frederick Roberts accepted the appointment.

▶

A German cartoon: 'Greetings from the War. The English soldiers in South Africa enjoy the attentions of both sides. From the Queen they are given chocolate, from Kruger they get a good thrashing.'

GRUSS VOM KRIEGSSCHAUPLATZ

Die englischen Soldaten in Süd-Afrika erfreuen sich allseitiger Aufmerksamkeit: Von der Queen bekommen sie Chokolade und von Ohm Krüger Wichse.

Wounded British troops being ferried across the Tugela River. To reach Ladysmith Buller's troops had first to cross the Tugela and then establish themselves on the hills beyond against fierce Boer opposition. The defenders of Ladysmith could hear Buller's guns to the south as he attempted to gain a lodgement across the Tugela.

British troops, out of range of the Boer trenches, wait on the veld during the Battle of Colenso on 15 December 1899. ◄

Friday, December 15

R J K MOTT SERVING WITH THE QUEEN'S REGIMENT WITNESSED THE OUTCOME OF BULLER'S LACK OF
UNDERSTANDING OF THE MODERN BATTLEFIELD:

'Roused at 3 a.m. and after scrambling in the dark to fetch and pack wagons and ammunition, I started with the latter to catch up the battalion; the baggage being parked separately. When I found it, it was deployed in eight lines of about 400 yards long, the men being extended to five paces; lines about 50 yards apart. At 5.30 one of the Naval guns opened. It was great fun watching the effect through glasses, and seeing where the shells burst. The lyddite effects were awful: a great, red-brown cloud of smoke; in fact, the 1st position looked exactly if it was on fire, so thick was the smoke and dust where the shells struck! The range was about 5,000 yards. The enemy would not expose his gun positions; so, at about 7 a.m. we were ordered to advance – Hildyard's brigade in the centre; Queen's and Devons in the firing line, W. Yorks and E. Surrey in support. Hart's B'de was ordered to cross at the ford, but unfortunately they missed it and got to a deep place. Barton's and Lyttleton's B'des in reserve. The moment the Infantry advanced, "whiz-z-z-pom" came the shells, right among us. Some did not burst, and of the first dozen only one of our men was hit. A big one pitched within 10 yards of me, but fortunately did not burst! I have got it and shall try and bring it home! It was from a 4.7 gun, and weighs 32 lbs. I have had it opened, and they say there is no danger left in it. Our fellows advanced to within 1,200 yards of the enemy, being rained on by shells and bullets all the time. A few got on another 200 yards into the village of Colenso, but further than that it was impossible to go, on account of the river. Some of the Devons were ordered to cross the railway line, but got no nearer the river than we did. The two batteries got much too close, and were absolutely put out of action very soon – every horse and man killed or wounded! Part of Hart's Bde. got across the river, but ran into an ambush and were driven back. No attempt was made to get round the Boers' left, and at about noon the order was given to retire to camp.'

A Boer laager at
Colenso.
◄

Saturday, December 16

GUSTAV PRELLER OF THE BOER ARTILLERY WAS GRATEFUL FOR AN UNEXPECTED PRIZE
AS THE FIGHTING DIED AWAY:

'I rode off early, before the sun had risen, and it appeared that the enemy was quiet. We returned to the tent. We were hardly there before the bombardment commenced, we saddled our horses again and rode back, but had a hard time getting through the fire zone of bursting projectiles behind our position. The enemy advanced against us in thousands in four large columns, coming directly towards us with the wagons and guns all in front. He also advanced to the right upon the Free Staters Ermelo, Zoutpansberg and Swazieland Policemen to the left upon the Boschrand occupied by Muller and Joubert's men. When they got about half way the infantry extended, one regiment after the other, the men were at intervals of 50 yards, and later on covered the whole plain in long lines. Two batteries with caissons coolly advanced until they got just immediately on the other side of the town (Colenso) and started to take up a position there. Then the burghers opened fire and so did Lood with the guns. In a short space of time the guns were shot bare, nothing being left alive. Then the infantry tried to storm the position along the railway, but were ten times repulsed with heavy loss. Enemy bravely tried to recapture the guns but they only just managed to get two of them away. They tried again but all the horses were knocked down and the men got away as hard as they could [It was during this episode that Lord Robert's son, Frederick, was mortally wounded]. Two hundred (more or less) of the enemy's infantry succeeded in reaching the guns and some the town also, then another battery took position and opened fire on our left, later on this one also retired. In the meanwhile the attack on the left and right was repulsed with heavy loss to the enemy and towards midday he was in full retreat with his wagons and everything. Field Cornet Kock and others crossed the river and reached the guns and captured 142 British there. The Standerton and Ermelo men also captured some. Before sunset we were richer by 10 Armstrong guns with ammunition (12 caissons) and thanked the Almighty for this great miracle. The enemy's loss in killed is estimated by various people at 1,000 or 1,500 and many wounded. We lost five killed and nine wounded. Visited the battlefield and the terrible sight is deeply engraved on my memory, the dead were still lying all over the field and the splendid horses in heaps. Wired to H. and the Volksstem giving an account of the fight.'

world opinion and foreign volunteers

Britain's handling of its relations with the Boer republics had long been unpopular in Europe, particularly in Holland, France, Belgium, Germany and Russia where anti-British feeling was strong. Once war had broken out, however, European assistance to the Boers was to come from individual volunteers and not overtly from governments. No nation was, in the last analysis, prepared to risk British retaliation against its own colonies for the sake of the Boers. Germany, for example, exploited the anti-Boer hysteria at the start of the War to highlight Britain's diplomatic isolation, thereby hoping to persuade the government to join a defensive alliance. To this end the Kaiser visited Britain in November 1899.

The disparity in scale between the respective military strengths of the British Empire and the Boer republics inevitably lent the emotional appeal of the under-dog to the Boer cause. This proved to be a strong incentive to many of the nascent republicans of Ireland and Europe and far more people volunteered for service with the Boer cause than were actually able to reach South Africa. The 'volunteers' also included military observers incognito, eccentrics and outright adventurers. The Boers made no effort to raise volunteers in Europe and on arrival in the Boer republics the volunteers were surprised to find that their intentions were regarded with suspicion and that their presence was resented by many.

Canadian infantry storming a kopje. A maple leaf badge can just be seen on the helmet flash of the soldier nearest the camera.
◄

General Kolbe (left) and Colonel Maximov. Maximov was a Russian serving with the Boers and was shot at close quarters during the battle at Mount Thaba.
▼

These feelings even embraced the foreign ambulances that had been created to assist the Transvaal Red Cross in its work with the sick and wounded. The volunteers who arrived at the battlefront numbered roughly 1,600 and came from America, France, Germany, Holland, Ireland, Scandinavia and Russia. They were of differing backgrounds and military capabilities ranging from aristocracy to professional soldiers. Proportionately the volunteers suffered much heavier casualties than other sections of the Boer forces. At Elandslaagte, a Boer defeat, General Ben Viljoen described the battlefield as 'a dreadful spectacle of maimed Germans, Hollanders, Frenchmen, Irishmen, Americans and Boers lying on the Veld'. After this failure Joubert was so disillusioned with the volunteers that he was on the verge of sending them back to Johannesburg declaring 'I won't have them here any more'. Contrary to Joubert's opinion a number of foreigners were highly professional soldiers who brought specialist skills to the Boer cause. Major Friedrich Albrecht, a German employed by the Orange Free state since 1880, used his military expertise in the training of the Orange Free State Staatsartillerie, even specifying a blue uniform in the German style.

Roland Schikkerling, a member of a Boer Commando, recorded his impression of a group of Irish volunteers: 'We had, standing near us, a small body of Irishmen and Irish Americans. They were lively boys, and the finest of company. This party adapted themselves to our conditions sooner and more easily than any of the foreigners with us. Where the German and the Hollander, nearer to us in blood perhaps, felt and looked out of place, you could not pick Patrick out of a herd of the wildest Boers. There were fieldcornets bearing the names of Kelly and O'Brien. This little band of men could curse like heretics, and their profanity was at times quite picturesque... At Elandslaagte many Hollanders and Germans were present at the taking of an enemy train loaded with much liquor. A portion of them, among others, was soon drunk and lying broadcast on the veld around the station.'

Even before war had been declared offers of military assistance from the Empire had begun to arrive in London. These generally involved the provision of troops for service in South Africa and often included units with training or roles that were to prove particularly suitable for warfare on the veld. Sometimes entire units volunteered for service against the Boers and a squadron of New South Wales Lancers on their way home from training in England jumped ship at Cape Town and offered their services. From Australia and New Zealand came the offer of mounted infantry units; from Canada an entire infantry regiment; from the Federated Malay States the provision of 300 Malay States Guides; from Nigeria the services of 300 Hausas; and from Hong Kong 50 men and four Maxim guns. By 1902 the total of troops from the Dominions alone that had served in South Africa amounted to 30,170.

► **An English Tommy standing facing front with clothes, topee, etc. labelled with 'Chamberlain'.**

the role of the black African

The War of 1899–1902 touched the lives of black people in South Africa in many ways. In towns such as Mafeking, Ladysmith and Kimberley it brought danger, fear, upheaval, economic loss and at times humiliation. Occasionally the War brought opportunity but only for a minority. More generally, the disruption of the labour market once hostilities began caused widespread poverty and led many Africans to readily accept the offer of work with the British forces.

The black population of South Africa in 1899 vastly outnumbered the whites. The population of the Transvaal, for example, included an estimated 366,000 white citizens and 734,000 natives in December of that year. In the Cape the population totals were 382,000 white and 1,315,000 black. In addition to the black population the coloured and Asian communities in South Africa numbered approximately 500,000 and 100,000 respectively.

Among the educated and politicised elements of black and coloured society in South Africa the prospect of the defeat of the Boer republics by the British Empire was generally welcomed. The administrative and social treatment of the black population was far more liberal in the Cape and Natal than in the Free State and the Transvaal. The hope of many blacks was that if the Boers were defeated militarily, and the republics administered by a comparatively enlightened Britain, the condition of the blacks would rise and their prosperity increase. The Asian community in particular thoroughly

supported the British war effort and Mohandas Gandhi was among those community leaders who created an Asian ambulance corps for service at the front in Natal.

There was widespread fear among whites at the beginning of the War that some native black rulers might exploit hostilities and promote rebellion against both the Boers and the British. As a result military units on both sides were at first diverted to keep a watchful eye on black communities and the enlistment of whites in sensitive areas was neither as rigorous nor as extensive as in regions firmly under British or Boer control. In the event no African rulers followed the path of armed rebellion, preferring instead to seek the redress of grievances by established political means. This is not to say that there were no examples of African violence or unrest. Indeed the Boers were subjected to consistent African hostility which on occasion escalated to murder.

Rebellion would have proved a difficult undertaking with the vastly increased military presence in South Africa during the War and also because Boer and Briton were in broad agreement that blacks would not be armed on any scale or encouraged to fight in what was seen as a 'white man's war'. The British extended this view to include a prohibition against the use of non-white troops from the Empire in military operations in South Africa. Once the strain of war had begun to exert a sustained effect on the military resources of both the Boers and the British it became clear that Africans had a

◄

A black African despatch runner waits while a British soldier conceals messages in his clothing. The runners provided a vital component of British communications, especially when it came to the need to carry messages into and out of the besieged towns.

large part to play in supporting the war effort of both sides. From the start thousands of Africans undertook military duties in support of the forces of both the British and the Boers in administrative, logistical and labour roles. As well as non-combatant service blacks also served as armed members of at least one of the Commandos and the British used armed Africans soldiers in the guerrilla phase of the War in block-house garrisons and during sweeps. Native chiefs were also encouraged by the British to patrol their borders against incursions by the Boers and to deny passage to Boer Commandos along strategic routes running across their lands. In return they were assisted with supplies of arms and munitions.

Where manpower was scarce, as in Mafeking, Africans were recruited into local defence organisations, and they were especially useful during the sieges for intelligence gathering and for the running of dispatches through enemy lines. As the War developed into a guerrilla campaign more and more Africans were employed with British columns as scouts and increasingly they had to be armed as the Boers tended to summarily execute blacks suspected of working with the British. The approximate number of armed Africans in British service is difficult to quantify but estimates have ranged as high as 30,000. The number of Africans and coloureds used by the Boers in a combat role was much smaller, though many gave excellent service on outpost duty around the besieged British garrisons.

▲
British Intelligence with a group of black messengers.

▶
Black farm workers who fought with British.

the siege of Kimberley

Of the three British-held towns that found themselves under siege as the Boers advanced into Natal and Cape Colony, Kimberley was in a military sense probably the least important. In a wider sense, however, it possessed two major attractions for the Boers. First it was the site of the De Beers diamond mines and second that imperial tormentor of the Boers, Cecil Rhodes, was inside the town. Faced with these twin attractions the Boer command abandoned its strategic rationale and allowed its Commandos to become embroiled in a four-month siege. The Boers did not even make a sustained attempt to take Kimberley by storm, preferring instead to compel its surrender through artillery bombardment.

The task before the town's commandant, Colonel Robert Kekewich of the 1st Loyal North Lancashire Regiment, was the defence of an 11-mile perimeter with a garrison that comprised a Regular army element of 400 men of the Loyals, a company of the Royal Artillery and the Royal Engineers, plus 2,000 volunteers raised by De Beers and 1,500 mounted Cape Police. Kekewich regarded the De Beers volunteers as something of a problem as they provided Cecil Rhodes with an opportunity to interfere in the conduct of the defence. Before Boers arrived outside Kimberley in strength on 15 October 1899 Kekewich had taken the opportunity to construct a chain of field fortifications around the town.

◄

A drawing room in Kimberley 'sandbagged' against the effects of shellfire. As the Boer bombardment grew more effective it was often the practice to sandbag both the exterior and interior of buildings.

Kimberley had a total population of approximately 50,000 of whom over 15,000 were natives. The speed of the Boer advance meant that few families had been evacuated before the enemy cordon closed. There were thus literally thousands of women and children caught up in the siege. With this size of population a major problem of any long-term isolation of the town was bound to be the supply of food and water.

The bombardment of Kimberley had begun on 7 November at a distance of 4,750 yards, well outside the effective range of the defenders' seven-pounders. Many shots fell inside the town killing women and children, much to Mr MacLennan's fury.

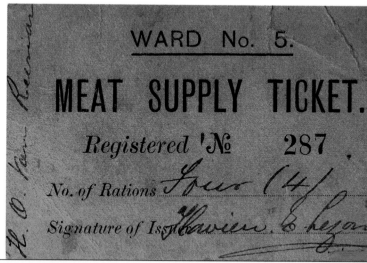

WARD No. 5.
MEAT SUPPLY TICKET.
Registered № 287
No. of Rations *Four (4)*
Signature of Iss...

Monday, October 16

AT THE VERY START OF THE SIEGE, WHILE THE BOER INVESTMENT WAS STILL FLUID, **MR H V MACLENNAN**, AN ENGINEER AT KIMBERLEY'S WATERWORKS, PERSUADED COLONEL KEKEWICH AND HIS MANAGER MR FORD THAT HE SHOULD BE ALLOWED TO ATTEMPT TO SLIP THROUGH THE BOER PATROLS TO ONE OF THE TOWN'S PUMPING STATIONS. IT WAS TENSE WORK:

'Just as I was leaving the office the Colonel passed. Ford asked him if there were any Boers about the mid station and he said they were all around that part. Ford at once said I was not to, but I got around him and told him I would be very careful and another thing I said, "We want water in Kimberley, and we have 1,900,000 gallons in the mid reservoir; why not pump that into Kimberley?" Martial law had been proclaimed. I had to get a pass from the town commandant to get outside Kimberley...When I got within two miles of the mid, I knee haltered my horse and crept along the koppie to the left of the mid. I got within 1,000 yards of the station and watched it for some time, but could not see anything like a Boer. I went back to my horse and rode right into the mid. I rung up Mr Ford and told him everything was right, so he sent one of the engine drivers and as there were three boys at the mid, we soon got up steam. It took us three days to pump the reservoir dry. Mr Ford would not allow us to stay there overnight, as the Boers might take it into their heads to give us a look up, so we left every night at 6.30 p.m. and out again at 6 a.m. The second days pumping was exciting as some Boers came over the rise and had a look at us. I stopped the engines and got the horses ready so that we would be able to clear out if they came. They stayed watching us for about an hour and then left, so we started pumping again. That same afternoon, two boys came from the river station (not waterworks boys) and told me the Boers had taken all my things and smashed up everything they did not care for...They also told me that the Boers were going to blow up the water works.'

Too late, the Boers cut Kimberley's water supply on 18 October.

An earth and sand-bag redoubt constructed by the British as a defence point against Boer attack during the siege of Kimberley. ▶

A TYPICAL REDOUBT
KIMBERLEY
(DURING THE SIEGE)
BOER CAMPAIGN
1900.

F.H. HANCOX,
PHOTO.

Monday, November 13

BEFORE THE BOERS ARRIVED **DE BEERS** HAD ENSURED THAT KIMBERLEY WAS WELL STOCKED WITH SUPPLIES AND BY 29 OCTOBER THERE WERE STILL 70 DAYS' RATIONS AVAILABLE. AS THE SIEGE LENGTHENED KEKEWICH TOOK STEPS TO RE-PROVISION. HE ALSO ATTEMPTED TO OVERCOME THE INDIFFERENCE SHOWN BY THE TOWNSFOLK TO THEIR OWN SAFETY DURING BOMBARDMENTS:

'About 60 cattle were brought in to-day by natives; I have offered a reward for each beast, and natives will I hope be able to drive off a few of the enemy's occasionally. In the early morning a reconnaissance was arranged by Lt. Col. Scott Turner of all the Mounted Troops. They started at 3 a.m. in the direction of Carter's Farm and the Lazaretto; very few Boers were seen, and some of their guns may have been moved; none could be seen although the advanced patrols got within 800 yards of the works the enemy kept well out of sight, but immediately on our men returning, they sent men forward into the position we had just left; there was no firing. About 70 shells were fired by the enemy to-day from the positions near Lazaretto and Wesselton – very little damage done. A cab driver received a compound comminuted fracture of the arm, and his horses killed. Notwithstanding the many cautions I have issued in the newspapers and by other means to the inhabitants they are still very careless indeed about shell fire; they could easily go to places quite out of danger but they seem to enjoy seeing the shells burst and natives at once run and dig them out, and sell them for good prices in the town.

There is quite a brisk trade going on in shells and fuses. I have to-day completed arrangements for the better protection of the large numbers of natives in the compounds in case of shells falling on them; they will be taken down the mines (if they will go there) or to other places of shelter which have been erected behind old debris heaps; at night they will be taken back to the compounds.'

The Norval's Pont railway bridge after it had been destroyed by the Boers. The bridge, over the Orange River, was 1,632 feet long and the Boers dynamited the centre spans. The bridge was quickly repaired to enable the railway to carry supplies through to Roberts in Bloemfontein.
▶

Saturday, December 9

ON 9 DECEMBER, **MACLENNAN** FOUND HIMSELF A TARGET FOR THE BOER GUNNERS DURING ONE OF THE REGULAR SALLIES BY THE DEFENCE:

'Was out with Capt. Cumming in the morning, when we saw the mounted men under Lt Col Peatman supported by the L.N.L. regiment and D.F. artillery go out by way of Kampers Dam, but had to retire. I was in the fight all day. I nearly got done for. The fight was over; our men had retired. I was standing in the open holding my horse and talking to Lynch, who was in plain clothes. When all at once the 9 pounder from kampers dam let bang. The shell fell about 200 yards to our left. They tried another over us. I said to Lynch, "they seem to be firing at us". Lynch got on his horse and rode to where the last shell fell. "Bang", another from the same gun. It went bang into the ground, not more than four yards in front of me, covering me with dust. I picked it up and found it to be a shrapnel shell. It must have gone off after it went into the ground, as the bullets are all gone. If that shell had burst in the air, as it should have done, myself and my horse would be no more. I have got the shell and will send it home.'

the siege of Ladysmith

Once hostilities began the British forces at Dundee, Glencoe and Ladysmith were insufficient to secure the frontier of Natal and were therefore dangerously exposed. A retirement across the River Tugela was, however, felt to be inadvisable psychologically and also because it would lead to the loss of Ladysmith and the destruction or capture of the extensive military supplies carefully assembled there. The flurry of British attacks on the Boer advance into Natal could not stop General Joubert's Field Force covering the last few miles towards Ladysmith on 29 October 1899. A reconnaissance conducted by General French with the 18th and 19th Hussars discovered nearly 12,000 Boers closing on the town, and it

was clear that unless decisive action was taken Ladysmith would soon be surrounded. To the north of the town on Pepworth Hill the Boers had already emplaced one of their six inch 'Long Tom' guns. In Ladysmith, General Sir George White, the British Commander-in-Chief in Natal, made plans for a dawn assault on the Boer positions. With the failure of this attack at Lombard's Kop on 30 October and the precipitate withdrawal of White's troops into Ladysmith, panic spread through the civilian population in the town. The supposed security of White's protection now looked little more than a chimera, and the night trains leaving for the south were packed with people fleeing Ladysmith who had left their

A birds-eye view of the siege of Ladysmith. A British observation balloon floats over the town. Such stylised views of British colonial battles and campaigns were produced as a commercial venture and proved to be highly popular.

▶

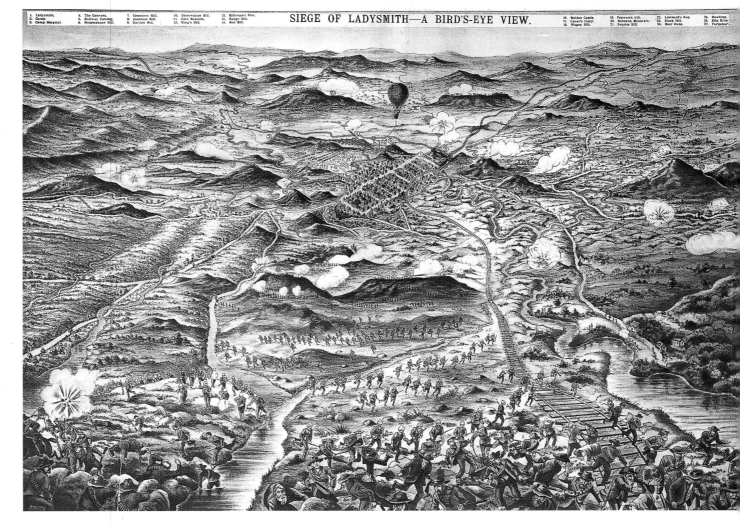

SIEGE OF LADYSMITH—A BIRD'S-EYE VIEW.

1. Ladysmith. 4. The Convent. 7. Cemetery Hill. 10. Observation Hill. 13. Rifleman's Post. 16. Maiden Castle. 19. Pepworth Hill. 22. Lombard's Kop. 25. Dewdrop.
2. Camp. 5. Railway Cutting. 8. Junction Hill. 11. Cove Redoubt. 14. Range Hill. 17. Cæsar's Camp. 20. Bulwana Mountain. 23. Black Hill. 26. Klip River.
3. Camp Hospital. 6. Helpmakaar Hill. 9. Gordon Hill. 12. King's Hill. 15. Red Hill. 18. Wagon Hill. 21. Sunrise Hill. 24. Boer Guns. 27. Farquhar.

Thursday, October 19

THE BOER ARTILLERYMAN **GUSTAV PRELLER** RECORDED HIS IMPRESSIONS OF THE SCENE HE SURVEYED AT LADYSMITH:

'A long straggling dorp [small town or village] at the foot of a rocky ridge. To the east extends a level plain through which twists and turns the Klip river. As far as Bulwana Kop is in our possession. First named ridge divides the town from the military camp, in itself a small town of zinc buildings W. of the town. North of the military Camp a series of ridges runs from West to East and form with aforementioned ridge a V. in the corner of which the M. tents are now pitched. North of the plain between the town and Bulwana Hill are some more stony ridges now strongly entrenched by the enemy. To the South of the plain before mentioned is Platkop likewise in possession of the enemy, and to the East also ridges in which are schanzes [redoubts or entrenchments] like small Kaffir kraals. East of the town, on the plain, we are nearest to the town, 6,000 yards. Probably trenches near the town. Since the siege started we have approached 7,000 yards nearer.

Our positions: At a distance of 6,700 yards north of the town near the Hoofdlager there is a Long Tom, together with other guns. From there at about the same distance, all the prominent kopjes, of which there are many here, are in our possession, all higher than the town. From thence our cordon extends westward along a series of ridges – here a portion of the Freestaters. Further west of the town where the main road from Maritzburg crosses ridge and where the road turns off and a fight took place, all ridges occupied, and further round Platkop to a very prominent flat peak south of the town but a little distance removed, is the main body of the Freestaters. From there a series of uneven red ridges to where the railway and river pass through poort, and then Bulwana Mountain 6,000 yds to the east of the town with another Long Tom and other ordnance, from where town is easily covered. Town deserted. Now and then a man on horseback through the streets. In the centre two Red Cross flags still wave. At the foot of Bulwana Mountain many hundreds of tents – during the day hardly any movement to be noticed in the camp covered with high gum trees – large number of slaughter oxen in circle 12,000 yds in diameter. To North of Bulwana Mountain, Lombards Kop, a high peak, also in our possession with plateau thereunder.'

Tunnels and dug-outs in the bank of the Klip River below the camp of the Imperial Light Horse. The tunnels were later destroyed by flooding. ◄◄

A Boer howitzer at Ladysmith surrounded by its crew. ◄

Friday, October 20

GUSTAV PRELLER TOOK PART IN THE BOER ATTACK UPON MAJOR-GENERAL SIR PENN SYMONS,
FORCE AT THE BATTLE OF TALANA HILL (OR DUNDEE):

'Never to be forgotten day. About 2 o'clock our advance guard got into touch with the English outposts and we heard firing. After waiting a little the burghers divided and stormed three of the kopjes in sight. We waited a little while and then were informed that the kopje in front of us (a flat oval kopje) was unoccupied and had been taken. We immediately advanced and ascended the kopje and about a quarter to five the first Krupp was in position and about 15 minutes after opened fire on the English camp which could be clearly discerned in the growing light, at about 4 to 5,000 yards. At the 5th shot they also opened fire. Meantime there was terrible confusion in the enemy's camp, the well directed shots bursting between the tents. The cavalry and infantry trekked out from the camp and took position behind some ridges. One battery took up a position in the camp and one to the left thereof. Later another battery took up position against us. In a few minutes it was made so warm for us on the Kopje that the cannon fire on our side was suspended. The English fire was good but the range of the shrapnel was not so good as it might have been, otherwise the position could not have been held for a minute. After about an hour and a half the guns were withdrawn and the British Infantry attempted to storm the kopje from two sides but were repulsed. Meanwhile the cannons were removed from the kopje and taken eastwards to another kop, but later brought back again. The Hussars had meanwhile got behind us on the level ground and Lood ventured a sortie with two Maxims. A heavy fight took place on the plain and a Maxim captured with two officers and two men. About 250 English fell, 50 or 60 burghers in hospital. According to returns of Commandants and Field cornets 106 of our people killed and wounded. English general (Symons) mortally wounded. The Hussars were pursued and several killed. The Maxims returned and the retreat was sounded. We then retired but not before Lood had placed a couple of well directed shots among a company of Hussars to the right of our position. It began to rain and it became bitterly cold.'

belongings behind and their businesses untended. By 2 November 1899 the Boer net had closed and all telegraphic and rail communication between Ladysmith and the south ended at 2.30 pm. The defenders of Ladysmith, now fully encircled by up to 20,000 Boers, continued to defend the town's 14-mile perimeter with their garrison of 12,000 men. The daily Boer artillery bombardment was largely ineffective once the sick and wounded had been moved out of the town, and the civilians had taken up residence in man-made caves in the banks of the Klip River. The British force at Estcourt to the south of Ladysmith maintained intermittent communication by searchlight, heliograph and pigeon post, and dispatched an armoured train to Colenso only 15 miles from Ladysmith's perimeter.

The Boer investment was not the tightly-knit cordon of troops and strong points that would be seen in European warfare, and while there were skirmishes and assaults on both sides they were comparatively few and far between. The main ingredients of siege warfare in South Africa were artillery bombardment and severe boredom. A Boer Commando under General Ben Viljoen cut the railway between Glencoe and Ladysmith at Elandslaagte and captured a goods train. A second Boer column under the command of Lucas Meyer crossed the Buffalo River and advanced to within striking range of General Symons' garrison at Dundee. A third, and the largest, Boer column under the command of General Joubert occupied Newcastle and then pressed on towards Glencoe junction.

The SS Avondale Castle en route for Delgoa Bay in Portuguese East Africa was intercepted in international waters by HMS Partridge, and escorted to Durban where £25,000 destined for the National Bank of the Transvaal was removed and placed aboard HMS Tartar. Nearly 5,000 political refugees, who were to all intents and purposes completely destitute, arrived at Lourenço Marques. The British Consul was allocated £5,000 from the Mansion House Fund to relieve their plight while shipping was arranged to transport them to Durban.

A Boer laager on the veld outside Ladysmith.
◄◄

Boers on sentry outside Ladysmith.
◄

Thursday, November 2

IN LADYSMITH **BREVET-LIEUTENANT COLONEL S H RAWLINSON** WAS PRESENT AT THE TRAGIC OUTCOME OF AN ARTILLERY DUEL WITH THE BOERS:

'6.15 a.m. the 4.7 Naval gun began firing at Long Tom who was battering us a good deal. The Naval 12 pounders also opened fire but they could not get the right range and dropped very short indeed sometimes. We went up and watched the practise till breakfast time. The enemy 6" gun ['Long Tom'] shot beautifully. Put two shells right alongside the 4.7 gun and one of these landing about a foot to the right of the right gun support took off poor Egerton's leg at the knee, smashing also his other foot. He was taken off to hospital, both legs were amputated but he died in the evening from the shock. He refused to take cover with the rest of us. The jack in the box game was rather amusing – one could always see the 6" gun fire and as the projectile took 14 seconds to arrive we had plenty of time to get under cover when we saw the flash. The whizz bang then found us comfortably ensconced between rocks so that no damage was done. However, Egerton insisted on standing alongside his gun and not moving to take cover.'

Ladysmith — Nicholson's Nek — Oct! 30th 1899.

INDIAN BAKERY SIEGE OF LADYSMITH
BOER WAR 1899-1900

T OF SHELL FIRE SIEGE OF LADYSMITH
BOER WAR 1899-1900

In the light of the demoralizing defeat at Talana Hill and the increasing pressure from the Boers, General Sir George White ordered General Yule, Symons' replacement, to retire on Ladysmith. After a four days' gruelling march in appalling weather Yule's force finally joined the garrison at Ladysmith. During the Battle of Talana Hill it had suffered a total of 446 casualties.

The British requested that the Boer government should allow the United States Consul at Pretoria to transmit a weekly list of the British prisoners held there with a note of their state and health. The High Commissioner, Sir Alfred Milner, gave permission for Captain Scheibel of the German warship Condor to observe arrangements at Cape Town for the disembarkation of British troops and the conditions on board transports.

Communications with the besieged towns were increasingly exercising the minds of the British command. General Buller received a suggestion that communications could be opened with Ladysmith through the use of Cardew's buzzer (an electronic code sent via the railway lines) and instructions were issued as to its use. Another solution was provided by the Royal Navy. Sir Redvers accepted a navy searchlight and crew from the Naval Commander-in-Chief, and asked that it be despatched to the Orange River.

Thursday, November 9

GUSTAV PRELLER WAS INVOLVED IN A CLASH WITH THE GARRISON AT LADYSMITH:

1 | The scene in Ladysmith on 30 October 1899 ('Mournful Monday') as Sir George White's troops retire after the failure of their attacks upon the Boers at Nicholson's Nek and Pepworth Hill. White was shattered by the disastrous outcome of his plan and two days later the Boers completed their isolation of Ladysmith.

2 | The ovens and fuel supply of an Army bakery at Ladysmith.

3 | The effect of a near miss from a Boer artillery shell during the siege.

'In the morning early while we were still sleeping a heavy cannon fire commenced on all sides, but the enemy's fire was mainly confined to the north of the town in the direction of General Joubert and the Pretoria people, between the position of our men and the town, where later on heavy musketry fire developed interrupted by the booming of guns. We battered those points where we detected or suspected the presence of the enemy and now and then got a shot from the big English gun. Where the shell burst we saw various colours of smoke – greenish yellow and black... At 10 o'clock a terrible musketry fight developed to the South of the town (probably the Standerton and Utrecht commandos) and for some time the fight continued thus on both sides of the town. On the South it waxed as hot as I have ever heard. The British volley firing could be easily distinguished from our irregular fire, varied with cannon fire from both sides and our Maxim fire. This fight was confined to and extended along the plateau right in front of our position. The fight to the north of the town lasted about two and a half hours. The enemy later on opened fire with about eight guns, as it appeared, from the plateau on to our people below. Their fire was hot and rapid, but the effect, as it appeared later on, very slight. (three Standerton men wounded) Capt P. then opened fire on them with Creusot and later on the big gun, also fired on them, and silenced the British fire. We however received information, and could see, that our people were stuck up behind a ridge in front of the enemy, and could not move. Groothaus also let us know that the shield of the Krupp and the spring of the Maxim were damaged. Repaired later on. No further mishaps. Burghers escaped in darkness although we saw the enemy's cavalry manoeuvring to cut them off. Big gun placed a fine shot in the British schans about sundown. General left for the council of war. A peaceful night.'

Thursday, November 30

AFTER A MONTH OF SIEGE WORK **GUSTAV PRELLER** WAS FINDING BOTH THE ROUTINE AND THE WEATHER VERY TRYING:

'A very sickening routine seems to have set in now. In the morning we rise, walk on the ridge with our telescope, and take a view of the country in front of us, until the sun gets warm – then we take breakfast – then the monotony sets in. From 10 o'clock starts the terrible heat – the sides of the tent are buttoned up – and we are either sitting talking, reading, writing, or lying down sleeping until dinner time. After dinner there is still less movement, for then the heat is intolerable. The same routine again, only we undress ourselves now as far as possible. In the afternoon, we ride some distance this time to the station near the Red Cross Hospital. The day further passed off peacefully.'

The elevated view from a sandbagged defence position at Ladysmith. ▶

Wednesday, December 20

AFTER NEARLY TWO MONTHS OF SIEGE LIFE **LIEUTENANT COLONEL RAWLINSON'S** THOUGHTS WERE
TURNING TO THE EVENTUAL OUTCOME AT LADYSMITH:

'2 p.m. Much cooler today. In the veranda of Christopher's home the thermometer registered 103° at 10 a.m. yesterday. Today at the same hour it registers 67°. We all feel much fitter in consequence but with these enormous changes we have to be very careful of chills. Sir George is not very well today he has a slight go of fever... I see the Boers have got two of our field guns up in the old emplacement on Gun Hill. I hope they have not got ammunition for them in any quantity – really it is a case of "save me from my friends" to have Bullers guns pounding away at us besides those which the Boers have already...

I keep on wondering and wondering what will be our eventual fate. In another month we shall begin to feel the pinch of hunger and by that time shall be able to tell pretty well what will happen to us. We must do one of three things:

1. Either we shall break out at all costs, or

2. we shall be relieved by Buller, or

3. we shall eventually have to capitulate on account of sickness and starvation.'

the siege of Mafeking

Of the three sieges in South Africa in 1899 the siege of Mafeking was the most famous. The image of a gallant and energetic defence maintained by the outnumbered garrison and the sufferings endured by civilian and native at the hands of a cruel and overbearing foreign invader, fitted well with the ethos of late Victorian Britain. Mafeking came to represent more completely than anything else that strange blend of patriotism and xenophobia which was Jingoism. Hysterical celebration on the streets of London and paeans of praise from the great and the good followed the eventual relief of the town in May 1900. The myth and substance of the siege came to represent special qualities in the British character: heroism, service, sacrifice, duty and stoical endurance. The siege shot the garrison commander Lieutenant-Colonel Robert Stephenson Smyth Baden-Powell to what today would be the equivalent of worldwide stardom. In the space of the siege Baden-Powell was transfigured from a man with an image that betokened the nickname 'Bathing Towel' to simply 'BP'. Yet Baden-Powell should never have been in Mafeking since he had orders to raise two regiments of irregulars for service as a guerrilla force to harass the Boers. Instead, at a time when the Cape government was opposed to any increase in the defensive strength of Mafeking, he took his men into the town and assumed command during the 217-day siege.

The defence

Mafeking's six-mile perimeter was defended by 1,600 men, (few of whom other than Baden-Powell and his staff were regular soldiers) including 500 watchmen and cattle guards. They were pitted against a force of between 5,000 and 8,000 Boers under the command of General Piet Cronje. Among Cronje's subordinate officers were J P Snyman and 'Koos' de la Rey. When the Boers arrived at Mafeking they found that the defenders had already been hard at work. They had constructed bomb-proof shelters, defence positions that were linked on a telephone network and mine-fields of dynamite. They had amassed food and equipment stocks and improvised an armoured train. Mafeking was a small but prosperous town with a population of roughly 1,500 whites and 5,000 natives from the Barolong tribe. The natives lived mainly in the nearby settlement of Mafikeng. On strictly military grounds, Mafeking could and probably should have been by-passed by the Boer advance and left to be mopped-up at a later date. In practical terms, however, Mafeking was important administratively and logistically to British control in South Africa. Although situated in Cape Colony, Mafeking was the hub of the administration of Bechuanaland and a railway centre en route to Rhodesia. Baden-Powell's adoption of Mafeking as a local defence priority also served to focus Boer attention on the town and the military stores it now held.

From its start the siege, after a few initial skirmishes, was a comparatively civilised affair which settled into a lengthy artillery bombardment and trial by long range Mauser fire. There was no full-bloodied assault on the defences and Cronje and Baden-Powell even tacitly agreed a code of conduct for the prosecution of the siege. There was to be, for example, no military activity of any kind on Sundays and this was strictly up-held by both sides. Cronje also tried to respect the Red Cross flags on ambulances and buildings as well as the non-combatant status of the women's camp and the convent, although the Boers were highly suspicious of some of the uses these areas were put to by the defenders. Baden-Powell did not hesitate to assail General Cronje with protests over any bombardment of these areas, the exact position of which had been clearly described to the Boers. Cronje retorted that as a number of his officers had clearly seem a Maxim gun being fired through the windows of the convent it was a legitimate target for his artillery.

Deadly souvenirs

Although the population had to rely upon caution and a degree of luck during the bombardment, only four white members of the population were killed by shellfire during the siege. They did, of course, have to spend time underground in bomb-proof shelters but even these could be described as being similar 'to the cabin of a yacht'. As Sol T Plaatje, a black African interpreter to the resident magistrate in Mafeking, recorded in his diary, many Boer shells failed to explode on impact and they became the raw material for a flourishing souvenir trade: 'I have not mentioned that when a shell was not well-charged it does not explode when it reaches its destination. People pick them up and sell them; and townsfolk pay for them as follows:

one-pounder Maxim Shell	@ £ 10-6
The new five-pounder	@ £ 2-2-0
A seven-pounder	@ £ 15-0
Au Sanna	@ £ 6-6-0

Prices are on the ascent as shells are becoming rare. ('Sanna' formerly sold at £3-0-0.) Yet even if 'Sanna' does explode people do get money for her fragments. The base only fetches 10/6d and the numerous fragments may bring the total for one explosion up to two guineas. These shells are therefore a boon in one sense.'

There was dissatisfaction among the town's population as the siege progressed, particularly in respect to escalating food prices and the apparent indifference of the British authorities to their relief. But while complaints about the quality of some of the food supplies were legitimate, the white

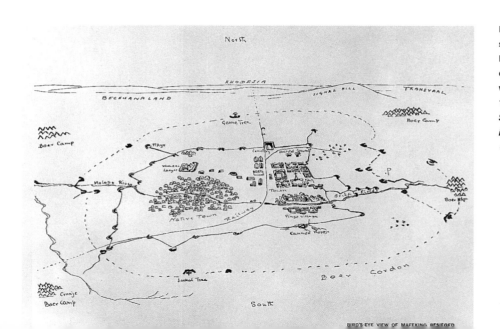

BIRD'S-EYE VIEW OF MAFEKING BESIEGED

Baden-Powell's sketch plan of Mafeking and its defences. The plan was published in 1907 in his book *Sketches in Mafeking and East Africa*. ◄

▲
A one pound siege note issued at Mafeking in March 1900. The siege notes were issued by the Standard Bank on the authority of Baden-Powell.

Private look-out in Town 1

Siege 1899 of Mafeking
Portions of shells fired by Boers into Woman's (Oct.) Laager. (Nov

population was never in real danger of starvation. On 15 November 1899 Baden-Powell could report that the white defenders of the town still had rations for three months, although the position for the natives was more problematic. The general health of the besieged, who totalled 1,074 white men, 229 women, 405 children, and 7,500 natives, remained relatively good throughout.

There was also friction between the Town Guard composed of 300 civilians and the few Regular officers in Mafeking. The members of the Town Guard frequently felt that they were shouldering the burden of the defence but received in return scant respect or appreciation from the military.

Sometimes the Boers stretched the bounds of the Sunday armistice a little too far for Baden-Powell's peace of mind as he recorded in his staff diary: 'Finding that the enemy come strolling without arms near to our lines evidently looking about for mines and reconnoitring – sent their Commanding officer a note requesting their immediate withdrawal to their own lines otherwise I should be compelled to break the Sabbath and fire upon them. I instructed my messenger to get into conversation with the Boers and tell them that we did not want to disturb the peace today as we were holding a holiday in honour of a big victory we had news of. Bands would play and fireworks in the evening.'

Baden-Powell was ever alive to the possibilities of positive propaganda and the need to stamp out rumour. As the siege progressed many of the population became convinced that 'BP' was managing the information they received. This possibility caused considerable resentment in Mafeking and the war correspondents who were present during the siege also came in for a good deal of negative criticism for what many regarded as their uncivil and loutish behaviour.

As the defenders of Mafeking were barely enough to man the perimeter Baden-Powell could not risk a major clash with the Boers in the open. He was fully aware, however, of the need for some offensive action by the garrison to keep morale high and to throw the Boers off balance from time to time. Baden-Powell therefore carried out a policy of small, brief raids which could be broken off quickly before the Boers could concentrate in response.

1 | An improvised look-out post in Mafeking during the siege. Timely warning of the firing of a Boer gun usually enabled the besieged to take cover before the actual arrival of the shell.

2 | Issuing wood supplies during the siege at Mafeking.

3 | Stage-coaches outside Dixon's Hotel in Mafeking. Baden-Powell's headquarters was next door to the hotel.

4 | A display of the parts and contents of shells that landed in the Women's laager in Mafeking. Collecting Boer shells was one of the main pastimes in the besieged towns; it proved a profitable activity.

Wednesday, November 15

BADEN-POWELL HAD TO TAKE ACTION WHEN THERE WAS STRONG SUSPICION THAT HOARDING OF FOOD SUPPLIES WAS TAKING PLACE AMONG SOME OF THE MERCHANTS IN MAFEKING:

'Finding some unexplained discrepancies in the returns of merchants stocks of food stuffs at the beginning of last month and this month, it seemed to me that false returns were being rendered. I therefore issued notice that if, on inspection, stocks were not found to agree with amounts shown any surplus would be liable to confiscation. This proposal caused considerable stocks to be remembered which had been omitted from the returns sent in. My idea is to buy up all Native food meal at reasonable rates and to resell to the Natives, thus keeping the price within their means and checking the issue. The amount issued to whites I should reduce by a 1/4 pound as 3/4 pound of meal will make over 1lb of bread when baking in small quantities. Possibly it may be desirable to buy up, similarly, a great part of the flour and meal and issue in rations to save waste and the expense of famine prices later on. It would always be saleable – probably at enhanced prices.'

1 | British defence positions offering only a low profile to Boer snipers.

2 | A Boer artillery piece is loaded ready to open fire on Mafeking.

3 | Baden-Powell with officers of the Protectorate Regiment posing at Ramath-labama camp.

4 | A Boer position outside Lady-smith protected by barbed wire and a sandbag redoubt.

Thursday, December 10

ALONG WITH THE OTHER OCCUPANTS OF MAFEKING **SOL PLAATJE** TOOK HIS EASE ON A SUNDAY, OFTEN IN A PHILOSOPHICAL TURN OF MIND:

'The usual gaiety and merryments took place in the afternoon. There being no danger I took the pony and went out for a ride around 'disputed territory' and saw the Boers so close that I nearly felt inclined to go over and have a chat with them as they were seated on the ridges of their trenches looking at games played so merrily round our camp with longing eyes; this however is a serious crime and I cannot bring trouble upon myself in that manner. They undoubtedly wonder of what stuff we are made, to look so little the worse for this long Siege. I wonder whether they have forgotten that while Cape Town and many important colonial towns have been seats of Dutch governments and still wear Dutch names, Mafiking has since its creation never been cursed by being a Boer Laager, despite strenuous endeavours to make it such. It still bears the name given it by Tau's band of Barolong, who came from Lake Ngami in about 1750. They were a peaceful lot of men, yet they plundered everybody who dared interfere with their migration, and earned for themselves the title of 'Baga Rungoana le Bogale'. To return to our subject: these West Transvaalians ought to remember that Mafeking has always held her own against becoming Dutch and the only Boer who ever owned Mafeking was the one who swore by the honour of the King. It is a pleasant day; fair and cloudy, with an occasional shower every now and then.'

BOER FORT AT MAFEKING

FORT DER BOEREN MAFEKING

Q 575

COPYRIGHT MIDDLEBROOK DURBAN

VAN HOE P. RETO

Thursday, December 14

ALTHOUGH THE RISK OF DISEASE WAS USUALLY MORE OF A POTENTIAL DANGER TO THE DEFENDERS THAN THE BOER ARTILLERY FIRE, **SOL PLAATJE** RECORDED THE TRAGIC EFFECTS OF THE BOER SHELLING IN HIS DIARY:

'"Sanna" was quiet all the morning and commenced duty in the afternoon. The first shot made straight for poor Sibale's house. It was full of people – women and children – including Uninikazi, Mrs. P. Sidzumo. It pulled and shook the whole house upon them: pieces of shell or the house cut off her toes, shattered her legs and injured her face and head. The left leg was broken below the knee (and the thigh completely shattered). The other people remained alive in the debris. The poor husband, coming to see the remains of his house, was met with the ruins of his wife just pulled out of the debris. He became so senseless that he returned to the fort hardly knowing what he was doing until they told him that his wife wanted to see him. He jumped up in joyous bewilderment – for he had first imagined that she was dead already – and had a look at her before she was moved to the hospital. This was 3.45 and she died at 6.00 in the evening, leaving the husband and a little girl to mourn her loss.

We are very hard up for news. More despatch runners went out last night but returned to say they found the Boer lines impassable. We had always received two despatches every week. Now we have not received any for ten days and we really feel the strain.

Mrs P. Sidzumo was buried at 3 o'clock this morning. She had been in the Stadt yesterday afternoon and her husband came to call her back to the scene of yesterday's disaster. They went to the location together. When her husband proceeded to the trench she remained at her ill-fated home, and waited unconcernedly for the hour of this sudden tragedy. The little girl is not cognisant of her bereavement and plays about well at her Granny's place.

There was a fight at the Natal border in which General Joubert's forces were completely disorganised and large numbers of them killed, General Joubert himself being taken prisoner. We have heretofore received nearly all our news by telegraph, from the Boer Laager, whence it was conveyed by our people into Mafeking. Mistakes have, of course, been made with regard to names, locations and numbers and casualties, but they may be excused on that score as they are no mathematicians or scholars of any kind. Now even if Joubert himself is not caught we will say that it is some very important personage whose arrival deserves considerable fuss in the Transvaal.

Even the Mafeking Mail, which regards the native as a mere creature, was this day wont to say: "Although the following statements from the Native sources may only be rumour retailed, so many of the reports brought to hand through similar intelligence have been corroborated by official report received some weeks later, that we feel disposed to give more credence to a Kaffir ipse dixit than we formerly have done."

Anyhow if official intelligence is to be relied upon there were, at the end of last month, 10,000 Troops in Ladysmith and General Buller was advancing with 25 000 more. If truth is not stranger than fiction, what then prevents such large armies from catching the old General? I cannot make out why we are not getting any despatches, for we have people other than letter-carriers going out and coming in. There must be something radically wrong in it.'

"OH WHAT A RELIEF! QUITE LIKE OLD TIMES"

OGDEN'S GUINEA GOLD

Mafeking relieved at last.

Tuesday, December 26

SOL PLAATJE RECORDED THE RESULTS OF ONE OF BADEN-POWELL'S HARASSING RAIDS IN HIS DIARY:

'Early this morning we were aroused by the sound of big guns, muskets and Maxims towards Game Tree. It lasted for nearly an hour, then all was quiet again. It was a good number of the garrison endeavouring to capture a Dutch fort at Game Tree. FitzClarence figured among the ringleaders again and everyone was sure that – bullets failing – he would capture the Dutch fort at the point of the bayonet, but they unfortunately found it a tough business. They got up to the fort and were preparing to jump right into it amongst the Boers. But the walls were so high that only a few managed to get on top. Even here they could do nothing as the trench was too well roofed and the Boers, who meanwhile had their rifles through the loopholes, played havoc with them until they hoisted the Red Cross. FitzClarence alone got inside and stabbed two or three. They shot him once but he proceeded to bayonet another when they shot a second time and he dropped down – though not dead. (Three who went to the door of the trench were taken prisoners.) He is now in the hospital improving. I think [that] the wounding of FitzClarence incapacitates an eminent 'moguli' from taking part in future operations against the Transvaal, when the Troops cross the border. The Boers never hit so hard a blow on Mafeking since they besieged us. Altogether we lost 23 men killed and 26 wounded. The rest of the day was quiet.'

the war at Christmas 1899

Both combatants began the War with a great deal of confidence, though their optimism was largely born of ignorance. Many British participants and observers believed that the War would be over by Christmas 1899 and that the result would be victory for the fighting men of the British Empire. Instead it was now abundantly clear that the British had seriously underestimated both the fighting quality and the resilience of the Boers. Equally, the republics had no clear conception of the military strength that was about to be turned against them. The Boers were also extravagantly hopeful that they would find ready and powerful allies in Germany, Holland, France and Russia. With the exception of the support of

several hundred foreign volunteers, who at times could be more of a hindrance than a help, military assistance from the European Powers had failed to materialise.

The failure of the Boers

Strategically the advantages lay principally with the Boers at the start of the War. They held what were essentially the interior lines of communication and could thus potentially switch the Commandos to decisive points more quickly and effectively than the British. They had also prepared well for the conflict in terms of munitions and they were able to arm their forces

Weihnachten 1899 vor Ladysmith

◀

The Boer forces investing Ladysmith celebrate Christmas 1899 in high spirits and with a good deal of optimism.

adequately as they were raised. Their rapid progress into Natal and the Cape together with their early tactical victories drew further manpower and Afrikaner support to their cause. The Boer Command had the further advantage of two months' active campaigning at the start of the War before the British were able to deploy any kind of decisive strength on the battlefield. Yet by Christmas 1899 the Boers had effectively lost their opportunity to defeat the British forces in South Africa and secure an early peace on their terms. By tying down their strength in the futile investment of the beseiged towns the Boers allowed the initiative to pass to the British. The Commandos were neither trained nor equipped for the static and painstaking nature of siege warfare where engineering skills and firepower counted for more than marksmanship or mobility. Although the besieged British garrisons were concerned at the prospect of civilian casualties and by the risk of defeat through lack of ammunition or food reserves, they were not overly worried that the Boers would conclude the sieges by a rapid military breakthrough. In effect the besieged towns were almost mutual prison camps as some 16,000 British and local troops in the three garrisons occupied the attention of 25,000 Boers plus the majority of the republics' artillery resources. That the Boers fell into a strategic trap which was fatal to their chance of victory was due to a number of factors.

▶
British casualties are evacuated by train.

Christmas 1899

THE FREEDOM FOR THE INDIVIDUAL TO TAKE AS MUCH OR AS LITTLE OF THE WAR AS HE WISHED WORKED AGAINST THE EFFECTIVE DEPLOYMENT OF BOER STRENGTH. IN HIS DIARY **GUSTAV PRELLER**, THE BOER ARTILLERYMAN, SUMMED-UP THIS CONTRADICTORY APPROACH TO WINNING THE WAR AND HOW THIS DICHOTOMY, WAS IN FACT ONE OF THE COMMANDOS MAIN TACTICAL STRENGTHS:

'Having had to move about with our guns, like toys, this happened more freely with our burghers, who in every respect are considered extremely capable of making rapid movements, from a foreign point of view no order seems to exist, and the first thing they do is to pass remarks about the same. He who wishes, fights, the others do nothing, this however is entirely wrong. Thousands of our men are at home or in the laagers, it is too true, that if these people who are still in their homes after what has happened, were brought here, they would not amount to much, which the General knows, and consequently they are allowed to remain at home or wherever they are. Towards the end of December the Acting Fieldcornet of Pretoria informed us that they were as many as 2000 burghers fit for active service in Pretoria alone. If the officers do not keep a watchful eye over this, many of his men will remain at home when he gives orders to saddle up, many close their eyes to this knowing that they then only retain the pick of their men.

This then is the second purification which the commando experiences, and this is the reason if it was still being sought for why Boers were on Majuba, and why nearly everywhere in the hottest flights a comparatively small number of Boers delivered the fight, and stood against overwhelming force for hours with a bravery which even commands respect from our enemies, rest assured however, that it is only the pick of our nation and the flower of our troops who fight, for the purifying process is only known or seen by volunteering. If one or other plan is made and the enemy must be taken back in a manner different from the usual way (or the fixed position) then orders given to the Commandants and Fieldcornets to be there in a certain time with a specified number of men, provided with 300 rounds of ammunition and provisions for three days before it is considered that the expedition will be necessary or ammunition will be required. In as short a time as is possible everything is in order, three days provisions includes also macintosh,

and if possible blanket, if not the macintosh is ample and does service in case of rain or cold. They march out, and if it be necessary put on a spurt, which one can only realize when you are an eye witness to the same, if not the mounted commando moves with the utmost precaution, slowly, making use of all natural and other protection and ready to act at any moment, everyone rides as he chooses, smokes, talks freely and cheerfully, etc.'

Notwithstanding the continued tactical effectiveness of the Commandos, in strategic terms the Boer conduct of the War was to become increasingly passive. By December 1899 the tide of Boer conquest was beginning to ebb and the anticipated rising of Afrikaners in the Cape had failed to materialise. Before Buller had done anything of significance the strategic initiative was swinging inexorably towards the British as their strength continued to grow.

Prominent among them was the practical autonomy afforded to the individual Commando and the stress placed on the initiative of local commanders. By encouraging a fragmented view of military operations this worked against the implementation of a war-winning strategy and the effective exploitation of success on the battlefield. The Boer Command had also shown a distinct reluctance to achieve victory at any price. With no more than 90,000 men available for military service in the republics, mounting casualties could not only jeopardise the effectiveness of the Commandos but also the existence of the State. Thus when a Commando encountered serious and sustained opposition its senior officers would feel justified in pulling out of combat.

The failure of the British

For the British the first three months of the War were a chastening experience. Not only were they roughly handled in the major clashes of the campaign, but while their soldiers displayed considerable heroism their senior officers repeatedly demonstrated the tactical limitations of their experience. Their overwhelming reliance on frontal attacks in the early months cancelled out the British soldiers' courage and fortitude.

Tactically the Boers had enjoyed uniform success. The individual and collective strengths of the Commandos – marksmanship, mobility, field craft and flexibility – had confounded the British on the battlefield time after time. Even where the British could claim a local victory, through the eventual withdrawal of a Boer force as a result of sustained pressure, the respective casualty figures often told a different story. In both brief and more sustained actions the Commandos were usually able to inflict a casualty ratio on the enemy that was close to 4:1. During the opening months of the War British troops, whether victorious or defeated, thus paid a heavy price. It was, however, a price the British could afford to pay. The Boers, after their initial successes failed to persuade the British to make peace, could not sustain even a comparatively low rate of casualties indefinitely and still win the War.

► **Winburg Commando in Pretoria. The Boers believed that the voluntary aspect of their Commando recruitment meant that the soldiers within it were more passionate about the cause, and thus better soldiers.**

the British offensive

the strategic position

As 1899 drew to a close neither Briton nor Boer could look back on the first three months of the War with much satisfaction. The Boers had won a string of victories on the battlefield but the results of their endeavour were essentially local and transient. The British had suffered setback after setback but they, of the two combatants, could look forward with the greatest degree of optimism as it would be their strategic rationale which would be imposed upon the War in the coming months. At the year end, however, few British soldiers were feeling in an optimistic mood. Letters from South Africa reverberated with the tragedy of the battlefield as name after name of comrades and friends who had been killed or maimed filled the pages.

The humiliation of 'Black Week' (10–15 December 1899) had meant that Buller's removal as Commander-in-Chief in South Africa was a matter of course. Field Marshal Lord Roberts of Kandahar, Buller's replacement, met with Lord Kitchener of Khartoum, his Chief of Staff, at Gibraltar on 26 December. During the voyage to Cape Town Roberts and Kitchener finalised a plan of campaign for dealing with the Boers.

Climbing Spion Kop. 109

▲
British troops taking up firing positions on the slopes of Spion Kop. Throughout the battle Warren remained largely ignorant of the desperate predicament of his troops on the western summit.

Warren's advance

A new year, a new campaign

By January 1900 Buller had to a large extent overcome the failure of self-belief that had followed 'Black Week', and he still retained the support of an overwhelming majority of his officers and the respect and affection of his men. Christmas did much to boost morale after the setbacks of December, and the festive period was celebrated in some style throughout the officers' messes of the Natal Field Force and with sports and entertainments among the ranks. However, after three weeks of inaction, and with the Boers apparently equally comatose, there was a growing feeling in the Field Force that it was time to attempt to seize the initiative from the enemy. Before Buller could show whether he was capable of responding effectively to this challenge, the Boers struck at Ladysmith on 6 January with a hard-pressed attack centred on Wagon Hill and Caesar's Camp. In beating off this assault, which continued for over twelve hours, the defenders suffered more than 420 casualties including 45 officers. The possibility that Ladysmith was on the brink of collapse spurred Buller to action and in forwarding General White's report of this engagement to the War Office he added a note: 'I start as soon as possible. For some time I have feared that, in Ladysmith, all has not been very well.'

Sir Charles Warren and the 5th Division

Buller's spearhead in this fresh advance upon Ladysmith was to be the recently arrived 5th Division commanded by Lieutenant-General Sir Charles Warren. A Royal Engineer, Warren came to his command via service in South Africa, Bechuanaland, Egypt and Singapore, an unsuccessful candidature for the parliamentary seat of Hallam in Sheffield, and three years' tenure as the Chief Commissioner of the Metropolitan Police during which he failed to apprehend Jack the Ripper. Fifty-eight years of age, Warren was a soldier full of colourful and original ideas but he lacked recent experience of warfare, logistics and administration. He was also a thoroughly disagreeable character who succeeded in alienating all around him, and he did not get on well with Buller.

Spion Kop

In launching another attack against the Boers on the Tugela, Buller chose to ignore the words of counsel from the Commander-in-Chief, conveyed by telegraph, advising that any thought of decisive action should be postponed until further reinforcements had arrived in South Africa. Rather than

Friday, December 22

COLONEL J W HUGHES HALLETT OF THE SEAFORTH HIGHLANDERS AT THE MODDER RIVER:

'Not much news and not much heart to give it if there was. We are stuck here for the present as we have not sufficient force to go on with. This is a horrible hot place and so dusty. We are within sight of the enemy three miles off and are entrenched here. No news of Kenneth. Personally I have absolutely no hope of his being alive. I have written Mrs Kenneth by this mail. Sergt. Peter Thompson went down by train to Capetown yesterday. He is very cheerful poor chap. He was shot through both legs high up, but is going on well. Sergt. Trussell is also doing well. You might write a line to their two wives to tell them. Fluffy will I fear always be lame, the bullet went right through the foot smashing all the small bones. Waterhouse will I hope pull through, but I fear he is very seriously wounded. Wilson had a wonderful escape. The bullet hit a knife just over his heart and split, wounding him in 3 places. Baillie and Clive are very slightly wounded in the foot and ankle. Chamley is badly hit in the left arm and chest. How *any* of us escaped is to me a mystery under that awful fire for 10 hours from three sides, and all for nothing. All because Lord M. blundered, not poor Wauchope. I know they will try to blame him, but I have done my best to make things quite clear. I hope now the worst is over and we shall not be called on to sacrifice ourselves for nothing. Our time must come soon though things look black at present.'

pouncing on the enemy with speed and secrecy, Buller transferred his army and its entire supply column at a lumbering pace, and in full view of the Boers, westward from Colenso to Springfield. His target was to be either Trichard's or Potgieter's Drift and he planned to take the Boer positions by direct assault. Heavy rain turned Buller's route into a morass of mud which brought men, wagons and horses to a slithering, sprawling halt. At times only the few steam-traction engines which accompanied the column could make steady headway. The movement from Colenso to Springfield of food, ammunition and equipment in 324 wagons (each making a double trip), which started on 10 January, took seven days to complete; ample time for the Boers to realise what was coming and take appropriate action. Buller's plan was to launch Warren's Division on a five-mile march to cross Trichard's Drift in the belief that this would turn the right flank of the Boer positions at the hill of Spion Kop. Once they had turned the position the 15,000 men of the 5th Division would, it was hoped, be able to advance into the plain beyond. It was not Buller's original intention that Warren should capture Spion Kop, merely that he should outflank it.

As Buller had moved from Colenso so had the Boers. While they contemplated Warren's fastidious preparations to cross the Tugela, the Boers used the three days (17–19 January) it took to prepare the springboard for the British attack to entrench their men and mount their guns. In order

to roll-up the enemy flank Warren's troops found that once they had crossed the Tugela they had to cross ground dominated by the heights of Tabanyama and Spion Kop. This would be suicidal if the Boers were strongly established with artillery on either plateau. Warren was operating without adequate maps of this ground and he did not reconnoitre the Boer positions. He had also chosen not to support an advance by the Earl of Dundonald and his Mounted Brigade which had reached Acton Homes and thereby already effectively turned the Boer positions controlling the road to Ladysmith.

On Monday 22 January Buller, in a rare intervention in the conduct of the battle, told General Warren for the first time that he must take the 1,740 feet high Spion Kop and hold it. At 11 pm on 23 January 1,700 men of Warren's command began to climb the hill, without the assistance of guides or the advantage of prior reconnaissance. By dawn they had driven the Boer picket from the plateau of Spion Kop, but as the British troops attempted to dig trenches through the solid bed rock they encountered only 18 inches below the surface they could see little of their surroundings because of a thick white mist. As the mist began to lift the British troops realised that their shallow trenches were not on the forward edge of the plateau but set back, thus affording the Boers dead zones from which to mount attacks. When the mist finally cleared it was immediately obvious that a difficult

Ambulance wagons conveying casualties after Spion Kop while in the foreground British troops man a trench overlooking the veld.

▼

situation was in fact a disastrous one. The British 'trenches', located on the western half of the plateau, were overlooked to the east by a hill named Aloe Knoll and the Boers began to pour concentrated rifle fire into the British troops causing terrible casualties. Throughout a day of tragic confusion and muddle Warren did little to bring effective aid to the men on Spion Kop. Tortured by thirst and unable to bring proper aid to the wounded, men died by bullet or artillery shell, fell asleep in the midst of the fighting through exhaustion, and clung to whatever natural cover they could find. With his men in this deadly situation Colonel A W Thorneycroft ordered the evacuation of Spion Kop under cover of night. During the day the British had suffered over 1,000 casualties to little avail.

Ironically, at the moment when Thorneycroft ordered the evacuation of Spion Kop the Boers were also in the process of pulling their men off the heights. The intensity of the battle coupled with the few tentative outflanking movements made by the British during the day had caused considerable panic in the Boer ranks. For a time there was the possibility of a general retreat from the Tugela and only Louis Botha's personal intervention with his men held the defence together. As it was, Spion Kop was unoccupied by either side for nearly two hours during the night of 24/25 February. Buller, far from dismayed at Warren's failure to hold Spion Kop, ordered a general retreat back across the Tugela.

Vaal Krantz

Buller was anxious to break through to Ladysmith before Roberts and Kitchener were in the field. This at least would restore some lustre to his tarnished reputation. Accordingly, having tried to defeat the Boers on the right and centre of their position he now attempted to do the same on their left at Vaal Krantz. If the British could move with speed the auguries for the attack were good. Many of the Boer Commandos, believed that after Spion Kop the British would make peace, and had taken leave. Buller's attack on 5 February faced only 4,000 Boers and victory seemed assured. Speed, however, was not part of Buller's conception of the battle and by the time the main attack went in the Boers, undeceived by a feint attack, were massed exactly at the point where the British had signalled they were about to cross the Tugela. Worse, Buller ordered that the advance be halted mid-way through the attack thus committing the leading brigade to an assault on Vaal Krantz by itself. Even as the regiments of the brigade gained a foothold on the crest Buller ordered their commander Major-General Neville Lyttelton to withdraw. Lyttelton ignored the order but eventually on 7 February, and in the absence of any enthusiasm from Buller, the realisation that the original plan was failing was unavoidable and the British withdrew and retreated to Chieveley. This time Buller's defeat cost of some 400 British casualties.

Monday, January 22

PRIVATE W A PYE, WEST YORKSHIRE REGIMENT:

'Paraded under arms about 4 am. Our Brigade was on Convoy Guard. After breakfast we had a bath in the Tugela. Had to lay about in the blazing sun all day. Felt properly done up. Fighting was going on in front of us which we could see plainly... In the afternoon, we were ordered to go to the front. We were not so long before we were in the firing line when it come on dark, we were moving about the best part of the night getting into position for morning. It was a terrible march up the hills. Every now and then one would fall over a boulder or else into a hollow. Then it commenced raining we got wet through... At daybreak we were in the firing line, firing away as hard as we could go. We had our Maxim gun with us. We remained in the firing line till about 2 pm when we were relieved by the Border Regt. The enemy's bullets and shells were, pouring round us like rain. We relieved the Border Regt again about 6pm and held the position till about 8am the following morning... Making about 49 hours in position and under fire. The average number of rounds fired by each man of the Regiment was about 500 and our rifles were like bars of hot iron.'

Boer dead lying on the battle-field of Spion Kop. The Boers suffered some 300 casualties compared with British losses of 1,200.

◄

Wednesday, February 24

PRIVATE JAMES MCGOWAN, B COMPANY THE KING'S OWN (ROYAL LANCASTER REGIMENT):

'Dear Ted,

I have received the parcel for which I am much obliged to you. You will have seen from the papers about the four days battle 20th to 24th. The last day was the worst for our Brigade as we lost about 1,000 killed wounded and missing. We marched all night and got to the top of a hill on which the Boers had an outpost. They fired a few shots and then retired to their entrenchments, but at daybreak they commenced a regular storm of shot and shell until dark, men fell in all directions, and had to lie, as it was death to stand up. If you wanted to shift you had to crawl on your stomach. We got no food or drink all day, wounded men asked for water which we had not got. We have not had our clothes off this month, and do not know where we going next. I do not think that in spite of all the troops we are making any progress towards the termination of this war. They will have to alter their tactics or they will be outwitted by the Boers who are so clever at concealment. Tell me if you can how this war is going. We have heard that supplies of food have reach Ladysmith but do not know if this is true. With love, your brother Jim.'

When Buller called off the attack on Spion Kop the Boers assisted British medical orderlies and stretcher-bearers in the task of retrieving the wounded from the battlefield.

►

SPIONKOP AFTER THE BATTLE

NA DE SLAG

Friday, February 26

LIEUTENANT R J K MOTT, THE QUEEN'S (ROYAL WEST SURREY REGIMENT):

'We seem no nearer to the relief of Ladysmith! I wonder if we shall be able to manage it at all, and what will be our next move? You see, the whole of the North side of the Tugela is commanded by a high range of hills, stretching the entire width of Natal, and as the Boers have fortified the whole place, and can move their men, who are all mounted, very quickly to a threatened position, it is like attacking a fortress for us. I think we shall have far more men by attempting to relieve Ladysmith than there are in Ladysmith, and I believe it would be better in the end for Sir George White to cut his way out. Of course at present the war outlook is very serious, but we must remember that the Free State and Transvaal will be far easier places for our troops to fight in than this natural defensive ground of Natal.'

Roberts' re-organisation

Lord Roberts was respected by the troops, and his partnership with Kitchener was a key factor in Britain's success.

Roberts and Kitchener arrived at Cape Town on 10 January 1900 and immediately started the process of preparing the South African Field Force for an advance that was to penetrate deep into the Boer Republics. Roberts was now aged 67, and he had lost his only son at Colenso in the December fighting, but Kitchener who was only 49 would effectively act as Roberts' second in command. Although Roberts and Kitchener had widely differing temperaments – Roberts being approachable, kindly, and genuinely concerned for the welfare of his troops while Kitchener was stiff, aloof and ruthless – they formed a fluent and effective working partnership. One result of 'Black Week' was an expression of the Nation's determination to see the War through to a victorious conclusion. The enthusiasm of volunteer soldiers to fight against the Boers facilitated the despatch of militia battalions, yeomanry regiments and units such as the City Imperial Volunteers for service overseas. By the middle of February 1900 the strength of the British forces in South Africa had grown to 179,846 with more troops (4th Cavalry Brigade and 8th Division) on their way from the United Kingdom. Of this force approximately 128,000 were Regular troops and 1,000 had been supplied by the Royal Navy. Even with this strong influx of numbers from the UK, less than 20% of this force were mounted troops. The Boers, as they had had throughout the war, possessed a marked advantage in speed and mobility whenever they chose to employ it.

Logistics and mobility

As the Field Force grew in size so the incidence of disease, and particularly typhoid, among the troops became a commensurate problem. By the beginning of February Roberts was urgently calling for more 'civil surgeons' to be sent to South Africa from town and country hospitals in the United Kingdom, and for additional personnel to man another field hospital. The general health of the troops was affected principally by a lack of vegetables in their diet and by the scarcity of fresh water on the veld. As a result men marching long distances or engaged in battle would drink from polluted rivers without regard to the severe risk to health that these represented. Logistics had also been a problem in some areas with wagons carrying food and equipment often lagging hours or even days behind the troops they were meant to supply. This was the case particularly with some of the civilian supply contractors who understandably did not feel that they were bound to endure Boer artillery and rifle fire in order to get supplies to the troops. As a result of this, men on active operations could, at times, find themselves going without a meal, or even as much as a dry biscuit, for over 36 hours.

The first and major alteration brought about by Roberts and Kitchener was in the reorganisation of the transport and supply system used by the Field Force and set up by Buller.

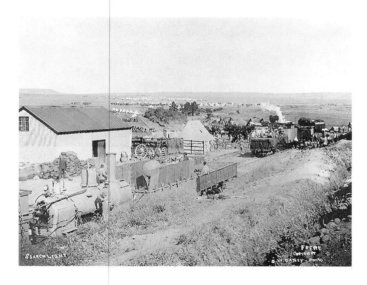

◄

A searchlight mounted on a British train. Searchlights were used by the British for signalling and, during the guerrilla phase of the War, for illuminating the veld in front of the blockhouse line.

►

Bullock handlers and drivers with Roberts' column break for a meal.

Kitchener switched from a supply system that worked principally at regimental level to one which was centralised on transport depots run by the Army Service Corps. This led to considerable chaos, and a partial return to the former method of supply using transport controlled by the regiments had to be tolerated. Roberts was more successful in turning the thoughts of his troops, and in particular those lately arrived in South Africa, to the task of preparing to meet the Boers, tactically, on equal terms. Roberts increased the proportion of mounted infantry in the Field Force and formed a cavalry division under General French. He began to tackle the lack of suitable maps through the Director of Military

Intelligence and issued a pamphlet to the troops, *Notes for Guidance in South African Warfare* which stressed the tactical and personal skills required to beat the enemy. For Roberts, fire and movement, individual marksmanship and the brave seizure of the initiative were the ways forward. In future the Field Force would prepare carefully for each operation and, while carrying out as thorough a reconnaissance of the enemy as possible, would seek to shroud its own intentions in secrecy. Roberts even went so far as to keep his own journey to join his troops on the Modder River a closely guarded secret. In a generous gesture Roberts left Buller in command in Natal.

the British advance

While in England Roberts had not been reticent about airing his views on the progress of the war in South Africa or upon Buller's lack of experience of independent command. Now that his turn to settle with the Boers had finally come he chose to adapt and develop the strategic plan which had been outlined before Buller's campaign had begun. Roberts planned to base his operations solely on Cape Town and the railway which ran from there to Kimberley, before turning east to advance upon Bloemfontein and Pretoria. With this plan Roberts threatened not only the respective capitals of the Republics but also Boer communications across the whole of their battle front. The first target, however, was the relief of Kimberley.

On 8 February 1900, when Roberts reached the Modder River, he had some 37,000 men and 113 guns available for operations against Cronje. The dash for Kimberley was to be undertaken by the Cavalry Division supported by infantry (6th and 9th Divisions) and a brigade of mounted infantry. The Cavalry Division rapidly out-distanced the infantry in an epic march (11–15 February) which saw it swing east from Ramdam before, in an ingenious and daring manoeuvre, riding through the centre of Cronje's defensive position at Klip Drift. French and his troopers eventually reached Kimberley on the afternoon of 15 February thus ending the siege (*see* page 98).

British field artillery firing on Boer positions during Buller's abortive assault on Vaal Krantz at the beginning of February 1900.

▼

After Vaal Krantz, Roberts realised that Buller had completely lost his nerve and he urged him to remain on the defensive in Natal. Buller cried out for reinforcements but the troops now arriving at the Cape were destined in the main for Roberts' push into the Boer Republics. Displaying admirable patience, Roberts agreed that Buller might make forward movements provided that they did not compromise the safety of his Field Force. Buller, exhibiting a mounting grasp and confidence that surprised his staff, decided on a fourth attempt to break through the Tugela positions to Ladysmith, this time by moving east and sweeping in a wide arc around the left flank of the Boers at a line of hills called Monte Cristo. On 12 February Buller's troops began a series of assaults on hill features which took them progressively nearer to Ladysmith. By 20 February the Boers had given up hope of holding the south bank of the Tugela and, although they were to give the attacking British troops a stiff reception at Wynne Hill and Inniskilling Hill, their resolve was weakening under sustained pressure. The constant and accurate fire of the British artillery, coupled with infantry attacks which at unit level exhibited both dash and intelligence, had worn the enemy down. By 28 February Buller had broken the Boer defence and the enemy was in flight from the Tugela. On the evening of that day two squadrons of Dundonald's mounted infantry entered Ladysmith.

British mounted infantry from the Leicestershire Regiment move up in January 1900.
▶

Wednesday, February 14

HOWARD DENT, CIVIL SURGEON WITH ROBERTS' FIELD FORCE:

'The wounded from Reusberg are in bad state. Several wounds septic and one man at least hit by an explosive bullet. One trooper of Australian contingent was wounded by fragments of stones thrown up – he had dropped 11 Boers consecutively as they were getting over a wall. Tonight taking in 40 wounded from Reusberg and 40 from Modder... In one case some *Buckshot* have been extracted. Anaesthetised for amputation of arm for gangrene following gun-shot of forearm – bullet must have expanded, exit wound tremendous size – vessels destroyed, done on Monday last.'

British troops unharnessing dead horses from a supply wagon. Nearly 670,000 horses, mules and donkeys were procured during the War at a cost of £15,000,000. The majority were purchased in South Africa but many thousands were obtained in North and South America, Austria and Australasia.

▶

SAPPER WALTER PELLS, A ROYAL ENGINEER, SERVING WITH FRENCH IN HIS DRIVE ON KIMBERLEY:

'After all the troops arrived here besides us, were formed up we were 30,000 strong, which formed the relieving column for Kimberley. This column which was under General French, where everyone are mounted men, so as to be able to move quickly if required. Us, 'C' Troop Pontoon were the only dismounted troops in the whole column, but we rode in our pontoons. We again changed mules here, this time for artillery horses and drivers so as to be able to move as fast as the remainder of the column. We were only about six miles from the Boer position here...'Arrived at a place called Klip Drift, on the Riet River, at about 4pm. After the Boers retreated the day before yesterday they made for this place which they strongly fortified in the direction they arrived here and the way they thought we should have come in. That was the reason we did not come by the main road, but we went around about way, and so we arrived quite the opposite way to what they expected us to, and took them by surprise and captured their laager and a number of prisoners.

We covered 90 miles between here and Ramdam, besides working and fighting. We found the river fordable, so all we had to do was to cut the banks down for the cavalry and the artillery to go across. After this we left the column here, as we were not required again with them, this being the last obstacle between here and Kimberley which was only twelve miles from here.'

British infantry resting on the veld during an advance in February 1900. ◀

Sunday, February 25

LIEUTENANT R J K MOTT, THE QUEEN'S (ROYAL WEST SURREY REGIMENT):

'We have been having a terrible time and poor Hastie has been killed – the most loved of our Officers. On 14th February we moved from our beautiful Blaaukrantz camp to Hussar Hill; bivouacked there for one night; and then occupied another small hill E. of it, where we stayed 2 nights. Next day we carried out a reconnaissance towards Cingolo, which we occupied on Saturday the 17th after slight opposition. The Queen's had to make an all-day flank march through awful country, in terrible heat and without food or water. On Sunday we attacked the left of the Boer position. The Queen's and W. Yorks gallantly assaulted the highest and steepest parts – called "Monte Christo". The brigade of Rifles took Green Hill. The Boers retreated very hastily across the Tugela, having been under terrible artillery cross-fire previous to being charged. They left their laagers standing and burned their provisions. We captured lots of ammunition and some ponies. Next day we occupied the Boer laager and shelled the remaining Boers off

Hlangwani. On Tuesday we occupied Colenso, and the Queen's crossed the river on Wednesday morning. After breakfast a shell or two landed among us, but nobody was touched; a piece of shell narrowly missed me and my pony. Since Wednesday we have been giving the Boers a heavy bombardment, and gradually advancing Northwards. We cannot, however, silence their guns, which are splendidly sited and magnificently handled; their shooting is excellent, so is their sniping, even at a range of 2,000 yards! We are losing men rather heavily, but doubtless so are they. Our men are having a very trying time; I have to be on the go half the night, taking rations up to them: cannot go in the daytime as our oxen would be too good a target. Tracks are difficult to find in the dark, and the Regiment keeps changing position, and the sniping is too close to be pleasant. Poor old Hastie was killed by an explosive bullet; he was dead before they could get him to hospital. Warden was dangerously wounded by a shell in the face; he will probably recover, though

he must have a fearful face – he is a pitiful sight. Whinfield has been slightly wounded, and so has McNamara. The fighting has been going on for 8 days and 6 nights – and every day good fellows are being hit. Early this morning all our guns recrossed the Tugela, and were to proceed Northwards and again cross by a punt made by the R.E. The object is to catch the Boers by enfilade and reverse fire. If we can take the high ground North of Pieter's station we shall have turned their left flank, and should be able to get into Ladysmith soon. Frank Middleton [Dorset Reg't] has been badly wounded in the thigh; I am going to see him at Chieveley today, if I can. I never told you that, in the attack on Monte Christo, Sillem, Mangles and Bottomley were wounded, but not badly, I am glad to say; Sillem is the worst. It is terrible, the way the Boers pick out Officers; we have had 2 killed and 14 wounded up to date in all battles.'

the relief of Kimberley

Kimberley had the honour of being the first of the besieged British garrisons to be relieved, but this did not occur until 15 February 1900.

As they waited patiently for the breakthrough that would pierce the Boers' cordon, the defenders of Kimberley were resigned to a daily diet that included a large proportion of enemy shellfire, a diminishing proportion of food in issued rations, and a small but regular proportion of casualties. In such conditions the overall health of the population suffered and a growing number of cases of mild scurvy were

Thursday, January 24

LIEUTENANT-COLONEL ROBERT KEKEWICH, THE GARRISON COMMANDER:

'At about 4 a.m. this morning enemy commenced a heavy bombardment of the town, and between that hour and 9 a.m. threw about 150 shells into the town. The only casualty I have heard of is that a white woman was killed in her house.

Enemy appears to be firing 9 guns:

1 from Smidt's farm;
1 " Kampersdam
3 " Carter's ridge (2 being cordite)
1 " Alexandersfontein (Cordite)
2 " Wimbledon ridge
1 " Olipantsfontein Kop.

I am trying to arrange that Kaffir Beer be issued to all, but there is a difficulty in getting it brewed quick enough, and I have little Kaffir corn to spare for this purpose.

Enemy continued the bombardment of the town, Beaconsfield and the Premier Mine, and counting those fired in the morning from 300 to 400 shells must have fallen, about half of these were at Beaconsfield. Two women and a dog were killed. We have really been very lucky. The two cordite guns from Carters ridge are the most dangerous and have a longer range; shells from them have fallen into Belgravia a distance of about 8,000 yards.
The commissioners I appointed consisting of Col. Murray and R. Duncan estimate the numbers drawing food supplies are as follows:

Defence forces	4500
Europeans, Cape coloured	28468
Asiatics	1520
	34488

Natives including 2100 in De Beers Compounds and 850 in convict station	22276
	56764

These numbers are arrived at from the various food supply depot registers, and De Beers and Military returns. On the 6th Dec the Mayor, Mr. Rhodes, the Medical Office of Health and others calculated the numbers as 44,400, and as about 7,000 De Beers compound boys have left about 37,000 only should now be in the town. Owing to all the available men to take it being employed on the Defence works I have been unable to arrange for a Census to be taken. I shall now much as I regret it have to reduce the ration of bread stuffs slightly.'

noticed, particularly among the Town Guard. Repeated sorties were made to capture some of the Boers' supply of cattle grazing outside the defences, but red meat alone could not fulfil the dietary requirements of either fighting men or civilians. These problems were of course on a large scale since, with a population of over 50,000, Kimberley had the greatest concentration of civilians of any of the besieged British towns.

While the large population of Kimberley was a disadvantage during the siege in terms of supplies and casualties, the fact that so few people had left the town meant that the myriad skills to be found in the business and industrial community could be put to good use. Mr George Labram, De Beer's Chief Engineer, had used the skilled labour resources of the diamond company to construct a four-inch gun during the siege with which to hit back at the Boers. Sadly Labram was killed by a shell from the Boers' six-inch gun while in his room at the Grand Hotel. To escape the deadly firepower of this weapon some 4,000 men, women and children went down into the De Beer's mines after Cecil Rhodes had sent placards round the town urging them to do so. While it undoubtedly saved lives, Rhodes' initiative caused not a little panic and also considerably complicated the feeding arrangements in the town.

February 1900

MR H V MACLENNAN ENGINEER AT KIMBERLEY'S WATERWORKS:

We are having an awful time now. The Boers have a six inch gun firing into Kimberley from Kampusdam. 100 pound shells are no joke. Everyone is under ground. Lynch and myself have to be on duty, in case of fire. Called out for a fire owing to a 100 pound shell going through the house. Had to get the water on; the whole house burnt down. Saw a woman and child killed by a 100 pound shell. It was an awful sight. God help the first Boer I get in my power. The Boers have now killed poor Labram. I was with him for two hours just before he died. He just went upstairs to wash his hands and I stayed below. Bang went the gun. We all waited to hear the burst, when it struck the very hotel we were in. You should see the dust that came down the stairs; everyone thought the hotel was on fire. I went outside to have a look at the damage, when I saw that it was Labrams room that had been struck. Poor chap he was in an awful mess. His head was nearly off. His heart was taken clean away and his left leg was just hanging on by a thread. I took his death badly as I knew him so well. He was buried on Saturday night at 8 pm and the brutes of Boers shelled his funeral. All the women and children went down the mine. Col Harris the Col of the town guard also went down the mine. Lynch and myself never went underground once and we slept in our rooms every night. Not many people in Kimberley did that.'

By the time French's Cavalry Division burst through the Boer positions around Kimberley 1,694 of the inhabitants had been killed during the siege. Of this total 134 Europeans and 433 non-Europeans were under the age of five.

5.30 A.M ON THE MARKET SQUARE
DURING THE SIEGE OF KIMBERLEY 1900
WAITING FOR MEAT RATIONS

F.H HANCOX   PHOTO.   — S 151.

Thursday, February 15

LIEUTENANT-COLONEL ROBERT KEKEWICH DESCRIBES HOW HE CELEBRATED GENERAL

FRENCH'S ARRIVAL:

'The enemy's 6 inch gun fired a few rounds into the town in the morning, and Alexandersfontein had a very hot time of it during the morning. Early in the afternoon I received a helio message saying General French was arriving with the Cavalry div. and 5,000 men, and asking which was the best route in. It was indeed glad news. I went out to meet him and unluckily missed him, and on my return found him at the Sanatorium. I have not heard details but it certainly was a wonderful performance of the Cavalry Div.

I at once sent out all the troops at my disposal to attack the enemy's works at Diebels Vlei, and the Intermediate Pumping Station.'

CASTING SHELLS — DE BEERS WORKSHOPS

The manufacturing capacity of De Beer's workshops in Kimberley was effectively harnessed during the siege to produce ammunition, ordnance, and pumping equipment to maintain the town's water supply.

▶

MR H V MACLENNAN HAS HIS WORK CUT OUT RESTORING THE TOWN'S WATER SUPPLY:

'At last the relief column has come. The big gun is away and we are safe and sound. I am going out with our men, as they are going to the mid station. They hope to get the big gun at the mid. The Boers may make a stand there. I may have some fun tonight. The relief column will be in tonight at 8 pm. It is now 4 pm and the mounted men and guns are to leave here at 5 pm. I will give you the rest of my news in another letter. I will leave this with the office boy to post, as I may not be back in Kimberley for some time, if they manage to clear the Boers from the mid station at once. Then I will be up to my eyes in work, as we must get water into Kimberley, as soon as possible. What awful luck, Ford's house and garden is too awful for words. The house, I don't suppose he can live in again. The garden is no more, a few trees are left in it, everything else is dead. The smell of dead Boers, horses and cattle is awful. Sanitary service is evidently not known to the Boers. God knows why a nose was given to a Boer, its no use to him. By this time there was a big fight going on at Dronfield. General French with 5,000 men and 40 guns were going for all they were worth. I had a good look at it, but did not stay very long, as I had to go in and tell Ford about the engines. He was pleased to hear about the machinery being all right. I left for the mid again, and got there about 4 pm very tired. The fight was still going on. At 6.30 pm our guns stopped firing, and our men went back to Kimberley. The men and horses were dead beat the horses more so than the men. From Modder River to Kimberley in 3 days time was rather much for them.'

Cronje's retreat

British troops carry out a river crossing with the aid of a rope lifeline.
▼

With Kimberley relieved Cronje fell back eastwards along the Modder River towards Bloemfontein on 15 September. Many of his Commandos retreated with their families and the Boers were accompanied by a vast train of wagons. While the British infantry followed in Cronje's wake, elements of French's exhausted Cavalry Division left Kimberley at speed early on 17 February in an attempt to intercept the Boers at Koodoo's Drift and hold them until Kitchener arrived. Cronje almost slipped through the closing British cordon but French clashed with the Boer column as they were about to begin crossing the river at Vendutie Drift. With shells from French's artillery falling among his wagons Cronje formed his Commandos into a laager near Paardeberg and began to dig in for a siege.

JOHN LANE WITH CRONJE'S RETREATING COMMANDOS:

'From one o'clock, we get on as hard as we can, no one seems to know where we are steering for, simply following the front wagons. Sometimes four wagons abreast in the veldt, into such holes that in day time I am certain would break the wagon. Here you pass, or rather have to get out of the way of a wagon, wheels fallen to pieces, men asking you to load up their stuff, which is impossible. The night is fairly dark, no moon. Men carrying their blankets, wearied, footsore, asking you for God's sake to load them up. I never imagined there were so many foot men, but I find out most had sent their horses to good grass on a farm about four miles away, never, poor idiots, dreaming they would have to leave the 'Positions', so certain were they the British must attack there, and so certain they were of driving the British back.

A man comes riding up and says Cronje has ordered a Laager to be formed under the large Peak ... and I am to push on with all haste. Informs me the British are in force alongside of us and behind on the other side of the river, just as he says this, there comes a whirring thro the air, one shell after the other, bursting over the wagon, it is about seven o'clock, a large body of our horsemen come galloping back, making for the Koppies, and are taking up positions, there is a Pom-pom and one Krupp with them...The British Artillery searching the Koppies with shrapnel. I make the boys do their utmost with done-up oxen, to get to the Peak, where wagons are uitspanned and there is some shelter. The British have good cover, as one is not to be seen; the shrapnels are bursting all over the show. I can see our two guns galloping behind the Koppies, first to one and then another. They don't seem to be able to locate the British, the fighting lines seems to be extended three miles so far the British on the right side of the River, we on the left, i.e. going N. I see about two hundred Boers dismounting, leaving their horses at the bottom of the Koppies, climbing up in extended order, take shelter along top of Koppie behind stones and commence a heavy Mauser fire on other side, then shrapnel begins to fall like hail, not where the men are, but on another Koppie where I don't see any of our men. It is strange seeing the shells, put right behind a Koppie and you cannot make out where they come from. All along these Koppies I see being occupied by Boers. I see the two guns have taken a position and knocking up a sort of shelter. I cannot, so far, see anything of the British, only they are sending the shells pretty hot from somewhere and seem to have got the proper range. At nine o'clock get to Laager, which is protected by this big high rock, is about a hundred and fifty feet high and three-quarters of a mile long, and gives a splendid shelter, we are entirely out of view. The river is about a thousand yards off, and the British as far off on the other side. I uitspanned getting my wagon well up into the centre.'

Paardeberg: Cronje surrenders

For ten days from 17 to 27 February Cronje and his command of approximately 4,000–5,000 men, plus a number of their families, endured a siege on the open veld in which concentrated artillery fire was unleashed on a scale and intensity of duration seldom seen before in an operation by the British Army.

That the Boers were able to hold out for so long in the face of this battering by high explosive was due to the ingenuity and energy with which they entrenched themselves along the river. Cronje had formed his laager on the north bank of the Modder at Wolvekraal Farm some six miles to the east of Paardeberg Drift. The Boer positions extended for over two miles at a point where the river flowed through a cutting approximately 30 feet deep and varying in width between 90 and 300 feet. The river banks and the many dongas which ran into the cutting at right angles provided useful cover and a number of natural trench lines. The Boers extended this protection by building dug-outs in the banks of the Modder and by digging a network of trenches to supplement the defensive positions provided by Nature. The laager was ringed by commanding heights but the Boers were able to use the river cutting as a protected tactical route through their positions.

While Roberts was indisposed with a bout of influenza some miles away at Jacobsdal, Kitchener, rejecting the option of starving or bombarding Cronje into submission, decided upon an all out infantry attack on the laager on 18 February. Without allowing time for an adequate reconnaissance of the Boer positions or for his own intentions to be passed fully to his subordinates, Kitchener launched his troops on what was essentially a frontal attack. As with many such attacks in this war the British infantry could not carry their assault to success in the face of accurate rifle fire from Boers in concealed positions. Kitchener also had to deal with attacks delivered from the rear of his battle line by Boer reinforcements attempting to get through to Cronje. During the Battle of Paardeberg the British sustained over 1,200 casualties, the Boers some 300.

Saturday, February 17

JOHN LANE, AN UITLANDER SERVING WITH THE BOERS:

'In half an hour's time got up to main Laager. Everything in disorder. Horses, oxen and men all confused together, in the dark you tumble over an ox lying down, or run right into a span of oxen in a wagon. Men busy entrenching themselves about two hundred yards outside of Laager. Everyone doing the best he can for himself. They don't make one continuous trench, but each party from two to ten, who mean to stick together, make what they think the best protection, as the General has told them they will have to stick it out, till reinforcements arrive to relieve us!! The trenches are more or less in a line, behind are the wagons, then the River bank, with its numerous gullies and holes, washed out by the floods and any quantity of the usual thorn and willow trees growing on the banks and lastly the River itself. Spades, picks and shovels are sadly wanting and a good many make an attempt at a protection, simply by packing up stones and working up the sand with butt end of their Rifles.'

JOHN LANE:

'Just about seven o'clock the British opened the ball with a most terrific Artillery fire. Boers running to their trenches, others up and down the River bank, on the opposite side just the same taking place. We four have made no preparations, thinking we were safe behind the River bank. About ten yards from the wagon, there is a gully running into back of River, which will give us some sort of shelter from the shells. So into this S., Jock, one, Van S and myself, run quickly into. F. remains lying under wagon. We had hardly got into this hole, when lyddite and shrapnel were bursting all over in the Laager, just above us. The noise and shock of the lyddite is something awful. The first few minutes unstrung my nerves, especially when about the second shell burst just at the top of gully on the high ground, covering us with ground and killing four out of the eight mules tied to wagon, which made you feel queer.

This artillery fire kept on for an hour and a half. I don't think hell can be worse. We heard the cry "Dear kom de Engelsche" I knew what this was, the enemy are storming our positions we can see nothing of it, but hear the Mausers and small arms at it hard, the Boer guns, what we have of them, begin to pour forth now one continu-

ous rattle, above all you can hear the hurrahs and the groans of poor fellows who have "got it". The British storming over the open, the Boers in their trenches, well protected, only occasionally exposing their heads a small target compared to what the British gave, sometimes a full sized one. I think up to ten o'clock the British must have charged many times at all points but never got home, the Boers are too well entrenched. The loss on both sides must be considerable, especially on the British side... I see several of the Burghers dead and wounded. The fire is hot, shells now flying in earnest. The Zip, Zip, of the Lee Metfords as it goes close by you; sometimes in the ground sending sand all over your face, sometimes I imagined I was hit and said now I have got it. Men come running from the Trenches, saying ammunition was running short. I had to go over river, to show them where it was and got several boxes over under difficulties, the river strong and the boxes heavy, several boxes fell into River but suppose when it goes down will be able to get them again, or rather I should say the British I think will have that pleasure. Had hardly got into cover, when a Lyddite burst just on the top of us, painting us a nice olive green colour. About four o'clock, the British

commenced their charging tactics again, all round at every point. From here I went into a large trench dug out for the wounded, it is about forty yards long by ten feet deep and about two feet wide on top, but tunnelled in at bottom. In this hole, there were this morning now, about eighty men wounded, some badly, simply blankets to lie on, to get to see one at the further end, you had to pick your steps over the others and be very careful not to tramp on them, so thick were they packed, no doctors, wounds untended, blood clotted and bandages never removed. Several I knew I got some water and washed and put fresh bandages, torn from my shirt, where I could bandage, and tried to make them as comfortable as I could, but could not stop, if we cannot get better shelter and bombardment begins again, I am afraid, poor fellows will have a hard time of it. If I should get wounded I will watch being brought here. I remember my wife put into my portmanteau a sheet, so I run down and get it, tore it up into bandages, and leave it with a German who is attending the wounded, to use as bandages for wounds.'

As soon as Roberts heard the news of the outcome of the day-long battle he rushed to Paardeberg and overruled Kitchener's argument that the assault be renewed. Instead Roberts was determined to reduce Cronje to surrender by means of bombardment and starvation. To assist him in this process he had, in addition to 12-pounder guns and pom-poms, a battery of six-inch howitzers and the seven 4.7-inch guns of the Naval Brigade.

By 27 February the situation within the laager had deteriorated drastically. Wounded men were receiving minimal medical help, hundreds of dead and decomposing oxen and horses littered the Boer position, and food and ammunition were running low. As many as a thousand Boers had already slipped from the laager to make their way home or to Bloemfontein. And still the British artillery bombardment showed no sign of abating in its intensity. Morale was crumbling within the Commandos and there was no longer any realistic hope of either breaking out or being relieved by de Wet. The British cordon was by now too firmly established. Urged on by his officers Cronje took the decision to surrender unconditionally. In what was their largest defeat in the War almost 4,000 Boer fighting men went into captivity to spend the next two years in Broadbottom Camp on St. Helena or an even more distant exile in the West Indies and Ceylon.

General Cronje and his wife posing with some of their British guards during captivity on St Helena. ◄

A British troopship coaling at Durban after disembarking reinforcements for Buller's Field Force. ▼

General Cronje's laager at Paardeberg seen from Kitchener's Hill, 18 February 1900. Oil on canvas by Godfrey Giles. ▶

Monday, February 26

Percy *6ᵈ Lan* *'Ca*

JOHN LANE DESCRIBES THE DESPERATE SITUATION THAT FORCED THE BOERS' SURRENDER:

'A deputation has just gone over to see General re surrendering. The men refuse to stop in trenches any longer. The General has soothed them, so far, by promising to hold a Krijgsraad tonight and decide what to do. In a trench just to the right, eleven men were in it. About ten o'clock, a lyddite shell burst right in the centre, blowing seven of them to bits, the remaining four not getting a single scratch. It is simply awful. I expect we will be getting it worse every hour. At the Southern end I hear the British have advanced their trenches to within a hundred and fifty yards of ours. Small arms firing was going on hard all morning. The Burghers are afraid of a charge being made and keep up an incessant fire, if the British should get thro' there, they will sweep this side of river, force us back on their trenches to

the North. Once the Berghers get or are rather driven out of their trenches, the British artillery will simply play havoc with us. This afternoon the British artillery have been going at it strong. If this is anything like what "hell" will be, then, I fancy everyone would do his utmost to keep out of it. Burghers praying to surrender, entirely undone, gloomy looks, haggard appearance, men not having any sleep for nights, some nothing to eat, having no clothes to change. This makes a man feel bad. About eight o'clock all the Commandants and officers we have left, go over to the General for the meeting of the Krijgsraad (Council of War). Before they left this side of River the Burghers simply stormed them, saying they would not fight any longer. If Cronje did not surrender they would take upon themselves and go voluntarily

over to the British lines. Nothing to eat, stench, men lying unburied, fever and dysentery, have brought us to this. Firing still continuous, every ten minutes there is a salvo of artillery, on South side small arm volleys going. Knots of twos and threes moving around, waiting to hear the decision of "Krijgsraad"... About ten o'clock the word is passed all round from one trench to the other in silence, the word "Surrender", this must be the decision of the Krijgsraad. You hear no remarks, but everyone gives a sigh of relieve, as for myself, I say "Thank God".'

The surrender of General Cronje to Lord Roberts at Paardeberg on 27 February 1900. This dramatised rendition of the scene bears only a passing resemblance to the actual meeting between the two leaders.

▶

Tuesday, February 27

JOHN LANE:

'At daybreak, Kaiser, Secretary to General Cronje, went over to British lines with white flag with the offer to surrender, no conditions asked. As he was passing where I was standing, he said "This day's work costs us the Independence of the Transvaal". Shortly he returns again, to bring Cronje himself. The General rides over on horseback, dressed in top coat, big wide awake hat and the inevitable big riding whip (with which he has laced many a Burgher). On passing he gave orders that white flags were to be put up at instances of a hundred yards all along trenches on this side This was the last I saw of Cronje at Paardeburg. I looked over to the Laager side. There I saw flying on the desselboom of a cart (the cart being tipped up) a tremendous white flag (almost as big as a sheet). All over the place, nothing but white flags. I thought of the day when Cronje said he would never hoist the white flag "it was only Britishers did that". Circumstances alter cases. He also boasted to me on several occasions he would never allow himself to be taken prisoner. Orders now given, everyone to lay down his Rifle and cartridges at certain places on river bank, on the sides of the different trenches. This occasioned a general rush, some putting them nicely, others just throwing them down. At this time all firing had ceased, not the sound of a shot.

So ends my part in the Great Boer War of 1899, 1900, and now I am a prisoner of war in the hands of the British.'

the relief of Ladysmith

When Buller's advance troops reached Ladysmith on the evening of 28 February 1900 they were shocked to find a garrison of exhausted, gaunt men, many with their clothing threadbare, turned out to greet the rescuers. Behind them stood emaciated women and children worn out by the siege but overjoyed that the misery of the last months was at last over. The final weeks of the siege had been a fraught time for the defenders in which the stress of a daily bombardment had been exacerbated by hunger. The relief food wagons did not arrive until 2 March the day after Buller himself triumphantly entered the town. Satisfied with the effort that had been made to reach Ladysmith Buller was happy for his generally fit and healthy Field Force to rest. He rejected all appeals from his own and General White's officers that a pursuit of the Boers and their vast wagon convoy should be carried out. After the repeated failures to get through to Ladysmith since December 1899 Buller was now increasingly referred to by his officers as 'Sir Reverse'. It was also a shock to many of those on Buller's staff to learn about the telegram their

Guns of the Naval Brigade in action during the advance to relieve Ladysmith.
▼

Commander-in-Chief had sent to General White at the end of 'Black Week' urging that the garrison of Ladysmith surrender. White's officers were scathing in their criticism of Buller and with the relief of Ladysmith they now had the opportunity to air their views on his competency as a senior commander.

The collapse of the Boer siege had been dramatic. Amid panic, especially among the wagon drivers, the Boer forces raced northwards to put as much distance between themselves and the Natal Field Force as possible. Significant amounts of equipment and supplies had to be abandoned and as always after a defeat a proportion of the Boer strength slipped away and made for home.

On 1 March 1900 there were just over 10,000 men of the garrison of Ladysmith available for duty with another 2,700 sick in hospital. Only a small percentage of the garrison was in a condition where they could be counted as an addition to Buller's strength for field operations. The garrison had been besieged for 119 days and its relief was a signal for congratulations from around the Empire.

The citizens of Ladysmith line the streets of the town to welcome the relief force.
►

Monday, February 19

LIEUTENANT C.E. BALFOUR, THE KING'S ROYAL RIFLE CORPS:

'We are on very short commons now indeed and all feel very hungry always and it's beginning to make one feel a little weak though... We have rather ups and downs of spirits according to the news that comes in but taking it all round there is the greatest confidence and cheerfulness in everything going on alright. They must give all of us a fairly long rest as the men are in a pitiable state of weakness, with ragged clothes, very little boots left and I'm sorry to say covered with vermin. The town now is absolutely sucked dry and there's nothing but the bare ration to be had and very little of that. You would be amused to see how carefully all our food is made out to us in equal shares down to sugar, tea, etc, so that there should be no possibility of one man getting more than another and it's far more satisfactory so, for then there can be no grousing... My poor Colour Sergeant who was wounded on Wagon Hill died a few days ago after keeping alive for a month with 2 bullets through his head! (A fact.) The worst feature now of course is the sickness for the men are so weak that if they get enteric they just die off like flies.'

Wednesday, February 28

GUSTAV PRELLER OF THE BOER ARTILLERY DESCRIBES THE RETREAT:

'The enemy were master of the bloody battlefield and we had to flee. O terrible word: God, how have I not prayed never to see this. All was lost here. Back for home. The people are tired, it is said they have had to endure a lyddite bombardment for 14 days and are fagged. They appear to have no idea that with returning home they are also selling everything, everything that is dear to them. We slept very little that night. At 12 o'clock we arose and began to fix everything straight for departing. A lot had to be left behind, seven tents not even opened were burnt, and clothes were left lying. Terrible it was, enough to make one grey... Near Long Tom there were no oxen, it rained and enemy fired wildly from the troubled town, whose saving was so near. Finally mules arrived... Finally (about 11 o'clock) Lood told me to proceed with the guns which were there (3 French) Maxim, 2 caissons, to Modderspruit and truck. It was a bitter and regrettable journey drenched to the skin, through mud and rain, all our positions already deserted. At 12 o'clock we passed through the deserted Head laager – everything as quiet as the grave, only yesterday it was activity generally. At 1.30 we reached Modderspruit but discovered no provision had been made here for the loading of the guns. Everything was topsy-turvy here and then stood ready to clear. General J. telegraphed that the guns had to come to Elandslaagte, after having outspanned for fifteen minutes we departed again through dark mud and slush. This little distance was if possible still heavier than the former was, besides this the way was blocked with wagons, cannons etc. When the day broke we arrived at Elandslaagte. Here was a terrible sight, wagons arrived in hundreds from all sides in streams, there were thousands already.'

Black Africans celebrating the relief of Ladysmith. ▶

LIEUTENANT FREDERIC CRESWELL, IMPERIAL LIGHT HORSE:

'My dear Mag,

I hear letters are going out this afternoon in about half an hour's time so scribble a line to say that I am very well, tho' very thankful that relief has come at last, as horse and biscuit and little of that was beginning to tell on the whole garrison. However thank God this place has held out all right, and the weary four months are over and that is everything. Success makes all the past seem like a jolly recollection almost, though it is saddening to think of those who were with us at the start who are gone and to think of all the suffering one saw at the hospital camp. I think it was worth all to experience the few moments yesterday afternoon when we first caught sight of the first of our troops come in (at the time unexpectedly). At mid-day we had news that Buller had drubbed them the

previous day and our people on the hills had seen big lines of wagons trekking, but we did not think the retreat was so precipitate. At about 5 pm Alfred Edwards, Matthias and myself were standing on a low kopje near camp watching our shell practise on the Bulwana, where the Boers were supposed to be moving their "Long Tom", when we heard sounds of cheering and turning our glasses to the Caesar's Camp heights we saw the Manchesters standing on the ramparts cheering wildly. We thought they must see some of our people on the heights beyond when suddenly Matthias said "Why here they are!" and there was a body of horse between us and Caesar's Camp having skirted that and right close up to town. They turned out to be A Squadron of our regiment which had remained behind at Estcourt at the

beginning of the war and some carabineers. So that the I.L.H. [Imperial Light Horse] had the honour of being the first in riding side by side with the Carabineers. As they crossed the drift into camp we gave them three tremendous cheers and then sang "God Save the Queen" and then more cheers. I think we all felt we had never cheered before. Now it is all over one can say "Thank God" and one feels from the very precipitate retreat of the Boers that a very big step in bringing the war to a close has been taken. Let us trust that at home our people will stand firm in their determination to make no terms. All the sacrifice of life will have been in vain if the Dutch are allowed any measure of independence. There must be only one flag in South Africa, if we don't want a recurrence of this war.'

the advance to Bloemfontein

The surrender of Cronje at Paardeberg and the British relief of Ladysmith plunged the Boers' war effort into crisis. Morale plummeted, resistance to British movements was no more than sporadic and the steady stream of men returning to their homes threatened to become a flood. President Kruger's appearance in Natal at Glencoe on 1 March 1900 and the force of his personality did much to restore confidence and make a defensive position along the Biggarsberg possible. In Natal, where the danger of a complete collapse of resistance was most acute, Kruger threatened to shoot any men taking absence without leave. These setbacks also appeared to rule out any prospect of intervention by a European power, an illusion which some Boers, including Kruger, still fervently hoped for. Joubert argued that the Republics should seek peace terms immediately. Many disagreed but a telegram from Presidents Kruger and Steyn was sent to the Prime Minister, Lord Salisbury, on 5th March offering peace in return for a guarantee of independence for the Boer Republics. Salisbury's reply six days later was uncompromising and ruled out independence for either the Transvaal or the Orange Free State. The British had already suffered 12,777 casualties thus far and on 7th March their advance on Bloemfontein resumed.

Lord Roberts had 33,504 men in the field in the Orange Free State and he advanced with one infantry division on the north bank of the Modder River and two infantry divisions and the Cavalry Division on the south bank. A turning movement and flank attack by the Cavalry Division turned Generals De la Rey and de Wet out of a prepared position at Poplar Grove and forced them to fall back. It was not possible to intercept the Boer retreat because of the ground after heavy rain and the exhaustion of both men and horses in the Cavalry Division. The British lost four killed and 49 wounded during the action. On 10 March Roberts had greater difficulty in pressing forward when his centre column met stiff resistance at Driefontein in an action that resulted in 430 casualties. On 11 and 12 March the British advance was unopposed despite the leading troops being only six miles south of Bloemfontein. On 13 March the British entered the capital of the Orange Free State with hardly a shot being fired. President Steyn had moved his Government to Kroonstadt.

Roberts lingered in Bloemfontein resting his troops, who had suffered a great deal of sickness and particularly typhoid, and restoring railway communications. The Boers used this breathing space to convene a council of war (Krygsraad) at Kroonstad on 20 March. Kruger, Steyn, Joubert and some 50 senior officers attended and decisions were taken which would alter the whole character of the War. Wagons and the laager were to be abandoned and all Commandos were mounted. Tactics would centre on attacks on communications, isolated garrisons, and sources of food and supplies. A fast moving guerrilla war would be launched as soon as possible. The Boers had regained their fighting spirit.

◄

The timetable for a special train conveying Lady Roberts to Bloemfontein in April 1900.

A wagon and its team carefully negotiate a river crossing.
◄

Boer prisoners under guard at Kroonstad in May 1900.
▼

Thursday, March 8

HOWARD DENT, CIVIL SURGEON:

'No fodder for the horses. 10,000 waggons in the convoy with 20 days supplies for the troops. Hear there was some sniping into the convoy coming with us at a farm where I fancied I heard bullets "ping" as we passed last night. Rumour is that there are no Kopjes between this and Bloemfontein and maps show practically none. Lord Roberts was on Kopje watching the battle and sent messages directing the different divisions by signallers. Balloon officer made splendid drawings of the Boer position. This place called Poplar Grove a few trees of that name round a farm. This evening report going that Steyn was on field yesterday and that the Free Staters want peace. Also that OW Steyn has said he would rather give in than let buildings of Bloemfontein be blown down. A convoy of sick to be made up; tomorrow

morning early, hear that we are going to march ahead and do 20 miles. We are now just about 42 miles from Bloemfontein. Other divisions appear to be sending their sick to us and filling our hospital to the great annoyance of the C.O.

Hear a great many tales of the looting of the trenches – first in seem to have got wines (which Boers took from officers mess brought up in Convoy they captured) whiskey, jams, tinned milk, flour and meal and quaker oats. We unfortunately just come in too late for these things. Great many cases of fever (malaise, headache, pains, diarrhoea and occasionally sickness) are in hospital – some tonsillitis. Some turn out to be enteric fever.

Mail left for England today and another came in – English stamps also to be had – wrote home. Got papers

today of Feb. 12. Lancet. Lieut Greer of Lincolns said that Joubert, Kruger, and Steyn were on field day before yesterday urging their men to fight – this he got from the head quarters. Also hear that 4 snipers on kopje near trenches where we camped two nights ago hit one man on broken down waggon. One C.O. of Regt. saw pair of boots on ground near a old burrow – took hold of them and found they were on an armed Boer who was down the hole.'

The grave of the Comte de Ville-bois-Mareuil, a Frenchman who commanded the foreign corps serving with the Boers after the fall of Bloem-fontein. He was killed during an encounter with British troops near Boshof on 5 April 1900. ▶

L HAMILTON FOX, 3RD CAVALRY BRIGADE:

'The march after to Bloemfontein was another event to be in, with the various camps on the road, and excitements by the way at Poplar Grove, Drie Dam etc. At Bloemfontein itself we had practically speaking no fighting, the Boers having left, and the authorities came out and handed over the town. We were, or rather our Squadron (F) of our regiment and some of the Remington Guides, the first to enter the town, and paraded through the principal streets. Of course many of the Dutch inhabitants had left, but those that remained seemed very glum, rather a different reception to Kimberley, though we were cheered greatly and run after with cigarettes by the English there.

The other day, last Thursday, we had some sport. Officers' horses races and mens Alarm Race, Tugs of War for both, Running Races, Eating Biscuit Race (didn't I wish they had one at Koodoos Drift) and a sing song in the evening, both men and officers contributing songs, quite a change. Then, too, we had a tin of tobacco 1/4lb. Navy Cut with "The Compliments of some Friends at Home" written on it. Yesterday we had The Queen's Chocolate issued out to us, and I have just finished all mine, very good, and am sending you home the box to keep for me, and one of my shoulder badges, which I have worn since Cape Town – very cheap badly cut ones they are but I thought you might like it as a keepsake. You could if you liked better get it plated and make a brooch of it, and after the war I will send you or if I come home for a spell will bring you some more – one that has been to Pretoria!

By the bye, keep the stamps and post-mark of this letter; Aunt Rose might like them. I also enclose a new stamp, as they are Free State stamps with the British postmark over as you will see, and also a bit of the ribbon off the chocolate box. I had a few bits of shells too, some from Kimberley got during the bombardment, and others, but the Boers I guess have them now as they were with our transport waggons. I don't expect the War will be finished for at least another 3 or 4 months, and it may be another six yet before we are disbanded, but I will try and write occasionally. You need not be the least bit anxious if you don't hear for some time, as one can't always write on the march.'

the relief of Mafeking

When Roberts captured Bloemfontein (13 March) it was barely a month since he had crossed the border.(12 February) into the Orange Free State. In that time his troops had relieved Kimberley, forced the largest element of the Boer forces fighting in the OFS into a disastrous surrender at Paardeberg, evicted one of the Presidents of the Boer Republics from his capital, and cleared the enemy from Cape Colony. When coupled with Buller's relief of Ladysmith this record represented a startling reversal of British fortunes on the battlefield. Casualties were often still high in engagements on the veld but the British were learning how to defeat the Boers even when they were entrenched. The effective use of

artillery to support short dashes by the infantry, the increasing application of flanking movements rather than frontal attacks, and the greater use of cavalry and mounted infantry now presented a challenge which began to show that there was no longer much future for the Boers in set-piece battles. Yet there was still the unfinished business of Mafeking.

The situation of the defenders of Mafeking began to deteriorate in January 1900. The physical consequences of the siege – hunger, sickness, and boredom – started to take an increasing toll of the garrison's spirit and optimism. The Boer artillery bombardment intensified and there were now almost daily fluctuations in the garrison's morale. There was a good

Thursday, January 18

SOL T PLAATJE WITHIN MAFEKING UNDERLINES THE HEAVY BOMBARDMENT THEY SUFFERED AT THE BEGINNING OF THE YEAR:

'Boers are using some marvellous shells just now. Experts say that they are very new and must be made in Johannesburg. I wonder if the gunners who fire them appreciate the idea that they are better and deadlier than the brand 'Made in Germany'. They seldom burst where they first land, but merely plough the ground for a little distance, then pump right up in the air again and start a fresh journey for one or two more miles before they reach their fag end. This afternoon they sent a shell in the direction of Market Square. It went through the office of the Mafeking Mail, frightened the compositors out of

their wits, went into D. Webster's next door, and burst just on top of Vere Stent's bomb-proof. A fragment pierced the wall of Dixon's bar, touched up the head of the proprietor a bit, and scattered the bottles all over the floor. This morning another paid an intrusive visit to the other end of the Market Square, and thundered into Lippman's store, completely ragging his office and the goods therein. Little Mr. Lippman was choked with dust when he came out, and could hardly apprehend the sympathetic expression directed to him by the bystanders. He was only coughing like 'kgomo ea ntaramane' for about

fifteen minutes. One piece hurt the arm of a young lady, fortunately not seriously, and the crowd of purchasers escaped unhurt. In the evening they fired two heavy volleys with 3 minute intervals between them; the second one was heavier than 'Sanna's' report.'

Mafeking's Relieved !

SHAKE.

Bedford
19/5/00

Dear Mr Potack.

We have shouted "Rule Britannia," we have sung "God Save the Queen"; we have toasted "Gallant Baden" half a score. We have sent our very best respects to plucky Mafeking, and have hoisted flags and bunting in galore.

With a wild and frenzied madness—born of joy—the Empire cheers; while we Britishers rejoice throughout the land. In this hour of jubilation I am sending just a line, with the wish that I could warmly shake your hand.

Yours exultantly,

Thursday, February 8

SOL T PLAATJE – AS SUPPLIES RUN LOW, PEOPLE'S DIET BECOMES MORE SPECIALISED:

'The people are now receiving oatmeal for food instead of grain which, it is feared, will run short if sure steps are not taken to save it. The oats were intended for horses, but as the horses could eat grass when things grow serious, it is being thought of as human food. There is a general grumble all round here also. The pang has been felt all round, just at this time when folks had appetites. I have developed a marvellously strong appetite. I long for food every evening at 10.00 p.m. and after taking my supper at 7.00 I nearly die during the night if I do not take a cup of cocoa and a few biscuits before going to bed. Things are getting serious and I consider myself lucky for having thought out the thing at the beginning and stuffed my pants with matches and such things as were likely to be called in when things grow serious. I trust I will not number among those who will eat horses if we are not relieved by the end of March.'

deal of inexperience apparent in the management of the food stocks within Mafeking and even the supply of ammunition began to run low despite the sterling efforts of the ordnance workshop in turning anything that might function as a munition into a weapon. Prices for items of everyday food and drink also rose alarmingly. A glass of whisky now cost 1. 6d. and horse flesh became part of the defenders' staple diet.

The relief of Kimberley provided a timely boost to morale and hopes of an early raising of the siege grew during March. It was also proving easier for messengers and cattle raiders to slip through the Boers' lines, thereby bringing some relief to the besieged on two key factors: news from the outside world and variety of rations. For the African population in Mafeking, however, starvation was constantly looming and locusts were eagerly devoured by the Baralong. Relief simply could not come too soon and there was a growing suspicion in some quarters in the town that Baden-Powell was keeping the siege going for the purpose of self-aggrandisement. In May even the Sunday armistice was broken by Boer shelling

and the activities of a raiding party, and on 12 May the enemy launched an attack that was meant to spell the end of Mafeking. With the siege over many of the civilians in Mafeking concentrated their thoughts on compensation. The British government did pay compensation but the awards were regarded as unfair and universally parsimonious. In particular the black Africans who endured the siege – the Barolong and the Mfengu – believed that they had been cheated as the promises made to them were not honoured, and they received little credit for their part in the defence. Indeed Baden-Powell went to some lengths to misrepresent the role of the Barolong in the defeat of the final Boer assault. The tensions and jealousies, rife among the besieged, continued to mould the myths that grew out of victory.

The assault failed but the fall of Mafeking was reported by a Reuters correspondent only five days before the town was relieved on 17 May 1900. The celebrations rang around the Empire and Baden-Powell became the hero of an era, despite the reservations of those who had endured at Ladysmith.

Tuesday, February 13

SOL T PLAATJE:

'The Boers have brought another kind of shell to bear on us. They have incensed the 9-pounder shells and they are very incendiary. Yesterday we saw a flame in the course of one of the shells [in the air] to where it exploded. The flame went out before it reached the ground. These shells struck at Mrs. Stenson's, and the explosion caused fire. That must be the reason why they have started shelling the Stadt – apparently to test its effect on the grass thatched huts. They continued the shelling till 10 p.m. and knocked off, presumably disgusted, for no damage was done, and they have become mild again. They are, I think, perfectly convinced that there is nothing in them, for if they were of any use, and if the flames were effective, they certainly ought to have seen the grass huts blaze away in the dark night. However, after one of those shells exploded, Manomphe's son-in-law, Thlaping, walked up, and while picking up a fragment, noticed that there was something like a cut diamond in the debris. He picked up this beauty of a thing. His nerve, however, told him that there was danger in it but, in order to do justice to his pluck, he took his left hand full of sand, and put this thing on it. The sand caught fire and burnt his hand. He chucked away this thing and rubbed his burning left hand with his right. The former ignited the latter, and he was soon tortured with pain. His only relief is to keep his hands in cold water – this does not help much unless fresh water is put in every three minutes, for the water becomes very hot after it.'

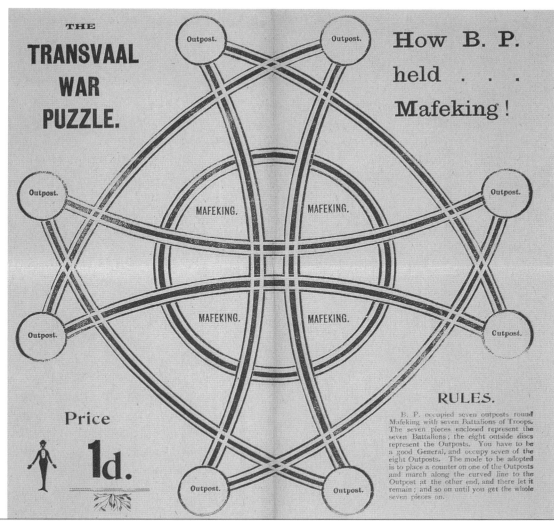

Friday, May 18

LIEUTENANT FREDERIC CRESWELL, IMPERIAL LIGHT HORSE:

'The inhabitants and garrison of Mafeking for a seven months besieged crowd are a very healthy well-fed lot and very different looking set from what were in Ladysmith. When Baden-Powell said just now, turning to us, "Some of you know what a siege is like and what its hardships are" I felt very much inclined to say "Yes, but I don't think any of you seem to know much about it". On the other hand the way they have entrenched themselves and the enormous amount of labour they must have put into them is very great and will tell the tale of the siege for many a long day to come. I was rather disappointed in Baden-Powell. He was so exaggerated in the speech he made to us, talked of our having given the Boers a real good dusting which was rot. However, no doubt he knows it was rot and thought it right to talk a bit of pretty pretty.'

the soldier's experience

As a fighting man the Boer was more self-contained than the British soldier, particularly after the start of the guerrilla campaign in the summer of 1900. Comfortable in his rugged, everyday working clothes the member of a Commando carried in his saddlebags sufficient food and equipment to make himself independent of re-supply, save for ammunition, for days at a time. The standard diet while on Commando comprised bread, porridge, and roasted, boiled or dried meat. Salted and air-dried strips of biltong made from venison or beef were a mainstay of the diet of men who operated away from the laager for any period of time. The Boer could care for himself and his horse and operate effectively for long periods, inspired only by his Bible, without orders from higher command. The lack of strict discipline and the general air of democracy within a Commando meant that its men would take a *laissez faire* attitude to their length of service at the Front. Many Boers came or went from the fighting line much as they pleased, especially if there was loot to be transported home or if the morale of the Commando was low. The stan-

dard of general health among the members of a Commando while on campaign was significantly higher than would be found in a British regiment, particularly as regards to typhoid. Conditions for the Commandos deteriorated significantly during the guerrilla phase of the War when the need for extreme mobility meant that only essential items for fighting could be carried despite the fact that men spent many nights in the open. Clothing fell to pieces, it was often impossible to get dry in the absence of fires, and rations became meagre, dull and repetitive.

The Boers were of course playing at home and Tommy Atkins' first hurdle was the need to acclimatise to the conditions of warfare in South Africa, a country which the vast majority of British soldiers had never seen before. They had the strength of the regimental system behind them and comradeship played a vital role in motivating men to endure what many other ranks came to see as a tedious and protracted struggle in a land whose inhabitants despised them. Inadequate training for the style of warfare they encountered on

Friday, January 11

GUSTAV PRELLER, BOER ARTILLERY:

'Many of the Artillery are now going barefoot, ragged clothes are the rule, the men wearing bits of sail-cloth and rugs. The food consists exclusively of mealie pap and beef, with barley coffee wherever it is to be had. A mackintosh is a rarity and rugs are scarce. How we are to get through the winter I do not know. Our whole camp consists of about ten tents including those of the officers. The weather is foggy and rainy. In the day time, when it is warm and sunny, the flies lay their eggs in our damp kit, and on these damp days they hatch out and become maggots. My box is in a loathsome state, the lock is so full of them that I cannot undo it.'

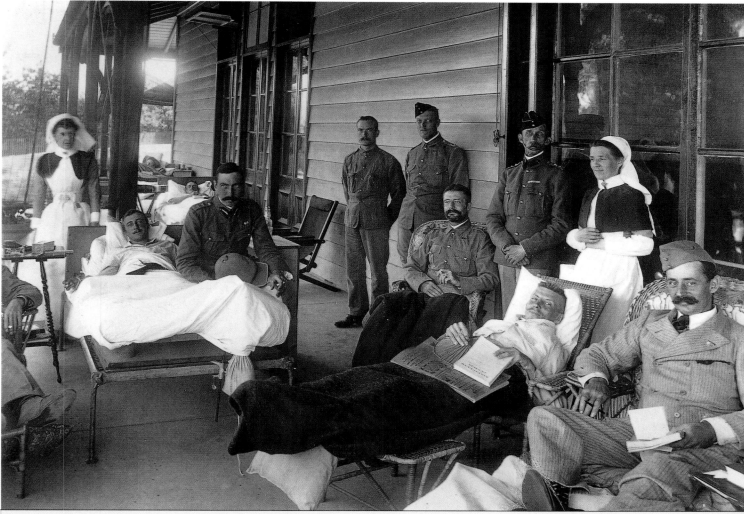

A British officers' hospital in South Africa with convalescent patients in the foreground. ▶

Friday, **January 26**

LIEUTENANT R J K MOTT, THE QUEEN'S (ROYAL WEST SURREY REGIMENT):

'On one of the days of the battle, I rode into Spearman's Hill camp, where there is a canteen, and bought 6,000 cigarettes: gave 800 to the wounded of the Brigade, and the Regiment bought the rest. Another day I got 70 bags of tobacco and 4,000 cigarettes for the Regiment. We have been roughing it the last 10 days, without tents or kit; only greatcoats and one day's supplies on the regimental wagons. Luckily, the nights have been dry, and the result is there has been practically no sickness – in fact, far the healthiest time we have had so far.'

Friday, March 15

R J K MOTT HIGHLIGHTS THE FACT THAT, DESPITE THE HARDSHIPS THE BRITISH HAD TO ENDURE, COMFORTS FROM HOME WERE BOUNTIFUL:

'Our camp is rather hot and glaring in the middle of a wide open plain and a mile from the Tugela but what our future movements will be no one knows. Lots of people think the whole show will be over in a few weeks and I shan't be sorry though I should like to be in the final show in the Transvaal. The most extraordinary number of presents have been sent to both officers and men and this war really does seem to have boomed poor Tommy. He's so loaded up now with caps and comforters, socks, shirts, pipes and baccy that if we were ordered to move suddenly he would have to leave half his things behind. The same with us. I am only supposed to have 35 lbs of baggage, but I'm sure I have about 150.'

campaign, coupled with leadership that was profligate of their lives, meant that British troops paid a heavy price in casualties for minimal progress in the opening stages of the War. If a Mauser bullet did not kill them then enteric fever (typhoid) might oblige instead.

The British soldier's exposure to sickness and disease began during the long, cramped and unhygienic voyage out to South Africa. It was not only horses which died at sea. Some troopships disembarked units that were riddled with food poisoning, diarrhoea and dysentery before they even set foot ashore. Thereafter difficulties of supply, the scarcity of fresh water on the veld and nights spent lying awake soaked to the skin or freezing on top of a kopje were not calculated to keep soldiers healthy. The battle against disease was not won, despite the strenuous efforts of the medical staff with the Army. Over 13,000 men died, mainly from typhoid, while 31,000 men were invalided home after suffering its ravages. The treatment of battle wounds and associated conditions was on the whole speedy and effective. The Royal Army Medical Corps, supplemented by specialist civilian surgeons and nurses, practised the best contemporary techniques of surgery and patient care. General anaesthesia, aseptic surgery and techniques such as X-rays meant that the wounded British soldier in South Africa had a much better chance of recovery than his nineteenth-century predecessors. The mortality rate among the wounded of the force that relieved Kimberley, for

example, was only 2%. British soldiers now carried field dressings into battle and these made a material contribution to the survival of men with bullet and shrapnel wounds.

Tommy Atkins showed repeatedly during the fighting on the veld that he could continue to function on half-rations or even on no food at all for considerable periods. But he was never happy about any loss of rations. His morale would suffer as a result for he was a fighting man who desired his creature comforts, and the quickest way to restore his confidence after a reverse was via his stomach. The canteen system established by Buller was psychologically at least a life saver to many soldiers as they could buy food or cigarettes to supplement their issue rations. British soldiers also received unsolicited presents, of both tobacco and clothing, from patriotic citizens back home, the most famous of which were the gifts distributed to officers and men on behalf of Queen Victoria.

An abiding taste for alcohol in all its forms is a quality which the British soldier has often cherished and he was no shirker in this respect in South Africa. Tommy Atkins supplemented his official rum ration with native brews, whisky, and alcohol removed unofficially from supply wagons and stores. Deaths from alcohol poisoning were not uncommon and at times officers found it difficult to discover enough sober men in their companies to man picket lines. It was one way of combating the tedium of soldiering on the veld.

Tuesday, April 16

L HAMILTON FOX, 3RD CAVALRY BRIGADE:

'Well, we have had good, bad and indifferent times since we left Cape Town Jan 27th... At Koodoos' Drift we really had the worst time as far as comfort (an important item as you know with me!) went, as it rained heavily and wet us through, and many chaps got sick, though I never felt really ill myself. Then rations and grub generally were reduced by more than half, to say nothing of the scarcity of tobacco (another useful item!). I well remember feeling very hungry and offering 1s. for a biscuit, but could do no business for love or money. Plenty of fresh meat of course, too much in fact as it made the chaps sick without sufficient vegetables and no biscuits. But that is over now and never likely to occur again, and considering the events that occurred at the time (namely the surrender of the Cronje and his force) well worth it; though even now we are of course to my idea and most others' ideas, not over fed by any means – but still alive, well and hearty!'

guerrilla war 5

the Boers embark on a guerrilla war

By the end of May 1900 it had been obvious for some weeks that fighting set-piece battles based on static defensive positions was not a style of warfare that the Boers could ultimately win. They might, and did, inflict local defeats on the British but there were now simply too many of the enemy out on the veld for battles won in detail to make any lasting impression on the overall strategic picture. Despite reverses the British continued to advance; at times painfully slowly but always forward into Boer territory. In contrast, a single defeat suffered by the Boers could lead to grave consequences for their war effort through the loss of vital munitions, a collapse of morale and 'desertions' from the Commandos.

Guerrilla warfare gave the Boers their only hope of maintaining armed resistance against the military might of the British Empire. To hold their conquests in the face of widely dispersed Commandos raiding across the length and breadth of the Boer Republics and into Natal and Cape of Good Hope, the British would have to disperse their troops in penny packets to guard installations, lines of communication and the civilian population of South Africa. The vastness of the country gave the Commandos both room in which to hide and the ability to strike unexpectedly with the advantage of a local superiority in numbers. They hoped that by cutting railway lines, intercepting supply convoys and overwhelming isolated garrisons they could keep their struggle alive in the minds of the British public and in the eyes of those European nations to whom they still looked for diplomatic or military intervention. The Boers might, by adopting guerrilla tactics, cause the British to despair at a mounting toll of casualties and to recoil from the human and financial cost of continuing the War. They would at the very least give the argument for an independent Transvaal and Orange Free State a currency which the British would find difficult to extinguish while fighting continued.

The conduct of the guerrilla war and the fountainhead of the enormous spirit which kept the Boer Commandos in action under what were often appalling conditions of danger and hardship, would now rest principally with four men: President Marthinus Theunis Steyn, Christiaan De Wet, Koos de la Rey and Commandant-General Louis Botha. In Marthinus Steyn the Boer cause had a man who would not compromise in his determination to fight 'to the bitter end', and in De Wet and de la Ray it had men who understood and could exploit guerrilla tactics to the full. In the Boer farmer, confident in both his horsemanship and musketry practice, they had a weapon that was ideal for their purposes.

▲

General J P Snyman (left), the commander of the force left to continue the siege of Mafeking in November 1900, and Philip Botha, Louis Botha's brother.

◄

National Scouts photographed in May 1900. The Scouts were raised in South Africa from ex-Burghers who were prepared to serve with the British. By the end of May 1902 the Scouts totalled 1,359 men.

Roberts' invasion of the Transvaal

By the end of May 1900 the Boer cause was in disarray. Mafeking, the last of the three British towns under siege, had been relieved on 17 May; the Orange Free State had been formally annexed by Britain on the Queen's birthday on 24 May; Roberts had invaded the Transvaal on 26 May; President Kruger had left his seat of Government for Machadodorp on 30 May; and on 31 May Roberts entered Johannesburg. The British were now close to the ultimate prize, Pretoria. Louis Botha decided not to defend the town and on 5 June the Boers surrendered Pretoria unconditionally to British troops. Boer demoralisation appeared to be almost complete and Louis Botha called a council of war to discuss whether the armed struggle should continue or whether the Commandos should surrender to Roberts. While the feeling of the meeting was still uncertain, a letter arrived from De Wet pleading with the Burghers to keep their weapons and use them to fight a guerrilla campaign against the British. For the moment the Boers still had an ample supply of weapons and ammunition buried across the republics, and they could afford to buy provisions and equipment with the funds rescued from the Transvaal Treasury by Jan Smuts.

For the British, who expected the War to be over within a few weeks at the very most, this new style of warfare was to come as a profound shock, though De Wet had given them an indication of what could be expected in actions near Sanna's Post on 31 March and at Reddersburg on 4 April. These engagements gave a clear sign that it was possible for the Boers to dominate the veld even while the British dominated the towns. Roberts' extended line of communication – Pretoria was some 1,000 miles from Cape Town by rail – was vulnerable to even small bands of men equipped with the means to wreck bridges, rails and rolling stock. With this renewed determination to fight on, Botha was able to gather together 14 artillery pieces and approximately 7,000 men. With them he formed a completely new defensive position some 12 miles east and north-east of Pretoria on a chain of hills near Pienaar's Poort. This position extended for up to 25 miles and straddled both the Delagoa Bay railway and the roads to Middelburg and Pietersburg. Although Roberts' offensive strength had been severely reduced by the need to deploy garrisons and mount guard along the railway, he could not afford to ignore this threat while he waited for reinforcements and watched the remaining Free State Commandos play havoc with his rearward communications. If the British were to control the Transvaal and have any hope of inducing the civilian population to maintain a state of neutrality, Roberts needed to capture or at least disperse this enemy gathering.

A contemporary British cartoon exploiting the discomfiture of the Boer leadership after the fall of Pretoria.

▶

Homeward bound. Over 72,000 British other ranks together with 3,000 officers were sent home to the United Kingdom as invalids during the course of the War.

◀

Lord Roberts (mounted in the centre) takes the salute as British troops march into Pretoria on 5 June 1900. ▶

CAPTAIN G T BRIERLEY ROYAL ARTILLERY:

'Having marched along the railway 90 miles, we are now at the Headquarters of Robert's Army, and feeling ready for anything. Tents are everywhere, the Army is resting after Kimberley and Paardeberg. Railway congested, men and horses dying like rats, chiefly on account of the awful rains on the top of hardships. The Boers are strengthening up North, or determining how much to leave behind in their flight. Lord Roberts is wondering how to get Burdett-Coutts, Hospital comforts, big guns, ammunition, horses and food, up in one train, and it is raining as it never rained before. Boers are at the waterworks and mopping up small detachments. Remounts are coming slowly, without which we are as powerless as a dead elephant. At Bloemfontein there is an air of enormous strength; it seemed that we could flood the country with troops from this place, but our troops afterwards disappeared into the veldt and were lost in space; and the feeling of strength did not reappear till Pretoria.'

British troops firing the one o'clock gun from Johannesburg Fort.

◄

Saturday, May 22

GUSTAV PRELLER BOER ARTILLERY:

'The families in the Artillery Camp have been in a state of panic since last month which rose to the highest pitch for some days and ended in a decision to quit the country. The enemy is now near Vereeniging in the vicinity and just beyond Klerksdorp. Reitz has suggested to the officers casually – to send their wives to Lourenco-Marques, and placed a special train at their disposal, which will leave on Friday 26th inst. They receive provisions as well for six months. For the burghers a circular is issued, that they must leave their families on their farms, after one has been busy day and night since the invasion of the O.F.S. pointing out to them the atrocities committed by the English soldiers, upon Boer women, houses and goods – this will positively have a very lamentable effect. The Government is preparing to shift its seat. Every day I see people of the Cabinet busy burning documents. To me and wife the very troublesome and difficult question arose to decide to-night – whether ?: There are four ways – or places one can go to – firstly remain here, while I went on commando – possibly to Lydenburg, and she here among the British – secondly with wagon and oxen if procurable here, along with me to Lydenburg, with which from the nature of the case difficulties are connected, thirdly, to Lourenco-Marques and its unhealthy climate, and the chance of the line being destroyed. Fourthly to Barberton, fifthly to Pieters-burg. Lourenco-Marques offers extreme difficulties, but the benefits are: safety, greatest supply in provisions, diversion and relaxation – the chance that com-munication will remain open with the commando and the chance that the cli-mate will have a beneficial effect on Hannie's state of health. Our house – our happy residence for two years, with all our goods, we will perhaps for a long time – who knows perhaps for good – have to say good-bye to, and both of us go meandering about nearly ruined. The plan exists to ask mother to come and stay here, meanwhile, while with a large family she could go nowhere else, and many – the majority of the inhabitants remain here – then our goods would perhaps be protected. The difficulties about remaining here are too great for H. No communication and amongst the enemy with the possibility of living becoming hard and expensive. After long consideration and reasoning we decide that she had better go to Lourenco-Marques along with the others. Time presses, a lot of preparations have to be made. Our arrear salaries we get paid out. £100, all that we shall possess.'

Lord Roberts'
advance to
Pretoria freed
several thousand
British prisoners
of war as the
retreating Boer
forces could not
provide for their
continuing
captivity.
▶

Lord Roberts'
advance to
Pretoria freed
several thousand
British prisoners
of war as the
retreating Boer
forces could not
provide for their
continuing
captivity.
▶

ION POSTA

APE OF

DE BON

S ONLY TO

Saturday, June 9

S V ROBINSON, CIVIL SURGEON:

'I was left at Devondale the second morning with 8 sick men. I had to see them off to Kimberley. Two of them had been at a rum cask and were comatose. One died on my hands about 1 o'clock and I had to bury him and read the R.C. service over him. The men made a very pretty grave. They made a cairn of white stones and I had a cross made of wood and painted his name on it. I got away at 2 a.m. with the others to Vryburg and got them off at 8.30 next morning for Kimberley... On the way up there was a special photo artist on the truck with me so we had a photo taken and I believe it will appear in the Graphic. So you might keep an eye on it. "A Soldiers Lonely Grave in Bechuanaland". We have at times been very short of water and one day we could not find any to drink at all. The Boers' wives and children are nearly in a starving condition. One woman had absolutely nothing in the house and no water. One farm was ruined and there wasn't a single living thing there and nothing except a few letters and a little grain. It is very flat up this side – very few kopjes. We go on tomorrow at 8 to Ventersdorp 4 days and then to Frederikstad 2 days more and then entrain for Johannes-burg. You will know much more of the War then we do. We just have the bare fact that Pretoria has fallen and that Kruger has gone.'

Diamond Hill

While Roberts was preparing to dislodge the Boers from their position at Pienaar's Poort, the Commandant-General's wife arrived at Pretoria with a request from her husband for an interview with the British Commander-in-Chief. Roberts hoped that this would be the prelude to the Boer surrender but Botha, learning of De Wet's occupation of Kroonstad, felt emboldened to continue the struggle.

On 10 June 1900 Roberts struck eastwards from Pretoria in an attempt to push Botha and his command away from the British flank and back towards the Mozambique frontier. The two-day clash which followed on 11–12 June was known to the British as the battle of Diamond Hill and to the Boers as Donkerhoek. Roberts attacked what was a very strong defensive position manned by 7,000 Boers with a force of approximately 11,000 infantry and 5,000 mounted troops supported by 100 guns and pom poms. Roberts planned to turn both flanks of the Boer position and then press the centre until it collapsed under infantry assault. On 11 June French's cavalry and mounted infantry brigades attacked the Boer left flank

while Ian Hamilton's cavalry and infantry assaulted the Boers on the right. Amid confusion in the British deployment both attacks met heavy resistance, the struggle only abating as night fell. On 12 June the British attack was renewed and Roberts' troops were engaged with the enemy at such close quarters and with such intensity that both the 12th Lancers and the Household Cavalry had to charge the enemy to relieve pressure on the infantry. When it was clear that the Boer centre was seriously weakened by the defence of the flanks, Roberts pushed his infantry forward on the 12th to seize Diamond Hill itself. With the centre of his position compromised, Botha was forced to allow his men to slip away during the night.

This was the last attempt by the Boers to defeat the British by conventional means in a set-piece battle fought from a strong defensive position. They failed and began a retreat to the east, the dispirited Commandos falling back along the Delgoa Bay Railway to Balmoral Station and Rhenosterkop. Several hundred Boers rode into Pretoria to surrender while others buried their mausers and returned to their homes.

The movement of troops and supplies across rivers was a constant feature of the geographically dispersed campaign in South Africa. Here men of the Essex Regiment are ferried across the River Vaal.

Monday–Tuesday, June 11–12

CAPTAIN G T BRIERLEY, ROYAL ARTILLERY:

'Started at 5 a.m. and after going six miles fought Diamond Hill. Of course we only saw a small part of the fight which was over a large front. The fight started as far as I was concerned by my Scotch Ammunition cart overturning into a donga; each one of the six mules went on its back and at that moment a Boer gun began shelling, the shells falling all round us; the transport gradually took cover in driblets where it could. I saw that General French who was a short way ahead, had run into a prepared trap. I left the maxims for a moment to see to the cart. I appealed to some Australian pioneers under Captain Parrot to look after it, they promised to do so. We went on & left it; I was ordered to join Pilcher, and waited in a wood for orders; we were made a target of by a Boer gun and I left the wood hurriedly as it was getting warm and I was doing no good. Meanwhile the transport had a bad time, it was shelled in detail. One of my men dismounted to pick up and examine a Boer shell which had just arrived; he was a 17th Lancer as most of the men were, and I told him casually it might go off at any minute. He dropped it. The Cavalry had taken up positions also Alderson's Mounted Infantry and we were in for a hot time. The Boers had about ten guns; this was their main left flank we had knocked up against. Their flanks were very strong compared with their centre which Roberts was attacking. At night fall we were very much jumbled up and French's and Hutton's men slept where they were for the simple reason they could not leave. I never had an opportunity of coming into action to-day being in reserve with Pilcher, it was also very difficult to move about...

In Hutton's Brigade Col. Pilcher was in reserve, and found it difficult to relieve Col. Alderson owing to the difficulty there would have been in Alderson's men retiring from the positions they held which were so close to the Boers only a few hundred yards away; in fact our positions were pretty much where our men had been forced to take cover when the fight first began. The Boers had good positions which commanded ours and were thickly wooded and it required reinforcements to dislodge them. In the evening, after dark, Pilcher went with his Mounted Infantry and I with him, to the front line. We replaced Alderson and I got ready for action with a maxim among some rocks ready for the morning. We all slept in the firing line that night, lost touch with our food and had nothing, but during the night got something at different places where we saw lights, which were no sooner lighted than they got fired at by Boers. The wood was a constant scene of fires being lighted and then extinguished owing to sniping into them... In the morning [12 June] all sat tight for sometime and after a careful reconnaissance found the Boers had retired. Their centre had been split by Roberts and as we had retained them so closely on the left they had to retire to avoid being bottled up; we followed for ten miles passing through the remains of a large laager and getting right into the bushveldt country, quite new to me.'

Tuesday, June 12

GENERAL BEN VILJOEN, WITH THE BOER FORCES:

'The battle continued the whole day; it was fiercest on our left flank, where General French and his cavalry charged the positions of the Ermelo and Bethel burghers again and again, each time to be repulsed with heavy losses. Once the lancers attacked so valiantly that a hand-to-hand fight ensued... On our right General de la Rey had an equally awkward position; the British here also made several determined attempts to turn his flank, but were repulsed each time. Once during an attack on our right, their convoy came so close to our position that our artillery and our Mausers were enabled to pour such a fire into them that the mules drawing the carts careered about the veld at random, and the greatest confusion ensued. British mules were "pro-Boer" throughout the War. The ground, however, was not favourable for our operations, and we failed to avail ourselves of the general chaos. Towards the evening of the second day General Tobias Smuts made an unpardonable blunder in falling back with his commandos. There was no necessity for retreat; but it served to show the British that there was a weak point in our armoury. Indeed the following day the attack in force was made upon this point. The British had meantime continued pouring in reinforcements, men as well as guns.'

Royal Engineers constructing a pontoon bridge across the River Vaal at Norval's Point.

►

Wednesday, June 13

CAPTAIN G T BRIERLEY, ROYAL ARTILLERY:

'Marched back to Kameel Drift passing this time through the back of the Boer position. This was most interesting and we saw what a very strong position they had selected, the area of it was very great, in fact many miles. We saw many traces of the damage done in the shape of blood, lint and cotton wool. Our strength was: French 600, Alderson 400 and Pilcher 250 total 1,250. About two-thirds had been left behind dismounted at Pretoria. On the way home my other gun went smash and I was very much worried, and absolutely sick of maxims in this rough country. What am I to do now?... Rested. General Alderson went away with his push to assist Baden-Powell who had entrenched himself near Crocodile River, against a possible Boer attack, and it seemed rather a curious thing for the hero of Mafeking to be doing and tickled our men very much.'

the annexation of the Transvaal

While Roberts and Kitchener had been securing their position around Pretoria, Buller, more or less left to his own devices, had been clearing Natal. By 13 June 1900 he had driven the Commandos out of the province, 242 days after the Boers had first invaded Natal. He then linked up with Roberts before eventually handing his post of second-in-command to Kitchener and returning, still loved by the ordinary soldier, to Britain in November. For the remainder of the War there were no grand campaigns leading to decisive victories and Roberts was never again to defeat a Boer field force. In July General Hunter succeeded in trapping 4,000 Boers under Commandant Martin Prinsloo in the Brandwater Basin, a mountainous area of peaks and passes. With the latter blocked by British troops, Prinsloo had little alternative but to surrender. The first major De Wet hunt, however, ended in failure when Ian Hamilton's command failed to secure Olifants Nek thereby allowing President Steyn, the Orange Free State Government and De Wet to make good their escape northwards. Following the annexation of the Orange Free State on 24 May 1900 and its change of title to the Orange River Colony, the Transvaal was annexed by Britain on 1 September.

The problem for Roberts and Kitchener as the open phase of the War came to a close was that their troops controlled only the ground on which they stood. Only where there were British garrisons could influence be exerted upon the citizens of the Transvaal and the Orange Free State. As garrisons were based principally in the towns of the Republics, this was where control could be imposed. In the vast spaces of the veld the occupation was as fleeting as the columns which moved across it in search of the Boer Commandos. The British grip on their own communications was fragile in the extreme, and both troops and supplies were liable to attack and capture almost anywhere in an area that covered nearly 500,000 square miles. Roberts' forces began to evaporate in an attempt to secure a theatre of war that was larger than France and Germany combined. The number of troops tied down in garrison or communications duty seriously degraded Roberts' ability to hunt down roving Commandos. In an attempt to reduce the extent of the guerrilla problem by separating the hard core of the Commandos from their less committed brethren, Roberts issued proclamations offering what was in effect amnesty for those Burghers, not of high rank, who would lay down their weapons and take an oath of neutrality. In return they would be allowed to return peacefully to their homes and would not be classified as prisoners of war or have their property confiscated. Counter proclamations were issued by President Steyn but a significant number of Free State Burghers did lay down their arms and take the oath. The permanency of this transformation from commando to civilian depended, however, upon the maintenance of British garrisons in occupied districts and upon the success of British arms in cornering the Boers fighting on the veld.

Lord Roberts (leaning on balustrade), photographed at his headquarters in Pretoria on 2 October 1900.

▶

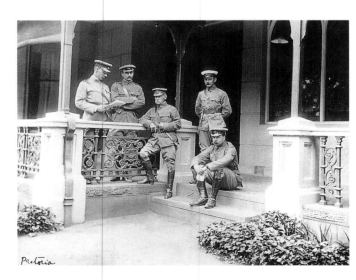

Thursday, August 2

BOMBARDIER R WAUGH, G BATTERY, ROYAL HORSE ARTILLERY:

'The battery remained in the Middelburg command for some time, being divided up into sections (two guns each) and quartered in different places round about the district, occasionally relieving one another. The following are some of the places we garrisoned: Pan (railway station); Doornkop; Bankfontein; Balmoral; Wonderfontein; Oliphants River and Gun Hill. While my section was at Pan attacks were often expected from Boer parties returning west from the scattered Commandos after the actions at Belfast and Lydenburg. Owing to the small number of the garrison at Pan the gunners and drivers occasionally had to take a turn in occupying the trenches at night; this is not the usual duty of an artilleryman but at times one is compelled to do things out of the everyday routine, especially on active service. This period was not one of inaction as reconnaissances were frequent and at times not over pleasant. Numerous rumours were frequent again as to the course of the war but none proved reliable, the only news which could in any way be depended on being that in the Home papers which arrived occasionally (if not captured by the enemy!).'

the guerrilla war

After the fall of Bloemfontein and Pretoria, Roberts assiduously promoted the view that the fall of the Boer capitals meant that the War had been won by the British and was therefore effectively over. While the phase of the War which involved major set-piece battles was indeed drawing to a close there was to be no end to armed clashes, to British defeats or to a continually mounting casualty list. In many respects the most difficult and controversial phase of the War for the British and Empire forces was only just beginning. The fact that the Boer leaders in the field – Botha, de la Rey, and De Wet – had changed their tactics from open warfare to a guerrilla campaign posed new problems for the British and when they introduced radical solutions this led to charges of barbarism being laid against their conduct of the War. Roberts' view in the Autumn of 1900 was that the struggle against the remaining Boer Commandos would now become essentially a police action which could be carried out in the main by auxiliary forces rather than by the Army's Regular troops. Consequently, in July 1900, the British Government decided that its Commander-in-Chief in South Africa should be shipped home to London and installed as Commander-in-Chief of the British Army. He would be succeeded in South Africa by his Chief of Staff, Kitchener of Khartoum. Like Roberts, Kitchener believed that the Boers were beaten and he had set his sights on fulfilling his most earnest ambition of

becoming Commander-in-Chief in India in succession to Sir William Lockhart who had died in post in March 1900. Kitchener was thus seriously put out when he realised that the War was indeed continuing, albeit as a series of guerrilla actions. The British Government was equally put out when it realised that the guerrilla campaign by the Boers would involve the commitment of ever increasing numbers of troops and a continuing drain on the Empire's financial and material resources. The Government, and to some extent the British public, now had other matters on their minds, and there was a growing feeling of ennui in relation to what was seen as the final pursuit of the Boers in South Africa. The Boxer Rebellion in China had broken out and the unfolding story of the investment of the legations in Peking meant that a new and even more exotic siege was available to fire their imaginations with heroic deeds from a lonely outpost of Empire.

Even when relatively static Roberts' Field Force required some 1,020 tons of supplies – clothing, food, ammunition and equipment – per day just to remain in existence. An impression of the sheer quantity of supplies involved in maintaining the Army on active service can be gained by a single request from the General Officer Commanding Lines of Communication made on 7 June 1900 for 4,000,000 lbs of biscuit, 2,000,000 lbs of preserved meat or Maconochie rations, 10,000 bottles of calves-foot jelly and 1,000 cases

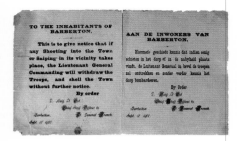

▲
A warning to the inhabitants of Barberton of the consequences of guerrilla activity in the area.

▲
Colonel Sir Henry Rawlinson's good luck card from the sergeants of the 2nd Btln Coldstream Guards, Christmas 1901.

1+3 | G J Scheepers, a Cape rebel and guerrilla fighter who operated in the districts close to the Indian ocean, was captured while immobilised at a farm with appendicitis. The British charged him with a number of war crimes including arson, the mistreatment of wounded prisoners and the murder of Africans and loyalists. His pleas of innocence were rejected on the basis of damning testimony from two of his Commando. He was found guilty and shot in public.

2 | General Pieter Kritzinger was luckier. He was acquitted at his trial and lived to a ripe old age.

SCHEEPERS
IVIE.H.ALLAN.
PHOTO.
GRAAFF-R!
COPYRIGHT

SCHEEPER'S TRIAL
(COPYRIGHT)

IVIE-H-ALLAN
GRAAFF-REINET
1901

During the guerrilla phase of the War the British became adept at the speedy repair of demolitions carried out on the railway by Boer Commandos.

▶

Wednesday, November 14

GUSTAV PRELLER:

'About 7 a.m. we turned out, 45 mounted men with a big Maxim, from the C.G. on the main road – Gen. Spruyt – here are about 800 men besides ourselves. Johannesburg (formerly Gravet), Heidelberg (formerly Comdt Spruyt) and Middelburg (still the infirm Comdt of Middelburg P. Trichard). While we were with the General Gen. Spruyt informed him that the enemy was advancing and asked if he should taken up a position. The C.G. answered that he was to take up a position and fall back on a kop east of Bothas near the farm of a certain Lewis Botha, where there was a little kraal, by which the C.G. ordered us to take up a position. We advanced immediately to the foot of the hill, dismounted at Kaffir village there and went up the hill as high as we could. The hill was not high but fearfully steep. When we arrived at the top we Middelburghers met our men retiring, we chose a position in a little kraal on the summit of the ridge, and saw the enemy about 5 miles away coming from Middelburg. They were on the road leading past the C.G. to Roos Senekal, but when they caught sight of us they halted, and turned in our direction, halted again and bombarded our kraal with lyddite (our big maxim had been left at the foot of the hill). The shells fell far beyond us. St. Coetsee went about 1000 yards forwards, before the bombardment, in order to shoot at the enemy's outposts, the enemy opened on him with field guns while the outposts returned fire, they came back. The English mounted men advanced, also Infantry, 2000 men more or less, and took up a position on a kopje on the right, and while their advanced guard and mounted men worried us with their Metfords at 1500 yards, they opened on us with a pom-pom. We were forced to leave our position, under a hail of bullets and shells, after having kept 2000 of Her Majesty's troops busy for about an hour with only 45 men.

Scarcely had we got a short distance with our horses, when the English appeared on the top and let us have it at long range Open order – no casualties – heavy shower or rain – everything wet – got wet through having no mackintosh – went back to the other side of Blokdrift Ceylons river. Many Boers fled further away with thousands of large and small cattle – many fat horses. The English advanced against us to-day from three points, one column from Machadsdorp or Dullstroom, destroyed our mills at Witpoort and burned everything there – a great loss for us – here in Mapoch's land there are only a few small water mills left. One column from Belfast trekked down into the low country and burned all houses which they came across, we saw four burning before our eyes, all belonging to Jouberts.'

▶
This is believed to be Hans Cordua, a 23-year-old German, who was arrested as the leader of an alleged conspiracy to kidnap Lord Roberts in August 1900. He was tried by a military court, found guilty and executed by firing squad.

▶▶
A British armoured train temporarily halted by Boer wreckers.

of champagne. While Roberts was at Bloemfontein, most of these supplies had to be brought forward along a single railway line. An army in this position was a target ripe for attack with guerrilla tactics. By the end of June 1900 Roberts was forced to deploy no less than 35,000 infantry and 8,000 mounted troops along the railway and in detached garrisons. What could happen to these line of communication detachments was amply illustrated at Rhenoster River on 7 June. The British post was guarded by the 3rd Battalion The Derbyshire Regiment and a party of Imperial Yeomanry. The Boers attacked them at dawn, drove in the pickets, killed 35 men, wounded 111 and captured everyone else. It was not of course a completely one-sided campaign. The British and Empire troops did secure successes against the guerrillas, taking prisoners, dispersing Commandos and disrupting the enemy's plans. It was only when their intelligence work and the quality of their scouting improved markedly that a cumulative degradation of the Boers' capabilities began to take place.

As the guerrilla campaign wore on there was a sense of increasing frustration at all levels in the Army, in the Administration in South Africa, and amongst the Cabinet at home. The tactics promoted by Kitchener to deal with the Boers after his assumption of command on 29 November 1900 were in many respects a considered response to this frustration and to the seeming impotence of his large forces to deal finally with the comparatively small numbers of Boers who were waging the guerrilla campaign. The tactics that emerged from Kitchener's headquarters – the use of concentration camps for civilians, the application of a scorched earth policy to the property of those armed and non-combatant Boers suspected of supporting the Commandos, the introduction of mobile columns, large scale sweeps across the veld, and barbed wire and block houses – would all play their part in defeating the Boers, but no measure by itself would prove decisive.

Amidst the defences of Ladysmith. ▶

Monday, August 26

GUSTAV PRELLER:

'It is summer already. Last week there was a peach tree in blossom, and the willows already display a pleasant green, which is gradually filling up the spaces between the dry branches. Nature is waking up and even the black ridges are assuming a green tint. The first cold showers of rain have fallen, preceded and accompanied by storms of wind, which howled drearily through everything. In the meantime we trek from one patch of grass to another in order to keep the animals alive. Our own food, mealies and meat, we get mostly from the Kaffirs in exchange for receipts or Government notes, but everything is very scarce. We grind the mealies in little hand or coffee mills. From time to time we get Kaffir corn instead of mealies and, whenever the necessary material are to be had, we make 'stormjagers' of a poor kind of it. Bread mealies are to be had here and there, and we make the best bread from them.

Our hearty longing for the summer is not unmixed with unpleasant anticipation whenever we think of the rains. A few cold showers have shown us how absolutely at the mercy of the weather we are, without tents, cloaks or protection of any kind whatever. Whenever the weather is bad we are compelled to make little shelters out of the corrugated iron from the burnt houses, which last have long since ceased to afford us any shelter, but we cannot always do this.

By day we live in the saddle, our home is wherever we off-saddle our bedding and commissariat we carry on the pack horses. The worst thing of all is the want of salt, of which we have not a bit left, and besides this tobacco, our only luxury, threatens to become scarce. We have already begun to limit ourselves to one or two pipes a day, and see no chance of replenishing our supply. Where we off-saddle there is our home; there the smoke of our little fire of fence posts or "bois de vache" soon rises into the air, and there our kettle hums merrily. We are worst off when we are without either mealie meal or meat, and have to roast hard mealies on a fire of their own cobs, to still our hunger.'

An example of a very effective piece of train wrecking by a Boer Commando. The Boers have loosened a rail and then pulled it across to meet the adjacent rail. ▶

Monday, October 14

GUSTAV PRELLER:

'When the enemy had retired we also returned to our old place on Prinsloo's farm, as we had done before at Middleberg farm and elsewhere. The enemy's camp remained at Tweefontein and his spies came as far as Elim, which did not make our brave officers any more careful. We stayed where we were; some nights our horses were tied up, others not. Some mornings we saddled and packed up at 4 a.m. on other mornings we did not. For these reasons we, Lood, Col. and I, left the threatened laager on Friday 25th October. The following Saturday, just before sunrise, came the attack. The night before they had been getting out mealies, the horses had been inspanned and only got in at midnight. Most of the men were still in bed. The confusion that ensued when the enemy rushed our piquet, which was sent out at daylight is hard to describe, although the same thing has happened so often before. A few minutes after the first alarm a maxim began playing on the camp, our horses were all over the place, only a few men had saddled up or brought their horses in. Some stood undecided, some ran hither and thither, others grabbed whatever came first to hand, saddle, blanket or pack, and ran for it under a hail of bullets. The English commanded the camp, which lay on an open flat from three sides, and if they had not first fired on the piquet, they would undoubtedly have captured everybody. Many jumped on their barebacked horses and galloped away. The little kit that the men had, and carried on their horses, everything that they could call their own, was left behind in nearly every case, an extra pair of trousers, rugs, a little box of salt, (with difficulty acquired by the boiling process), a piece of tobacco, pair of "veld-schoen" etc. Most of the men came away with nothing but what they had on their bodies and with no prospect of making up for their loss. On this Saturday and on the two following days sixteen of our men, including Capt. Kroon, were captured, as also were all, or nearly all, the spare horses and mules. As soon as our men were out of immediate danger they scattered, which was the cause of many being captured, and it took a week to get them together again.'

scorched earth

A Boer farmhouse set ablaze by British troops. The owners, given time to evacuate their belongings, disconsolately watch the destruction of their home.
▼

British soldiers guarding a store looted by a Boer Commando searching for fresh supplies.
►►

The Boer Commandos, organised in small, fast moving units that possessed an unrivalled knowledge of the countryside, appeared to be able to move at will across territory 'occupied' by the British. They lived off the land collecting food from farmsteads, clothing and equipment from un-garrisoned townships, and a wide variety of ammunition, weapons and material from captured British troops and looted convoys. They also obtained food from rural black African communities, by purchase in some cases, but more often by taking it. Kitchener's mobile columns criss-crossed the veld hunting the Boers but they were often ineffective due to poor intelligence, tactical ineptitude, and the seemingly phantom nature of the enemy. There was also simply not enough mounted infantry in South Africa to cover the ground in adequate numbers. Part of Kitchener's systematic approach to this problem was to seek to deny the Boer raiding parties any form of support on the veld. Removing the sources of re-supply for the Boer Commandos, Kitchener reasoned, would limit not only their mobility but

also the length of time they could maintain themselves in an operational state. Hunger, inadequate clothing, the absence of fresh mounts and a lack of ammunition could render them impotent almost as effectively as a clash with British troops. A policy of ruthlessly clearing the veld of known or suspected points of re-supply for the Commandos was therefore implemented. This went much further than the stratagem adopted while Roberts was still Commander-in-Chief, of destroying farms and slaughtering livestock purely as a reprisal for Boer raids in specific areas. Women, children and old people were forcibly evicted from their homes, which were then either cleared of anything that would give comfort to the Commandos or simply dynamited to destruction. At times the vast acreages of veld were set ablaze by both British and Boers to deny the enemy fodder for their animals. It was scorched earth in name and in fact.

GUSTAV PRELLER:

'The situation on the high veld is now as follows. There are no other commandoes on it besides that of General B Viljoen with the two pom-poms taken by General Muller about 600 strong. Nobody knows what has become of Ch. Botha's 3000 men. At the beginning of May the English marched out again from the railway and spread over the high veld in all directions, splitting up into small columns. Fifteen to twenty independent columns systematically laid waste whatever remained. Women were taken away, exposed to wind and weather in open wagons, and grossly ill-treated and insulted by the soldiers and officers. For example, a well brought up young lady, (Mrs. F. G. A. Wolmarans) was called a liar by a Provost Marshal, because she said she had no eggs in the house (which was the truth) and he thought otherwise. This happened with Gen. Bullock's column. Houses were burnt and plundered, and where the desired object could not otherwise be obtained dynamite was used (Is it their intention to send the women back?) Whole towns were plundered and laid waste, Bethal, Ermelo, Carolina, Piet Relief, the private houses as well as stores and Government buildings. Sheep were slaughtered in tens of thousands. Near F. C. Davel's, Bethal, 7000 sheep were tortured to death on four or five farms only. There are kraals full of slaughtered sheep and lambs; they are rounded up, secured in the kraals and butchered there. Hundreds live for weeks after with their entrails hanging out or their heads half off. The Kaffirs kill them weeks after the slaughter had taken place. Yet these methods are not confined to the smaller cattle. The wild horses are driven into kraals and shot there, brood mares, foals and all. On a farm near F. C. Davel's 260 head of cattle, young and old, were destroyed. These barbarous spectacles must fill every civilised man with disgust when he sees them. The most horrible forms of torture are made use of. On the farm of David Louw, Vryheid, (T. G. A. Wolmarans is my informant) they rounded up 3000 sheep in the dry grass and then set it on fire, with the most horrible results that human eyes have ever witnessed. Truth demands that I should make one exception when I accuse the English of these devilish cruelties. The New Zealanders (who have probably been but a short time in the country) have, as far as I can hear, never been guilty of such things, saying that they had not come to ill-treat women or to kill sheep but to fight, as men are accustomed to do. But to use an apt Arab proverb "the fire only injures the forest by means of its own trees" and so it is in this case. Hundreds of Boers, too degraded to have any idea of patriotism or of their duty as burgers have associated themselves with the English, many have even joined corps whose only object is robbery and plunder. Our noble minded enemy is not above making use of such people. They are paid out of the plunder and they – I blush to say it – are the ones who are guilty of the worst misdeeds of all. One of them, a certain Drostei, was captured when Muller took the camp, and a few days later he was tried and shot. Firstly the Boers, secondly the Cape Colony English Africanders and thirdly the English Africanders from Mashonaland are the worst enemies we have.'

A flock of sheep slaughtered by British troops on a Boer farm. Livestock by the hundreds of thousands was destroyed or confiscated during the War by both sides.

►

Thursday, October 17

ARTHUR TOMEY:

'On another occasion after a march of 20 miles we were informed that our halt was only for a couple of hours and that a further 17 miles was in front of us with a fight at the end of it. Night marches are always trying especially when the ground is rough and there is no moon and I remember his was an exceptionally dark night. We managed it somehow, but when we got into position at daybreak the Boers were in full retreat and we only captured four of them. We collared a few of their wagons however. It was strange that one of the captives had fought against my Regiment at Jacobsdaal, seven months before. He said he was about sick of it and not sorry to be captured.

Some of our work was very unpleasant. if we found arms or ammunition concealed on a farm we had to burn down the place and confiscate all cattle, stores, wagons etc and as the men were usually about or in hiding, and we had only women to deal with you can guess how uncongenial our work was. We brought in thousands of sheep and cattle and the district appears to be fairly quietened down although one of the most hostile in the country. On one occasion a small party of us were fired on from a farm, and after we had cleared the place out we found that a fine young ox had got shot. I don't know anything of butchering but I managed to take away enough meat to make a splendid meal for four of us.'

Sunday, September 22

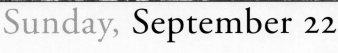

GUSTAV PRELLER:

'Now that our own food supply is getting so scarce we see what a service the English have done us in taking away our women folk. However severely the defenceless victims have had to suffer they would have had a much worse time of it, and made our continued resistence well-nigh impossible, if the enemy had left them among us ... Certainly the best of our men, who are now determined to stand fast for freedom, would have surrendered sooner than see their dear ones perish of hunger and want, and our cause would have been in a much worse condition than it is now. But the enemy's assertion that he was obliged to take the women away because we could not feed them, and that they went in voluntarily is untrue. When the women were taken away there were still plenty of supplies and, as far as I know, no woman has gone of her own freewill. On the contrary they have run all possible risks in escaping from the enemy. Here and there are still a few women, who have either returned from the enemy's lines, or succeeded in keeping out of his hands altogether, and these do invaluable service as nurses, seamstresses etc.'

concentration camps

Refugees

By November 1900 the British were faced with a refugee problem that was growing at an alarming rate. Boers who no longer wished to be involved in the fighting left their homes seeking protection from intimidation. Others, whose men were still participating in the War, left their farms because the British had destroyed them. For whatever cause they became refugees and the British had to attempt to meet their material needs or see them starve to death. At first Roberts had packed the families of Boers who were still fighting on to trains and sent them via the Delgoa Bay railway to join their men folk. It soon became clear that the Boers on campaign were not capable of feeding the refugees and at the end of September 1900 it was decided that special camps would be established. Although the British referred to them simply as refugee camps they were to become labelled as concentration camps. As such they accommodated not only refugees but also the families of fighting Boers who had seen their farms destroyed and eventually a significant percentage of both the white and black populations of areas in which Commandos regularly operated. The British object in establishing these camps was not entirely humanitarian for they were undoubtedly seen by

Thursday, September 19

Percy
6th Lan
Ca

HENRIETTA ARMSTRONG, IN IRENE CONCENTRATION CAMP:

'Now the women are told not to unpack. They may be sent away at any time, but in the meantime they are not supplied with fuel. Some of them were without anything warm to eat or drink for three days. The rain keeps on steadily. Two hundred families were brought from Heatherly district today. They tell a very pitiful tale of the treatment they have received from the soldiers. They first had to see their houses, crops, vehicles and furniture burned and destroyed. They were packed on the empty wagons. They had not gone very far, when they discovered the Boers. They drew all the wagons with women in front and put the men behind them. When the fight was over they brought the women as far as Pretoria in open trucks in this heavy rain, and shunted them off for the night. There they had to remain in their wet through clothing. At last the children began to get cold shivers. Then the mothers would not remain in the trucks any longer. They climbed over the sides and found an empty room. There they went with the poor drenched children for the rest of the night. What miserable objects they looked when they arrived here, homeless, sad and hungry. I always had all my kettles on the stove ready with boiling water when I knew some women were expected. But of course I could not supply them all, but as many of the worst cases as I could. The women who are packed up for Natal, are still here. Also without word. My God, how we feel now – what a merciless thing it was! I went to my quarters with such a sore heart. All the misery I saw in the Camp. When I got home they were just busy hoisting the beastly Union Jack opposite our mess marquee. Then I felt as if it was the last straw. But I dare not give in. The poor women require all the help we can give them. What would we do without the help of Doctor Neethling. He is doing everything in his power.'

1 | A Boer family photographed in Krugersdorp. Many Boer women were regarded by the British as active supporters of the enemy war effort.

2 | Camp inmates at Port Elizabeth celebrating President Kruger's birthday.

3 | Boer prisoners of war were encouraged to work on camp or civic schemes during their captivity and were paid for their labour.

4 | Accommodation for Boer prisoners of war at Broadbottom Camp on St Helena.

5 | A concentration camp at Springfontein under snow during the South African winter.

Kitchener and others as a way of removing Boer women, who were believed to be a particularly militant factor in Boer society, from the debate on whether resistance to the British should be continued. It was also felt that the prospect of prolonged separation from their families would encourage fighting Boers to surrender. Moreover, with their families in refugee camps, there would be little succour or information for the Boers on the veld, and the non-fighting or neutral Boers, who were subject to intimidation, could receive protection from the enemy in the camps.

Misery and suffering

Confining women and children together, mostly under canvas but occasionally in wooden huts in all weathers and with inadequate sanitary provision, was a recipe for disaster. Disaster duly came and it was from the start of 1901 that the unsavoury and notorious reputation of some of the camps really began. With the British military sweeps in the early months of that year the refugee problem began to run out of control. It has been estimated that in March 1901 there were approximately 35,000 white refugees in camps. Six months later in September the total figure had grown to 110,000. Despite the tripling of the number of refugees, the availability of camps did not keep pace with this human tide. From 27 camps in March the number had grown to only 34 by September. The largest camp was home to 7,000 refugees and several had between 4,000 and 5,000 inmates. The death toll had also risen alarmingly during this period from 250 between January and March 1901 to 3,205 in October alone, the latter representing an annual death rate of 344 in every 1,000 refugees. In addition, camps were established for black refugees.

The suffering and death that was for long an inseparable part of camp life was the result not of a deliberate policy but of want of system and inadequate preparation while the camps were under military control, and later while under civilian management from the attempt to deal with an ever

SOPHIE LEVISEUR DESCRIBES THE CONDITIONS FOR WOMEN AND CHILDREN WITHIN THE CAMP:

'You will a have heard of the stories of how awful the concentration camps were and how vilely the women were treated. Naturally, when the camps were started it was all done in such a hurry. There must have been frightful disorder; but as soon as possible things took a better shape, as men working in the camps told us. Naturally, taking the women and children from their houses was frightfully resented, and our poor women made things as difficult as possible for the authorities.

I know, for instance, that when Kit as a child had measles in the camp, her mother (who had, with her whole family, been put into the camp) hid her under the bed when the doctors came to search the tents for sufferers from the epidemic raging there at the time. This was a good way to spread the measles, and certainly could only have harmed the child and not the doctors. I remember a dear friend of mine, who with her five children was taken from her home to a concentration camp, telling me how they were put into a cattle truck with no opening but a small hole over the door. At night they were told to sleep on the bare floor without blankets or anything, and a private soldier came to her and said,

"Madam, would you mind your kiddies sleeping on my mattress? It is quite clean." She thanked him very much; and at another station, where no provision for food had been made for them, several of the Tommies bought with their few pence lemonade and buns for her children because they were so hungry. Right through the war one heard of the Tommies doing things like that.'

greater quantity of refugees without increasing the number of camps available to accommodate them. At first many camps lacked vital facilities – medical, logistical and sanitary – and the refugees suffered from shortages of suitable food, water, fuel, clothing and furniture. Consequently, large numbers of Boer women and children died in the camps from diseases – principally pneumonia, measles and dysentery – to which in their weakened state they had little resistance. These problems were compounded by the British view that the concentration of the refugees in a relatively small number of camps located on the railway would ease supply problems. In fact, of course, over-crowding merely reinforced the ease with which disease could spread through the camps. The isolated existence of the Boers on the veld rendered their families unsuitable candidates for the communal nature of camp life. Their suspicion and ignorance of urban medicine meant that well-intentioned schemes set up by the British authorities were effectively sabotaged by the Boer women themselves, to the detriment of their own children.

The black spot

Contemporary views on the conditions in the camps varied from observer to observer and from camp to camp. Lieutenant Malan, secretary to the Boer General Ben Viljoen, visited the Middelburg camp at the end of August 1901 at the invitation of Lieutenant-General Sir Bindon Blood. Malan reported that the refugees in the camp were happy with their lot and that conditions were satisfactory. Six weeks later the Fawcett Commission, sent by the British Government largely at the behest of the War Office to investigate conditions in the camps, found Middelburg to be badly administered

and generally in a far from satisfactory state. It was an Englishwoman, Miss Emily Hobhouse, who alerted the British public and government to the deadly conditions in many camps. Chamberlain and Milner were entirely convinced by her claims and steps were taken rapidly to put the camps in order. By May 1902 deaths in the camps had fallen to 190; an annual death rate of 20 in every 1,000 refugees. On 7 December 1901 Lord Milner wrote to Joseph Chamberlain: 'The black spot – the one very black spot – in the picture is the frightful mortality in the Concentration Camps. I entirely agree with you in thinking that while a hundred explanations may be offered and a hundred excuses made, they do not really amount to an adequate defence.'

The most telling condemnation of the refugee camps was the tragically high death toll. Altogether, 27,927 Boers died in the camps and of this total over 22,000 were under the age of sixteen. This even exceeded the toll that infection had claimed amongst the British Army where more than 16,000 soldiers died from diseases such as typhoid and pneumonia. The crucial difference was that the camp deaths represented over 10% of the total white population of the Boer Republics. In the 60 British camps holding over 115,000 black African refugees approximately 14,000 had died by the end of the War.

The military rationale for the camp system, to bring about the rapid ending of the Boers' will to fight was not achieved. Neither the deaths in the camps nor the separation of fighting men from their families brought the Boers early to the peace table, although it obviously weighed heavily on their minds. The emptying of the veld of sources of re-supply and intelligence did have an effect but only slowly and cumulatively.

Boer women and children arrive at a concentration camp proclaiming their defiance. When peace came there were still 17,964 women and 19,907 children in camps in the Transvaal alone.
◄

A Boer woman preparing vegetables for dinner at a camp in Port Elizabeth.
▼

mobile columns

Hounding the Boers

For the British to have a realistic chance of crushing the Boer guerillas they had to be able to match their mobility and speed across the veld. To do this they required fast moving, horse-drawn artillery that could keep pace with mounted troops and infantry who were fit enough to march all day and all night. Kitchener developed the use of mobile columns as part of his strategy for destroying the effectiveness of guerilla groups such as that led by De Wet. British columns criss-crossed the veld in response to sightings of armed Boers, to intelligence gained from black Africans and from their own scouts and to

De Wet's raids. In February 1901 De Wet crossed the Orange River and marched into the Cape. Kitchener immediately launched 15 mobile columns in a pursuit in a line over 150 miles wide. The chase lasted six weeks, De Wet constantly out-distanced or out-manoeuvred his pursuers until he was on safe ground. Part of the British problem in attempting to meet De Wet on equal terms was that they lacked the Boer skill for scouting and their intimate knowledge of the terrain. Often British columns did not even know where co-operating units were in the massive emptiness of the veld, communication away from the railway and its accompanying telegraph was difficult and there were constant false alarms.

A British gun team takes a river crossing at speed.
◀

Monday, June 29

ION POSTA
APE OF
DE BON
S ONLY TO

GUSTAV PRELLER:

'The English have now a new method of pursuit, when they see a Boer they gallop after him as hard as they can in order to capture him, a proceeding which has often got them into difficulties whenever they run across other Boers: then they will trek for hours at night, mounted, in order to surprise a party of Boers at day-break. It has become proverbial that at night it is not safe to be within three hours ride in front of an English column, while behind it half an hour is sufficient.'

Lieutenant Bonham-Carter's Troop of the 167th Squadron, Imperial Yeomanry.
►

Monday, July 29

BOMBARDIER R WAUGH, G BATTERY, ROYAL HORSE ARTILLERY:

'The Division moved out again on the 29th July and repeated our former tactics of chasing Boers, collecting cattle and sheep, burning farms and numerous night marches, with an occasional small brush with the enemy to liven us up… De Lisle was noted for the energy of his attack and frequent "all-night" expeditions, and consequent success in his endeavours. During our stay with him we were shifted around somewhat, but on the whole liked him very well, as he was pushing and courted success. If there was anything the troops disliked it was to proceed on a long march, and perhaps all through the night, in the cold and possibly without even cloaks, and then to discover that the expedition was fruitless and but wasted energy. But, on the other hand, if the venture turned out successful, no one grumbled at the additional hardships but were pleased to find that some of the hated enemy or their transport were captured, and their strength or mobility consequently affected.'

Monday, August 5

GUSTAV PRELLER:

'Now here in the neighbourhood of Silvermyn, Middelburg district, a column has marched from the eastern line to Carolina, we nearly fell into their hands. Another column from the southern line followed us for some days without knowing of us. We have to trek from one patch of grass to another, all the rest is burnt black. On many farms, where there is grass, the water is undrinkable, owing to the heaps of dead sheep in it. Fighting on the high veld is now more like hunting springbok than anything else. The English trek out, equipped with everything necessary for war, and chase us over the burnt ridges whenever they come across us, for we are scarcely anywhere strong enough to offer any opposition to such numbers. But the chase has its peculiar difficulties for them also, and not seldom they pay for it with their lives. So we look on the wild things about us with a certain sympathy, and with a sense of companionship in a life of distress.'

blockhouses

A blockhouse made
from corrugated
iron and stones is
finished high on
the veld.
◀

In January 1901 Lord Kitchener began to expand a system of strongpoints based on blockhouses set up initially in July 1900 to guard the Army's communications along the railway from Boer demolitions, particularly of bridges and track. At first they were substantial stone structures which offered considerable protection against attack by either small arms or light artillery pieces. As the purpose of blockhouses was extended to include their use as fixed points in a perimeter against which the Boer raiding parties could be driven and trapped, the urgent need to build more blockhouses led to their construction from corrugated iron, wood and sandbags. As part of Kitchener's tactics of anti-Boer sweeps and drives they made life for the Commandos both difficult and dangerous. Like a giant radar system the prefabricated blockhouses were sited with interlocking fields of fire, surrounded by alarm bells and trip wires, linked by signalling equipment, and physically joined by vast runs of barbed wire or trenches spread across the veld. Ultimately, some 8,000 blockhouses were

BOMBARDIER R WAUGH, G BATTERY, ROYAL HORSE ARTILLERY:

'The Division reached Kroonstad on the 1st December, but our stay there was but a short one and we moved out again at 4 p.m. on the 3rd. The same morning the Right Section of the battery joined De Lisle and the Centre Section Broadwood, thus leaving the Left Section and Head-Quarters with Bethune. Our route lay along the Kroonstad-Lindley blockhouse line which was then being completed. The construction of these blockhouses was a splendid move towards the completion of the war and done a great deal towards finishing it. They were not constructed, as some people supposed, solely for the purpose of stretch – but to furnish posts for the safety of convoys conveying supplies further into the interior than they could possibly have done with the ordinary small escort. It also enabled the columns to keep operating in certain districts without having to march right into a town, or station on the railway line, and then go back again to where they left. It may be mentioned that the country is not overrun with railways and a column may be working in a district 150 miles from the railway line.'

A British block-house near Bethulie. Watercolour by John Farquharson.
▼

constructed and 4,000 miles of barbed wire erected. The longest continuous line of blockhouses stretched for 175 miles from Wonderfontein east of Pretoria to Komatipoort on the Mozambique frontier. Increasingly the Boers' principal advantage — their ability to manoeuvre rapidly and then disappear into vast tracts of country — was denied to them. Duty in the British blockhouses typified the infantryman's life through the ages; long periods of complete boredom punctuated by moments of sheer terror and mortal danger. Each blockhouse would normally be manned by a garrison of six or seven men, in some discomfort, and in all 50,000 troops were assigned to blockhouse duty.

Friday, December 19

GUSTAV PRELLER:

'With Commandant Prinsloo through the blockhouse line. The day before, 18th Dec., Major Pretorius was surprised and captured with 33 men near Vlakvarkensfontein. This side of the blockhouses there are thousands of cattle trekking round about. Prinsloo has about 200 men, Naude has come in here with a hundred, so there are about 400 here altogether. We and Prinsloo trekked as far as Bronkhurstspruit. Here the Boers dispersed for some days under the Field Cornets and Corporals to fetch away buried property. The daily routine remains the same for all, as several columns have appeared in the neighbourhood. 3 a.m. Saddle up; 4 a.m. send out scouts; 5 - 6 a.m. trek, or off saddle; send out observation posts; look for Kaffir corn or mealies, prepare food, eat fruit, sleep. At sunset saddle up and go to another place. There make huts of corrugated iron, when obtainable, for there is a great deal of rain. Some horses already down with horse sickness... Occupied Neethlings farm again, sent out scouts who saw nothing. When it got light some of our men came upon a body of the enemy, who came out of Springs the night before, a wretched lot, worse than any I have seen for a long time. English came on to within three hundred yards of us and then trekked immediately back to Springs, followed by V. G. Tromp.'

sweeps and drives

During the guerrilla phase of the War British supply columns criss-crossed the veld delivering food and ammunition to garrisons and detachments. These slow moving convoys were intensely vulnerable to interception by the Boers.

▼

The experience of the American war in Cuba had shown that blockhouses alone could not be relied upon to defeat guerrilla activity. The area between fixed defences had to be swept frequently by mounted troops who could move at the same pace as the enemy. With his blockhouse lines in place, Kitchener organised carefully planned drives which swept through designated areas in which the Boer raiders were thought to be operating. Nothwithstanding this organised approach, the drives were often unsuccessful for there was simply too much space into which an alert Commando could easily disappear, even when it was pursued by several mobile columns all pushing it towards blockhouses or

entrenchments. The Commando leaders such as De Wet and Smuts became adept at avoiding British columns, and Smuts was able even to penetrate to within a hundred miles of Cape Town.

Drives were extremely successful in denying the Commandos easy access to shelter and sustenance, for as British troops swept through an area, often without making contact with fighting Boers, they fell back upon destroying the property and gathering in or slaughtering the livestock of hostile inhabitants. In one action alone on 31 March 1901 at Smaldeel, British troops under General Sir John Dartnell dispersed a group of 400 Boers and captured 80 wagons,

10,000 head of sheep and 3,800 head of cattle. Drives were also responsible during the summer of 1901 for sweeping the Free State Government, albeit without the Republic's President Steyn, into captivity. In the end the drives did contribute to the general process of wearing down the Boer will to continue with the War, but as Lord Milner noted in a telegram to Chamberlain on 31 October 1901 the results were highly disproportionate: '...we still employ 200,000 troops and 500 guns to deal with 10,000 men without any guns at all.'

Thursday, August 8

GUSTAV PRELLER, HEIDELBURG DISTRICT:

'Yesterday evening we arrived near Oliphantsfontein. An English column was marching along behind us and we had to trot. Yesterday evening at sunset we were at the place where there was some fighting last year at the occupation of Pretoria. In the event, together with the Commandants Prinsloo and van Niekerk we were surrounded by the enemy who only left one way of escape open, in the direction of Standerton, through which we got out at 3 a.m. this morning. Who will be able in the future to imagine or describe our night manoeuvres over the black ridges in the depth of a severe winter. By the feeble light of the waning moon, for whose rising we had to wait, we trekked along for hours; tired, asleep and worn out we hurried away from the danger which threatened us on every side. Behind and on our right we already saw the English camp fires, they were early on foot, and an hour later they were at the place which we had just left where they found nothing but the smouldering ashes of our fires. To the right and in front of us were grass fires lighted yesterday by the enemy. We march in silence, nobody speaks, and what should they talk about, even if they felt any inclination for conversation. Nothing is to be heard but the rolling of wagons and carts. We shiver from the cold; worst of all our feet are half frozen. At last the grey day breaks and a sharp wind springs up and makes our ears tingle. At last, quite numb with cold, we outspan with everything safely in rear of the enemy again. A few weeks ago the Germans who were with Commandant Mears received their passports for Europe. They got involved in a quarrel, which arose out of a trifling difference with a Burgher piquet [card game] and led to such unpleasantness that the case was brought before General Brits who gave his decision against them, whereupon they signified their unwillingness to fight any longer and betook themselves (about 15 in number) under the leadership of a certain Lieutenant Hengst to the Government, who paid them 2/6 a day, reckoned from the beginning of the war, and gave them an order on Dr. Leyds for another 2/6 a day and a bonus of £100 each, as well as a free ticket 2nd class to Europe.'

anti-war opposition

The British public ran through a wide gamut of emotion during the Boer War: indignation at the Boer ultimatum, pride as the Army sailed for South Africa, bewilderment and despair during Black Week, elation at the relief of Kimberley, Ladysmith and Mafeking, satisfaction at the triumphs of Lord Roberts, irritation at the guerrilla successes of the Boers. For a vocal minority of the public, however, outrage was the only emotion which characterised their response to the War. A significant segment of opinion in Liberal circles and amongst the Labour movement was solidly against the War even before it broke out, and protest meetings against British policy towards South Africa were held as early as the beginning of July 1899. At first the 'Pro-Boers' as they were generally and usually inaccurately described found the task of opposition to the War an uphill task. They were running against a tide of anti-Boer and anti-German jingoism that was constantly reinforced by the popular imperialism espoused by many organs of the Press. There were also divisions in the ranks of the Liberals and among the radical movements.

Some felt that the Boers could not be supported because they had hijacked the country from Black Africans; others that the War was a struggle for democratic enfranchisement and against the reactionary rule of the Boers. With the defeats of Black Week, 'Pro-Boers' came to be regarded as traitors and their meetings were broken up amid considerable violence, order only being restored in Scarborough after one such meeting through the intervention of the Army. Only with the occupation of Pretoria, after which the public began to lose interest in South Africa, was it really safe for the anti-war movement to raise its head above the parapet.

The tedium of the guerrilla war and the descriptions of the conditions in refugee camps created an opening for protest against the continuation of the War. Demonstrations were held and pamphlets circulated, this time with support from a number of newspapers. Yet many who felt opposed to Chamberlain's policies hesitated to express their concerns openly out of deference to the interests of national unity at a time of crisis in the country's affairs. The government was rankled by

◄

An Anti-war group in Battersea, south London. While these groups were troubled by the 'morality' of the War their essential case was that the conflict would ultimately destroy Britain's position in South Africa.

the criticism it received from the 'Pro-Boers', particularly in regard to the 'methods of barbarism' allegations levelled at it by Sir Henry Campbell-Bannerman, but it was not diverted from its intention of pursuing the Boers to defeat.

Bitter-enders and hands-uppers

The Boer camp had two extremes: the 'bitter-enders' who wished to fight to the last gasp, and those commandos and former commandos who simply wished to surrender to the British. The position of the 'bitter-enders' was epitomised by President Steyn who refused to surrender when the Orange Free State was annexed by the British and instead trekked across the veld with the Boer Commandos for the next two years braving all dangers and hardships. When the question of surrender was discussed Steyn raised his voice in protest at even the contemplation of such a step. In contrast, many commandos worn down by the physical and mental strain of a guerrilla campaign and tempted by British offers of amnesty

sought any opportunity to surrender safely. Known to the fighting Boers as 'hands-uppers', they represented a loss of many thousands to their rifle strength. General Viljoen had to deal constantly with disaffected Boers who, while not initially against the War, came to adopt a pro-surrender position. Writing of the Boer situation in July 1901 he outlined the problem:

'Matters were rather in a critical state, as treachery was rampant, and many burghers were riding to and fro to the enemy and arranging to surrender, the faithful division being powerless to prevent them. We had to act with great firmness and determination to put a stop to these tendencies and within a week of our arrival half a dozen persons had been incarcerated in Roos Senekal gaol under a charge of high treason... I often came across cases where fathers fought against their own sons, and brother against brother.'

As Viljoen implies, a number of Boers had laid down their weapons only to take them up again in the service of the British in units such as the National Scouts. These 'joiners' were considered worse than the 'hands-uppers'.

► Some of the Boer 'bitter-enders' (Bittereinders) who wished to continue the struggle against the British until an independent homeland was established. Their intense hatred of those who had collaborated with the British did not end with peace.

prisoners of war

The British advantage

The problem of the loss of combatants as prisoners of war was far greater for the Boers than it was for the British. The British lost troops as prisoners of war almost every day of the opening campaigns. The Boers lost the majority of their men taken prisoner in two large groups: after Paardeberg in February 1900 and after Brandwater Basin in July 1900. The British, as they advanced further into the Orange Free State and the Transvaal, had the advantage of occupying many of the locations in which their prisoners of war were being held captive. They were therefore able to free them, returning the fit to active service and repatriating the remainder to the United Kingdom. When British troops occupied Bloemfontein they liberated over 3,000 officers and men who had been captured by the Boers. During the first eleven months of the War 7,387 British troops had been listed as missing or prisoners of war, but by the end of September 1900 some 91% of these POWs (6,762 officers and men) had escaped

or been released from captivity. Statistics such as these were depressing reading for the Boer commanders but their highly mobile form of warfare made the problem of retaining prisoners almost insoluble, particularly during the guerrilla phase of the conflict. Indeed, British troops taken prisoner during guerrilla operations could find themselves liberated within a matter of hours or days as friendly forces pressed and harried the Commandos.

The Boers had no such advantage since their men, once they had left the prisoner of war camp at Green Point Common near Cape Town, were shipped by the British to areas of the Empire – Ceylon, India, Bermuda and St Helena – that were geographically remote from South Africa. There were also more than a thousand 'detainees' in camps in Portugal. Escape in meaningful numbers was thus made virtually impossible once prisoners reached their destination, even if they had not already given their parole. Mass escape while at sea was considered and Boer prisoners taken at Cronje's surrender at Paardeberg tried unsuccessfully to

Broadbottom prisoner of war camp on St Helena. Tented accommodation in camps was usually replaced by more substantial wood and stone structures as the War progressed.
▼

J L de Villiers in the clothing which he used to effect an escape from Ceylon.
►►

overpower their guards (a company of the 2nd Battalion The Royal Warwickshire Regiment) on the S S Armenian during its voyage from Simonstown to Bermuda in June 1901. Approximately 4,500 Boer POWs arrived in Bermuda where they were accommodated in 850 bell tents in well-established camps on the islands of the Great Sound. In all some 33,000 Boers had been taken prisoner by the end of the War, of which total 827 died in captivity. On 14 June 1902 there were 8,122 Boer POWs held in India, 5,652 on St Helena, 4,933 in Ceylon, 4,541 on Bermuda, nearly 7,000 in South Africa and 1,000 at sea.

Life as a prisoner of war

Conditions in the prison camps appear to have been at least adequate with the most vexing factor in the prisoners' lives being boredom. The British, in their administration of the camps, interfered very little in their prisoners' daily existence providing that good behaviour was maintained. Commandant

Peter Ferreira spoke for many Boer prisoners when interviewed in New York after his release: 'Really I do not think we have much to complain about in regard to our treatment. It is certain the British cared for us much better than we could possibly have cared for them.'

Statistically, the Boer prisoners certainly fared better than their families in the refugee camps in South Africa. In Bermuda between June and December 1901 only 12 patients died out of 950 admissions to the camp hospital. In the camps in India and Ceylon the extremes of the local climate as well as unusual diseases posed a threat to the prisoners but again deaths were within the limits of normal expectation. At the British camp at Diyatalawa in Ceylon the extensive outer perimeter stretched for five miles, and by March 1901 the camp housed 4,536 Boer POWs in 81 huts plus a number of officer prisoners. Each Burgher had a cubic space within his hut of 514 feet in which was accommodated his sleeping cot. The camp contained 22 kitchens and seven wash-houses as well four hospitals, a school, a two-acre

Saturday, May 3

MATTHYS JOHANNES UYS, BOER POW ST HELENA:

'Was captured on the 9th October 1901 on the Farm Mowbray Dst. Harrismith O.V.S. from there Harrismith stopped there a few days and was send to Tin Town, Ladysmith stopped there two and a half month and left for Durban were on the Roslin Castle for a few days and left with the Orient for St. Helena arrived here on the 22.1.02 and stopped on board till the 27.1.02 than

we arrived here in this camp at about sunset that evening very tired and disjusted, were treated very good by the old P. of War that evening next day we were asked to a consert of the (strevers) the following night we had a good consert in the orange zaal, which had been splendidly arranged by Mr. H. Fivaz, A. Ortlepp and Joe Tilly.'

recreation ground for cricket and football, two tennis courts, a swimming pool and a carpentry shop. The prisoners were encouraged to take paid employment on public works projects, and the Boers at Diyatalawa built a road, cleared sites for new buildings and constructed a number of reservoirs. The camp was guarded by 900 men of the 1st Battalion the Duke of Cornwall's Light Infantry using five guard posts of which three were equipped with Maxim guns.

In the full knowledge that they would not be detained long if captured by the Boers, though they would lose their weapons, equipment and items of clothing, some British troops had a tendency to surrender a little too quickly when surrounded. From 1 October 1900 King's regulations stipulated that when troops were taken prisoner a Court of Enquiry would be held to examine the conduct of the senior officer or soldier present at the surrender. From 1 May 1901 any officer or soldier raising a white flag in the presence of the enemy would be tried by a General Court Martial. The task of the Court of Enquiry was to discover whether a man had been taken prisoner through his own neglect or misconduct or as a result of the 'chances of war'. On this basis each man was exonerated or not as the Court determined.

Saturday, June 28

MATTHYS JOHANNES UYS, BOER POW ST HELENA:

'21 of us went for a Picnic at Sandybay on the 26th June 1902 the sea was very rough, and did not get any fish, had a Concert that evening, each one of us had to give a sougar resetation etc, it was terrible cold that night H. Fivaz and myself slept together after we all had a good bath in the sea on the morning of the 27th we had coffee and cakes and than all went out to fish, but as the weather was very bad and the sea too rough we failed, so we came back and had our dinner, than a rest and than all of us started for the sea to have a good swim... On the 28th we had a swim in the sea, very early in the morning, and then had breakfast ... we left for the camps, half way we stopped, and made some Coffee, had dinner and started for Genrl. B. Viljoens place where we had some Coffee and some of the party took whiskey and had a good smoke, and than we all started for the Camp happy and pleased with our outing, as it was a success with the exception that the sea was too rough for fishing, when we reached the camp, every one was glad to see us back and came for information and had many jokes, Re the poety.'

Prisoners in a camp
in Cape Town, 1900.
◀

Sunday, August 20

TROOPER J HAYWARD, SOUTH NOTTS HUSSARS YEOMANRY:

'The place where we are kept by the Boers is a open veldt for about 200 yards square with mountains all round it. It is a very fitting place to keep prisoners as you cannot see anything but Boer sentries who parade round it with loaded rifles. Mountains, turf huts & Catwire, the encloser is surrounded by Barbed wire fixed to poles about 8 feet high there are about 30 rows of this wire, so we could not very well get over it if we tried. At night the place is lit up by electric lights there are about 45 of these lamps all round the place so we are pretty safe here although several prisoners have escaped from here and got into the British lines. There would be more attempts made to escape, were it not for expecting being relieved by our troops who are supposed to be marching close to this place. There are the Irish Fusiliers, Suffolks, Glosters, Royal Artillery, Yeomanry. Colonials. New Zealanders, Canadians Australians, in fact nearly every core belonging to the British Army.'

the technology of war

Technology and tactics

The 40 years from 1855 to 1895 saw a revolution on the battlefield due to the impact of modern technology on war and tactics. The transition from muzzle-loading, percussion firearms to breech-loading, bolt-action rifles shooting smoke-less, centre-fire cartridges was completed. The infantryman no longer had to fight standing-up, shoulder to shoulder with his comrades. He could now load his rifle while lying down and could remain in cover when he engaged the enemy. Lines of troops no longer disappeared in thick clouds of smoke shortly after a battle had begun. The trauma of death arriving unseen through billowing white clouds had been replaced by the shattering experience of death striking unexpectedly from a totally invisible foe. Quick-firing, long range artillery was introduced together with automatic weapons such as pom-poms and machine guns. The result was a massive increase in firepower that was more rapid, more accurate and more difficult to suppress, and an associated and dramatic growth in the power of the defence. With weapons such as these the geographical envelope in which battles were fought was gradually expanded bringing with it problems of both communication and observation. In South Africa a slow but reliable solution to the former was still the despatch rider mounted on a strong, fast horse, but other methods of communicating requests, orders and intelligence were freely adopted by the British and Boers. Messages were sent by heliograph, telephone, electric telegraph and even searchlight. Although only the heliograph played an active role in battlefield communications, commanders on campaign could now pass information quickly to and from the Front, and even exchange intelligence with garrisons under siege.

Where once military communications had been tardy, inefficient and fraught with the probability of failure, they could now be almost instant. Where the Boers had deployed in a static defensive position, particularly in the set-piece battles during the advance into the Orange Free State and the Transvaal under Roberts, the British relied upon balloons for observation. Observation from a balloon enabled a commander to receive accurate reports on the enemy's current positions, and allowed the artillery to learn where its long range shells were falling so that inaccurate fire could be corrected as much as possible.

The strategic power of railways

In the vast expanse of South Africa mobility was the key to warfare. Tactically, for the individual commando or yeomanry trooper the horse provided the main means of closing with the enemy, but strategically the railway engine dominated the development of the War. For the British, only the railway could move sufficient food, ammunition, equipment, supplies and

1 | **An X-ray machine in use in South Africa to assist in the treatment of a British soldier.**

2 | **A sorting office for Christmas mail for British troops.**

3 | **Supplies of food stockpiled before issue to British troops.**

Balloons were employed by the British for observation of Boer movement and dispositions and for spotting the fall of shot of the artillery.
►

JOHN LANE, IN THE BOER LAAGER AT PAARDEBERG:

'I have not been able to have a wash since last night, I ventured down to the river. I had just pulled my shirt over my head, happening to look up, my eye caught sight of a big black thing, at first glance it seemed to be right on the top of me, I said, Oh my God, and fell flat on my stomach, thinking it would explode. I then got my senses about me and looked up, and Lo and behold, it was the balloon, appears for the first time since lying around Magersfontein... Some fellows shouted to me to hide away, "Poets kernel" they shouted, it does not much matter now, it is all up, they will now be able to find out every hole and position we are in and will pour in a hell of shells. The balloon kept up for about three hours, it looks very close, but is far out of range. Lots of our men kept firing at it. It is amusing to hear the talk of some of our Burghers so as "do you call this fair play" that damnable big round thing, spying our positions, we would not be so mean to do a thing like this. Let them throw away their big guns and balloons, come out on the flat with their Lee Metfords and we will show them what we can do with the Mauser...'

troops quickly enough and in sufficient quantities to sustain an offensive directed against the Transvaal and Orange Free State. Once the Republics had been occupied, only the railway could carry British reinforcements in strength to threatened areas as the Commandos roamed far and wide. For the Boers the railway was a magnet that drew them inexorably to what was seen as the 'soft underbelly' of British communications. Railways were intensely vulnerable to disruption by enemy action but they brought a speed to troop concentration which earlier commanders, used to moving their armies on foot or by water, could only dream of. The organisation and control of the 4,268 miles of railway in South Africa was in the hands of the Department of Military Railways officered by Royal Engineers and directed by Major Percy Girouard. The British had to fight for hundreds of miles of this railway before they could harness it to their needs, and there were occasions when it appeared that the outcome of the War would rest upon their ability to repair and protect the fragile but vital artery of the railway. By the end of September

1900 some 18,000 officers and men were required to operate the railways in the captured Boer Republics alone.

The Boer Commandos became expert at the business of railway demolition, using dynamite with abandon to demolish bridges, destroy culverts and wreck mile after mile of the permanent way. They also damaged water tanks and locomotives, blocked the line with boulders weighing several tons, ignited stocks of fuel, destroyed stations and cut telegraph lines. Despite this mayhem the British managed, for example, to convey 1,247,000 troops, 540,000 horses and live stock, and 1,058,000 tons of supplies over the Cape Government Railway between October 1899 and March 1901. In addition, the railway provided the means to run armoured trains into the battle area and to transport the sick and wounded quickly away from the Front in ambulance and hospital trains. When the Army left the railway, its supplies were transported in carts drawn by horses, mules and oxen. Occasionally a newcomer to the battlefield, the steam traction engine, lent a hand – particularly if the terrain was difficult.

Thursday, May 3

CAPTAIN G T BRIERLEY, ROYAL ARTILLERY, AT BRANDFORT DESCRIBES THE PROBLEMS OF LONG-RANGE WEAPONRY ON THE OPEN VELD:

'G' Battery shortly came into action against some Kopjes held by Boers. Hardback and I halted near the Battery wagon until ordered into action behind a small Kopje with some Mounted Infantry. We were forced to gallop over an open space commanded by a Kopje 1,500 yards away. They blazed at us for all they were worth whilst we were exposed. Hardback had one horse killed and a Corporal wounded through the thigh, and the men had three helmets perforated including my groom Gunner Turner. We got into action with two maxims, which we dismounted from the carriages and put on tripods, and soon silenced the Boers. We shortly afterwards went into bivouac, the Boers having retreated. Hardback and I both learned a great deal at this scrap; we had not realised the effective range of rifles, and how long it takes even at a gallop to get to a piece of cover which appears easily attainable at first sight. We were also, by being kept too far back at first, unable to see what was going on. An officer should leave his section under cover, and go and see for himself from a point of vantage, what is going on all the time, and when he is ordered to do anything, his orderly can take a message to his guns to proceed anywhere, and he can join them en route, keeping the fight in his vision all the time. If I had known for instance that there were many Boers on the Kopje which fired at us, which I could have seen from any high point, I should have put another thousand yards between them and us, whilst traversing the open space. We also got a glimmering of the danger of a maxim being brought into a zone of fire of equal range with small arms.'

A temporary bridge erected by the British to bypass the original railway bridge destroyed by Boer demolition. ▶

Friday, April 4

CAPTAIN J ROY, DERBYSHIRE REGIMENT ON SPECIAL SERVICE WITH THE MOUNTED INFANTRY:

'We are on the telegraph and can send a cable to England or a telegram anywhere in Africa. Its wonderful if you think of it. The nearest Railway is 70 miles off. If I wired today you would probably get it on the 6th.'

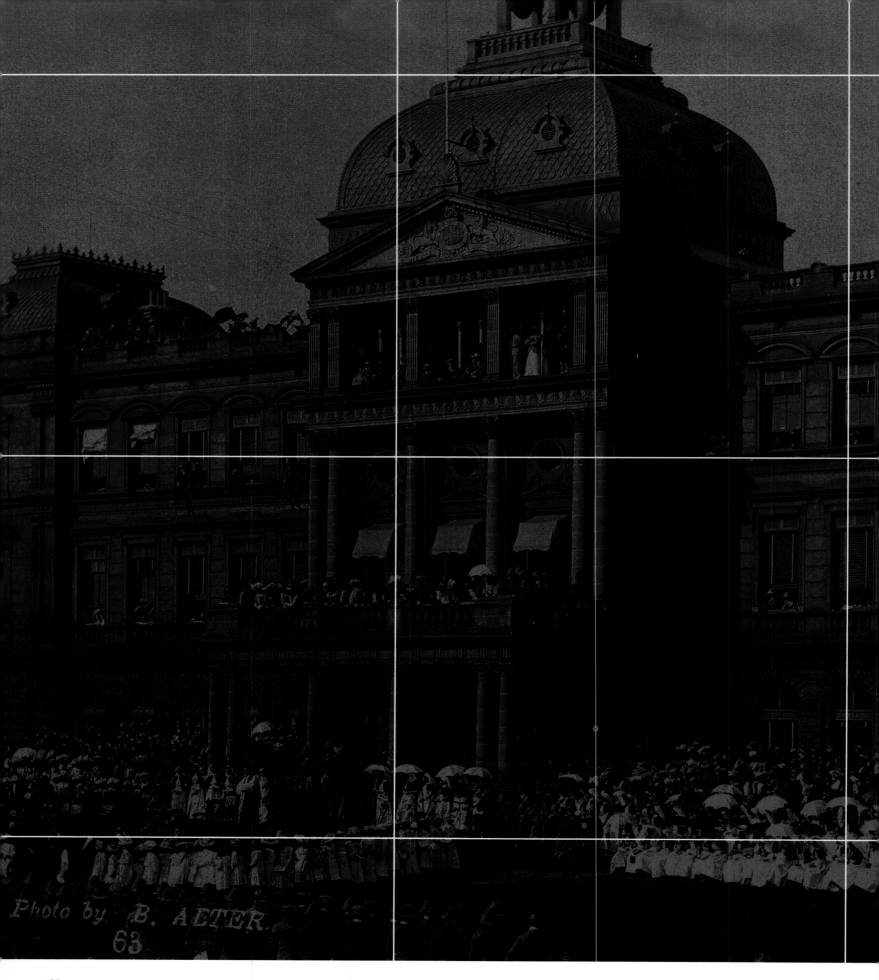

Photo by B. ALTER.
63

the road to peace

From the British occupation of Pretoria in June 1900 there was a willingness among leaders on both sides to air the question of peace. Indeed the British had concluded when they entered the principal town of the Transvaal that the War was effectively over since the Boers would have no alternative but to sue for an armistice. There were even a number of exploratory peace meetings during 1901 with emissaries as diverse as Mrs Botha and Mrs Joubert sallying forth to seek the views of the other side.

The British had made it clear, however, that the War was no longer, if it ever had been, a struggle waged for the Uitlander franchise, but an action aimed at depriving the Boer Republics of their independence. Throughout the first two years of the War the Boer command could demonstrate to their men that peace meant bowing to British rule. In addition, the British were demanding unconditional surrender, something which the Boer sacrifice during two years of war could not accommodate.

By the third year of the War the position of both sides on the question of peace was shifting. Boer and Briton were being worn down by a guerrilla campaign fought over enormous distances; Boer strength and resources were dwindling and their families still on the veld were close to starvation. Kitchener's troops were also approaching exhaustion. More and more of his seasoned regiments were leaving South Africa to be replaced by young, inexperienced soldiers barely out of training. The human and financial cost

of the War continued to mount but there was as yet little sign of normality returning, even to the Cape. While Boer Commandos continued their raids neither the mining industry on the Rand nor agriculture could regain their pre-war levels of productivity. The length of the War and Kitchener's draconian tactics for dealing with the guerrillas were creating political tensions in Britain, and the government wanted to see a discernible path towards peace.

In October 1900 President Kruger, exhausted by the struggle with the British, had left Africa for Europe, officially on leave of absence to raise active support for the Boer cause. Schalk Burger replaced him as acting President. When Kruger landed at Marseilles he was met by a cheering mass of 60,000 people and his onward journey to Paris was nothing short of a royal progress as ecstatic crowds marked his progress with flowers and celebration. While European governments might be unsure how to react to Kruger's arrival in their midst, their citizens were united in a vibrant surge of anti-British feeling. Throughout France there was only one cry on the lips of the crowds: 'Vive Kruger, Vive les Boers'. Similar scenes were repeated in Germany and Holland, even though the Kaiser refused to receive Kruger and his delegation. Across the Channel Lloyd George harassed the Government unmercifully, describing the War as 'damnable', 'senseless' and an 'outrage'. Among British intellectuals there was growing sympathy for the Boers and particularly for the wounded but defiant spectacle of Kruger in 'exile'.

An example of the colourful commemorative ware produced during and after the Boer War to celebrate Britain's triumph and that of her heroes.

Sympathy for those Boers still on Commando was spreading through the ranks of the British troops serving in South Africa, even as they harried their enemy across the veld. At Kitchener's headquarters there were officers who were by December 1901 decidedly 'pro-Boer' in their outlook on the War. To them the British demand for unconditional surrender was a nonsense. In their estimation it was clear that short of killing or capturing every commando on the veld, which might yet take several years, the only route to peace was to reach some form of agreement with the Boers. The civilians who wielded economic and political influence in the Cape were diametrically opposed to this view. Much of their opinion was exemplified by the High Commissioner, Lord Milner, who not only urged the government to sack Kitchener but also argued vehemently against peace talks with the Boers. He wanted nothing less than a complete and unequivocal victory which embraced the political exile of the Boer leaders. In the end the views of the Army prevailed over those of Milner and his circle, but only after a protracted period of negotiation.

The Peace of Vereeniging

On 23 March 1902, three days before the death of Cecil Rhodes, the Boer leaders indicated their willingness to discuss peace constructively. On 12 April Steyn, Botha, De Wet and Smuts met Kitchener in Pretoria and handed over a seven-point list of terms which were clearly unacceptable to the British government. On 17 April Kitchener and Milner put the British terms to the Boers, who then travelled to Vereeniging to discuss the offer with delegates from their Commandos. In May the Boers finally acknowledged that the restoration of their independence was not on the table and realistic discussions began. The negotiations leading to peace turned on three overriding questions: could an amnesty be granted to those colonial Afrikaners who had taken up arms and were therefore guilty of rebellion?; how long would elapse after peace had been signed before the Boers achieved self-government?; and what financial aid would be made available to those Boers who had to re-build and re-stock their farms? On the latter point the British agreed to advance £3,000,000. While an amnesty for the colonial rebels was refused, an undertaking was given that there would be no death penalties imposed and that the general punishment would be disenfranchisement. No time limit was put on the colonial administration of the former Republics and hence there was no date set for the restoration of self-government. On these principal terms the Treaty of Vereeniging was signed on 31 May 1902 and the Commandos finally laid down their arms and surrendered. The fighting was officially over but much of the political and social tension which had led to war – between Boer and Uitlanders, Boer and black African, and Burgher and Nationalist – remained.

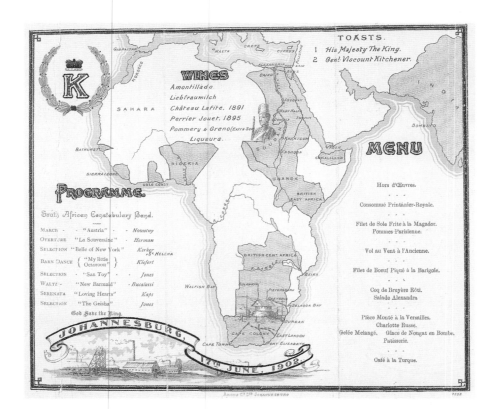

A dinner menu celebrating Britain's recently consolidated position in Africa. Johannesburg 17 June 1902.

A certificate from Cape Town recording the gratitude of its population for the services of the citizen soldiers who came from Britain to fight in the War.

▶

Wednesday, December 15

GENERAL BEN VILJOEN:

'At most times our outlook was gloomy enough, and our hearts were heavily weighed down by cares. I often found my thoughts involuntarily turning to those who had long and so faithfully stood shoulder to shoulder with me through all the vicissitudes of war, fighting for what we regarded as our holy right, to obtain which we were prepared to sacrifice our lives and our all. Unconsciously I recalled on this Christmas Day the words of General Joubert addressed to us outside Lady-smith in 1899: "Happy the Afrikaner who shall not survive the termination of this War". Time will show, if it have not already shown, the wisdom of General Joubert's words.

Just about this time rumours of various kinds were spread abroad. From several sources we heard daily that the War was about to end, that the English had evacuated the country because their funds were exhausted, that Russia and France had intervened, and that Lord Kitchener had been captured by De Wet and liberated on condition that he and his troops left South Africa immediately. It was even said that General Botha had received an invitation from the British Government to come and arrange a Peace on "independence" lines. Nobody will doubt that we on the veld were desperately anxious to hear the glad tidings of Peace. We were weary of the fierce struggle and we impatiently awaited the time when the Government should order us to sheathe the sword.'

the price of the war

The human cost

The human cost of the Boer War embraced both soldier and civilian, especially during the guerrilla campaign. Death in war comes not only on the battlefield from the action of bullet, shell or sword, but also from misadventure and most commonly from disease. Thus casualties can occur among troops and the civilian population at some remove from the Front. Even in the twentieth century accurate casualty figures for a prolonged period of warfare are notoriously difficult to compile. The attribution of civilian casualties to the result of war can be very difficult, particularly when they are filtered through propaganda. By 31 May 1902 deaths in action among British troops amounted to 5,774 while a further 22,829 had been wounded. Of the latter 2,018 subsequently died of their wounds. Deaths from disease totalled 13,250, accidents resulted in 798 deaths, and 75,430 officers and men were repatriated to the United Kingdom as invalids. Commonwealth units also suffered significant casualties on the battlefield. Of the 16,000 Australians who served in South Africa, for example, 518 were killed in battle and 882 were wounded. Out of 7,368 Canadians who reached South Africa, one third of them after peace had been signed, nearly 500 became casualties. The Red Cross Identity Depot, which fulfilled the role of a casualty office for the Boer Commandos, estimated that they lost 3,700 killed in action or died of wounds. There appear to be no reliable figures for the number of black Africans who died on the veld serving with the British and Boer forces. While the battlefield cost of the Boer War in human terms was grave, such totals of dead and wounded would be exceeded in the course of a morning's battle a little over ten years later.

The War had destroyed family life and on the Boer side even wrecked whole communities. The total civilian loss of life during the War is difficult to calculate with any strong claim to accuracy, but it is certain that the vast burden of this loss fell on the Boers. Civilian casualties outside the Boer population were mainly inflicted as a result of disease or by artillery and sniper fire during the sieges of Ladysmith, Mafeking and Kimberley. Figures for Boer deaths in the refugee camps have been estimated at between 18,000 and 28,000 though the higher figure is now generally regarded as correct. Black African civilians also suffered greatly as a result of the War, particularly during its guerrilla phase when black refugees died by their thousands in the camps.

The financial cost

Increasingly, as the guerrilla campaign dragged on, the Boers' war effort was supported by the British tax payer in the form of captured weapons, clothing, ammunition and supplies. By the end of 1901 Boer sources of supply were virtually non-existent and to continue to function in the field they

Monday, December 25

JOHN LANE, AN UITLANDER COMMANDEERED FOR SERVICE WITH A BOER COMMANDO:

'Christmas Day, the last one of the century. Rather a rum place for me to spend it, in a Boer Laager, facing the British Army, within range of their big guns... Today I cannot keep from thinking of my dear wife and children. It is hard to be compelled to be separated from them at this time, won't it be a happy time when we are all together again. I sent a telegram (we were allowed a free wire of ten words) to Wife. Wishing them Christmas greeting and peace on earth. When will it come?'

1 | The garrison of a British blockhouse on the veld.

2 | 'C' ward on board the British hospital ship Duuera.

3 | A Boer ambulance train.

A regimental memorial for the 1st Battalion Royal Irish Fusiliers who served and died at Ladysmith. Note that more died of disease than of injuries.

◄

plundered the many British supply columns which slowly wound their way across the veld. The cost of the War to the British was in excess of £220,000,000 and the British Chancellor of the Exchequer, Sir Michael Hicks Beach, was forced to raise taxation, both direct and indirect, to meet part of this expense. In 1900 income tax was raised from 8d to 1s in the pound and duty was increased on tea, tobacco, spirits and beer. In 1901 income tax rose to 1s 2d and duty was placed on the export of coal and on refined sugar. By the end of the War income tax stood at 1s 3d and additionally the Chancellor was forced to issue war loans totalling £135,000,000. There were also indirect costs to be paid through lost production on the Rand, the general disruption of entrepreneurial activity in South Africa, and increased spending in general upon the Army and Navy. The Boer War was by far the largest single military operation pursued by the British in the nineteenth century and it was the most costly. Usually Britain's colonial campaigns were exacting but small in scale and although the Napoleonic Wars saw upwards of 750,000 British troops employed, this total was cumulative over a period of 16 years. The Crimean War of 1854-56, which embraced a British Army of roughly 100,000 troops, cost the Nation £75,000,000 together with the loss of 19,584 officers and men who fell victim to the enemy and to disease. The Boer War was an indication of what modern warfare would mean for the economic and human resources of a nation.

Thursday, September 12

LIEUTENANT R J K MOTT, THE QUEEN'S (ROYAL WEST SURREY REGIMENT):

'I am "Commandant" here and have 2 blockhouses besides to look after. It is not a bad place, but up to now I have been very busy with alterations to the defences; the place was designed for defence by 100 men, but I only have 40; and the work is rather heavy, what with patrols and guards... The next excitement was last night when heavy firing was heard up the line at about 9.30. It appears that my patrol, a lance-corporal and 3 men, had met with 15 to 20 Boers, let them get within 100 yards and then let fly. They drove them back, and this morning found a dead Boer – the first a great many of us have seen. We buried him this morning, and I went out and read part of the Burial Service. He was one of de Wet's scouts, a very tall man – he was carrying despatches. He had 2 bullet wounds, ½ inch apart, between the eyes! One of my men, a little Cockney, when I ordered the grave to be filled in, said to me: "Beg pardon Sir, but 'e's got one of our greatcoats on – Can I go and get it out?" – !'

THE BEREFT BIRD.

NO ADMITTANCE.

Friday, April 11

CAPTAIN J ROY, DERBYSHIRE REGIMENT ON SPECIAL SERVICE WITH THE MOUNTED INFANTRY:

'Breakfast 5. a. m. and off at 6. We had to go on to the right as we were advance Guards – we pushed on and got into position about 7 a.m. Derby Coy. leading screen. 11th M.I. in support on each flank and rest support in the centre, about 7-30 they (Main body) started to move and almost at once my left flank sent in word there were a lot of Boers on the left. I sent back word and was just off to have a look when the Col. Von Donos came up and said they were Rawlinson's so I sent back word to this effect but another message came saying these were Boers and were attacking. I at once got the rest of my men up, told the Pom-Pom to come into action and sent to tell Col. Kekewich. They appeared just as I had done this and we were soon in the thick of it. They came on riding from the left and cut in between Advance Screen and ourselves. Really magnificent if it had not been such a hot place the Pom-Pom was in action but of course jammed and I went down to it to tell them to clear back to the rear and tinker it up. I kept riding round getting the men to shoot away and then went again to hurry up the Pom-Pom just as I told them to hurry up I felt a sharp bang on my left shoulder and like a red hot skewer pass through me and out in front. I knew I had been hit, the Col came up and I spoke to him and kept going about for another 5 minutes. I came across the Sergt. Major and said I was hit and felt bad, he caught me by the arm and took me back a bit. I just remember seeing the Dr. and then must have fainted as I next remember finding myself lying on the ground. They took my haver sack field glasses and revolvers off and then opened my shirt put a dab of cotton wool on the holes and I was taken off in an ambulance. When I got to Hospital I found Chaloner there and presently Penrose and Bull were brought in and I was told Hammond was wounded and out in the field, not a bad bag 5 officers out of 9 – 2 of these were away on the right. They gave me some Bovril and Brandy and I was soon fairly comfortable. Penrose another fellow and I were in a tent together, Penrose is hit through the right arm and flesh wound by right hip. The other fellow in 7th. I.Y. hit through right arm upper and lower and I fear bone is broken. Bull and Chaloner hit through the stomach.'

the effects on South Africa

With the signing of the Peace Treaty at Vereeniging the British and Commonwealth troops in South Africa melted away. As men were demobilised, disbanded and repatriated, British strength rapidly shrank from 250,000 men to 20,000. Almost 21,000 Boers who were still serving in Commandos surrendered and handed in their weapons. An active war zone had become virtually a demilitarised area in a matter of weeks. This was only possible because Kitchener rather than Milner had won the peace. Apart from the major issues, the British had not insisted on unconditional surrender, this removed the prospect of future Boer rebellions and secured a law abiding acceptance of British suzerainty by the populations of the Transvaal and Orange River Colony. However, differences in attitude among the Boer leadership towards the peace remained and De la Rey and De Wet, in particular, were hardly yet reconciled to assimilation within British South Africa. There were still further divisions in Afrikaner society at large. By the end of the War one in five of the Boers who were still fighting were serving on the British side in units such as the National Scouts. These hands-uppers, were anathema to the Commandos who simply regarded them as collaborators, and a number had been executed by Commando leaders while they were on missions to persuade the bitter-enders to make peace. Progressive Boer leaders such as Louis Botha and Jan Smuts were convinced that the self-inflicted wounds within Afrikaner society must be healed if nationalism was to flourish in the annexed territories. They made this their first aim.

Kitchener did little that directly interfered with the re-consolidation of Boer nationalism. As part of the peace terms set out at Vereeniging the British had agreed that prisoners of war would be repatriated, that the Dutch language would receive protection in the courts, that self-government would be tabled in the future, and that there would be no extension of the franchise to black Africans in the Transvaal and Orange Free State until after self-government had been introduced. This last provision, so doggedly championed by Milner at Vereeniging, meant that effectively there would be no

Sunday, June 15

CAPTAIN WILLIAM STEWART, MOUNTED INFANTRY:

'My dearest Father
I expect you have heard of peace by this time and all the conditions of it; they were just as good as anyone could expect. The Boers also seem to be pleased and say that they did not originally wish to become subjects of King Edward but now as they have got to, they will make the best of it and nothing will please them more than to fight for us in any war, European or otherwise, which we may embark upon. Most of them are quite cheery to meet and always pass the time of day when one meets them in the street but a few are surly and scowl at anything approaching khaki. There was a large parade last Sunday in Church Square [Pretoria] attended by 40 men and two officers from every corps in S. Africa... There the Archbishop of S. Africa gave us a Service which struck me as being an exceptionally good one as it could not injure the feelings of the Boers. The choir came in to the hymn "Onward Christian Soldiers" and went out to the tune of "Those in Peril on the sea"...'

Black Africans who were working with the Boers. The black and Asian populations were the greatest losers as a result of the War.
▶

franchise for the black population as there was little likelihood that a Boer government would willingly enact such a measure itself. It was an outcome that contradicted assurances given to the black population by British politicians at the start of the War and which laid down immense problems for the future.

Milner's failure

With the War over, however, Milner was determined to continue his work to establish British supremacy through the encouragement of immigration from the United Kingdom, through the paramountcy of English-speaking institutions and education, and by a programme of reconstruction that would deflate any resurgent Afrikaner nationalism. Behind these schemes would stand a rigorous and professional colonial bureaucracy that would impel the annexed territories towards a federal South Africa. Milner's schemes were buffeted by a succession of difficulties some of his own making, others the result of wider influences. Milner intended that revenue from

Tuesday, June 24

ALFRED STAFFORD, SOUTH AFRICAN LIGHT HORSE:

'Farewell to the life of a Warrior & Boer hunting. I depart for the New Goch G Mines three miles East of the Town to take up duties as an Amalgamator at £27.10 per month & quarters. There are quite a number of old Friends on this Property whom I knew in 1897 at the Van Ryn Estate G Mng Co. As regards Johannesburg the Town is beginning to look itself again, what is most noticeable are the neglect'd appearance of the Streets. Three years Rain, wear and tear no repairing has left them very rough but no doubt the new Town Council will get to work & straighten things up and make the Town look more presentable.'

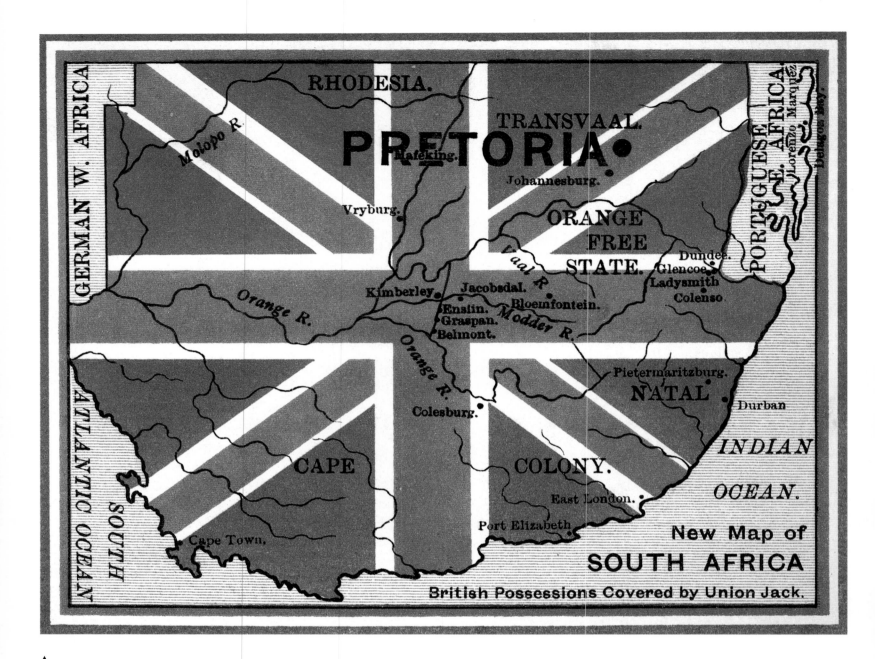

New Map of SOUTH AFRICA

British Possessions Covered by Union Jack.

▲

A contemporary map demonstrating the extent of Britain's possessions in South Africa immediately after the War. Within fifty years the descendants of the Boers who had fought the British would control all this territory.

▶

General Jan Smuts worked hard with Louis Botha to bend British plans into policies benneficial to Afrikaners.

the gold fields would pay for much of what he planned but a shortage of unskilled labour limited output and hence profits, and once British financial support ended the Transvaal economy went into recession. In June 1904 Milner acquiesced in the introduction of indentured Chinese labour to the gold fields and, in failing to prevent flogging as a stimulus to work, alienated opinion in Britain. At the same time both Uitlander and Afrikaner found his labour expedient profoundly unsettling and the Boer leadership took steps to re-establish their political strength to deal with this and other developments.

Het Volk

The positive Boer response to Britain's position was epitomised by Louis Botha and Jan Smuts, both of whom wished to be enlightened in their approach to preserving Afrikaner aspirations while working constructively with the British. These ideals were consolidated in a new political movement *Het Volk* or 'The People', formed in January 1905. Het Volk opposed practically all of Milner's plans and initiatives and was so successful in proposing and implementing alternatives that the High Commissioner's schemes soon lay metaphorically in ruins. Their actual ruin was brought about by economic recession and Uitlander hostility, and in March 1905 Milner resigned. The new Liberal government in Britain, headed by Sir Henry Campbell-Bannerman, introduced self-governing constitutions in the Transvaal and Orange River Colony and after elections in the course of 1907 Afrikaner governments were elected. Louis Botha became Prime Minister of the Transvaal at the head of a Boer administration which prized moderation. Stability and moderation also appealed to English-speaking opinion and Botha was able to effect a reconciliation that led to Uitlanders joining his Cabinet. In September 1909 Botha's policies were

crowned with ultimate success with the passage through the British Parliament of the South Africa Bill. This delivered a Union of South Africa composed of provinces represented by the four colonies. A Union government was formed in May 1910 with Botha as its first Prime Minister.

Non-whites were banned from sitting in the new parliament and African, Coloured and Asian protests were ignored in London. The War had left many black Africans in a state of near destitution with farming communities in particular wracked by famine. Although they received some help from the British government through rehabilitation and compensation programmes, they were paid at an even lower rate than the Boers. The defeat of the Afrikaners had not fulfilled their hopes for a greater share in land ownership, met their concern for better working conditions in the mining industry, or realised the aspirations of their chiefs for greater political autonomy. Above all, there was the sense of betrayal at the British failure to secure basic civil rights for the Asian, African and Coloured communities, who felt themselves to be worse off than before War had been declared.

Oath of Allegiance
(to be taken by all POWs before returning to SA):
I.. adhere to the terms of the agreement signed at Pretoria on 31 May 1902, between my late Government and the representatives of His Majesty's Government. I acknowledge myself to be a subject of King Edward VII, and I promise to own allegiance to him, his heirs, and successors according to law.

◀

General Ben Viljoen, Boer commander and witness of the War, who earned the respect and admiration of his British adversaries.

the effects on Britain

The reform of the Army

The ultimate extent and weight of the pressure placed upon the Boer Commandos by Kitchener's tactics and by the daily efforts of the British columns was amply demonstrated in the pitiable state of those Boers who were captured in the final months of the War. They were also demonstrated in the list of reasons the Boer negotiators gave for their agreement to surrender. As their first reason the Boers cited the destruction visited upon the Republics and the extent to which it had made the continuation of the War impossible. As their sixth reason the Boers pointed to the overwhelming military strength of the British which, they said, led them to conclude that there was no hope of eventual victory. Thus the Army had achieved the goal set out when Britain went to war. The Boers had been militarily defeated. Yet final victory could not remove the memory of the tactical ineptitude demonstrated by the Army's senior officers at the start of the War, nor the inadequacies of some of the weapons it deployed. In particular, the guerrilla campaign had seemed for much of the time to underline the tactical shallowness of British military thinking. With the Commandos of De Wet roaming the Orange Free State and with Louis Botha loose in the eastern Transvaal and De la Rey in the western Transvaal, British columns

◀

Medals for the Boer War being presented to British troops in Belfast.

Left: Queen's South Africa Medal. Reverse.

Middle: Queen's South Africa Medal. Obverse.

Far right: King's South Africa Medal. Obverse. ▶

CAPTAIN J ROY, DERBYSHIRE REGIMENT ON SPECIAL SERVICE WITH THE MOUNTED INFANTRY:

We had ordered dinner last night at 5-30 and at 5-30 came the order to march at 6. A bit sharp – I gulped down some Soup and a bit of Roast Mutton put some biscuits in my pocket and away we went. A good night for a march starry and clear. We went to get a Boer Larger. We got on well and at 2-30 halted till 5 and then on again. Dawn was breaking and the 3 columns split up. Rawly on the left Grenfell in the centre and ours on the right. We soon started fast, I was with the guns and they soon got done up. We went about 5 miles like this and saw nothing so it was a frost again. I hope Wools Samp-son does not often do this as it gets a bit monotonous going all night and getting nothing. We halted for ½ an hour and then started back. The M.I. being on advance and Flank guard. The Advance Screen sent word there were a lot of cattle in front and some Boers. So off we galloped only to find that they were some of Rawlinson's men that he had dropped with some cattle. An awful sell – we halted here for 3 hours off saddled and gave the horses a feed. The farm was also a store kept by an Englishman and his wife and they were the people who took care of one of the Derbies who was wounded in February.

They had him 6 weeks. I went to thank them and gave them a couple of sovereigns as a small present for their kindness. We went on again at 1. Adv. and Flanks. A day for the horses. They were quite done up when they got in. We must have gone 70 miles in 23 hours and had a lot of galloping in it. My two horses have eaten up well – I am dead tired myself – 20 hours in a saddle is tiring.'

Indian troops were not employed by the British in a combat role in South Africa, but they were used as stretcher bearers ◄

Sunday, June 1

ALFRED STAFFORD, SOUTH AFRICAN LIGHT HORSE:

'News is Heliograph'd to Camp, that Peace was declared last night "Hooray". Our Acting Sqdron Sergt Mjr on making his usual report to the Captain, remark'd "Good news this morning Sir" to which the Capt replied "Good news do you call it, may be for those who are connect'd with the Rand & Mining but I don't call it good news". Open confession is good for the soul and he is not by himself, numbers of Irregular Officers look upon the declaration of Peace in a dismal sort of way, this is not to be surprised at they've had a high old time during the past three years and now with the prospects of having to get around and hustle for a living looking them straight in the face their outlook is far from being rosy. "Ah well" every dog has his day and they've certainly had theirs.'

laboured across the veld after the Boers only to be left grasping thin air. If it was to compete on the battlefield with the much larger forces of the European powers, the Army needed a tactical and 'managerial' overhaul.

For the Army the Boer War marked a sea of change in how it was to approach the vital question of planning in regard to future conflict. One vital and concrete legacy of the War was the creation of a General Staff competent to deal with the myriad of detail that had to be settled before an army could be deployed in a twentieth-century theatre of war. At the same time the War Office was overhauled, the post of Commander-in-Chief scrapped and the Army's senior serving soldier designated the Chief of the Imperial General Staff. The General Staff would also be responsible for overseeing the training of the Army and as a result of the South African experience the standard of musketry was improved, a new emphasis was placed on concealment on the battlefield, and attention was given to the perfecting of fire and movement. The problems inherent in the use of cavalry on the modern battlefield were not taken to heart since most of the successful commanders in South Africa were cavalry officers. It was they who occupied many of the senior jobs in the Army down to and including the First World War, rather than more go ahead and up-to-date officers from, for example, the Royal Engineers.

▲

One of the many Boer War tribute medals presented by grateful towns, boroughs and institutions to returning British troops who fought in South Africa.

▶

Louis Botha, who became the first Prime Minister of the Union of South Africa in 1910, believed that the defeated Boers must work with Great Britain to achieve the best results for their cause.

Britain and South Africa

A number of historians have asserted that while Britain gained a victory in military terms in South Africa she subsequently lost the peace. The principal charge in support of this claim was that Britain had effectively returned the annexed Republics to the Boers once the fighting ended. This was certainly a point made repeatedly by Milner: 'I see things as they are, and recognise that it's a fool's trick to waste the energy and devotion of 1,000 men in trying to do the impossible, and to keep an Empire for people who are dead set on chucking it away. I could wrestle with Boers for ever. But British infatuation is too much for me.' The care and consideration with which the Liberal administration of Campbell-Bannerman treated the Boers was designed to ensure that South Africa became a friendly and loyal member of the Empire. While the Liberals miscalculated in so far as the Union of South Africa was dominated politically by the Afrikaner population rather than by the English community, they did succeed in forming a nation which Kitchener described as set fair to become 'a new America in the southern hemisphere'. That Union then became, until the middle of the century, an important economic and strategic linchpin within the Empire. When a Boer nationalist rising occurred in 1914 under the inspiration

Jan Christian Smuts successfully made the transition from soldier to states-man, and his later career mirrored the attempt to achieve effective Anglo-Boer co-operation.
◄

A commemorative fan displaying images of British commanders during the Boer War.
▼

of De la Rey and the leadership of De Wet, it was put down by their former comrades in arms Botha and Smuts. Boer had fought Boer and the winners were to serve with British forces in two World Wars. Kitchener's wish, expressed at a peace celebration in 1902, that one day the Afrikaners would fight alongside the British in defence of the Empire had been fulfilled.

The Boer War left a feeling of mutual strength and support through the Empire, which was particularly welcome given Britain's diplomatic and military isolation. The willingness of the people of the Dominions to view Imperial defence as something wider than merely home defence pointed to an inherent interdependence of the nations within the Empire. The Boer War gave sustenance to a growing sense of Imperial patriotism and demonstrated a desire to assist the Mother Country when danger threatened. This desire stopped short of accepting Imperial centralisation but it was a genuine and spontaneous feeling among many within the Empire. It was doubly welcome to Britain given the hostility that had been aroused on the Continent by her prosecution of the war in South Africa.

As a result of the Boer War Britain could meet the tribulations of a new century and a dangerous world with a greater degree of confidence in her wider security.

A jingoistic poster depicting the Transvaal on its knees before Boadicea. The Boer War instilled belief in Imperial strength throughout the Empire.
▶

the war in history

The lessons

The key to modern warfare had been amply demonstrated by De la Rey's tactical skill at the Modder River in November 1899. Notwithstanding the courage and fervour of the attacker the preponderance of advantage would rest with the 'invisible', entrenched defender thanks to the rapidity and weight of the firepower he could bring to bear. The other conclusion about modern war to be underlined by the fighting in South Africa was that cavalry no longer had a place on the battlefield. Except against an enemy who had already been thoroughly broken, the conventional cavalry charge was now a recipe for suicide. As mounted infantry, however, the horse soldier still had a significant role, particularly in theatres where there was ample room for manoeuvre. These important lessons had been apparent as early as the 1860s during the campaigns of the American Civil War, then largely forgotten while attention was concentrated on Moltke's campaigns in 1870, only to be underscored in the Spanish-American War of 1898, in South Africa between 1899–1902, and during the Russo-Japanese War of 1905.

In terms of the performance of troops in modern battle, the Boer War illustrated the need for leaders at unit level who were prepared to combine professionalism with the use of

◄
Had the Boer War been fought twenty years later it would probably have been won by armoured cars. As it was, horses were the key to tactical mobility.

their initiative. The British had also realised that the young male from the industrial cities was often not physically strong enough for the rigours of modern war, and that consequently emphasis should be placed on building up soldiers for active service. An embracing lesson of the British experience in South Africa was the need for an efficient and innovatory system for gathering intelligence prior to the outbreak of war. The British had been seriously hampered in the opening stages of the Boer War by a profound ignorance of the geography of the country despite their previous service there.

The Boer War confirmed a place on the battlefield for much of the technology with which European armies had experimented in the last decades of the nineteenth century. It also provided a further demonstration of the capacity of railways to mould strategy even where only a single line might pass through enemy territory. The railway gave a commander the option of maintaining his army over extraordinary distances and, in the use of armoured and ambulance trains, the ability to bring the power of steam into the front-line.

Total war

The Boer War is widely remembered for the 'methods of barbarism' allegations made against the British in their conduct

SOPHIE LEVISEUR:

'What a merciful war it was if we compare it to the wars of today. There was no firing on undefended cities. Of course there were nasty incidents, but the way the reactionary Boers talk is absurd: the English did burn down farmhouses, but they never shot a single one of the people in them, like the Germans did in this war, and many a time a farmhouse was burnt because some fighting Boers had fired on the English from a koppie nearby or from the house itself. What I never heard of is what Arthur Barlow said, that they had burnt whole towns, and surely we would have been told of that. Also the story of the concentration camps is frightfully exaggerated.

First of all, taking the women off the farms was an actual military necessity. The enemy were fighting in a country they did not know and went to the homes whenever possible. Naturally the womenfolk collected all information about enemy movements they could get hold of and warned our men; also they supplied them with food, and possibly ammunition. What army would have left them to do that? Of course, it was terrible for us, but, anyway, though the soldiers did dreadful things, as they always do in wars, no orders were given by Headquarters to shoot or kill citizens. No, it was as much a gentlemen's war on both sides as wars can be.'

of anti-guerrilla operations during 1900–1902. Although the War was conducted with commendable chivalry in so far as prisoners and the wounded were dealt with properly and humanely by both sides, the period of the Boer guerrilla campaign embroiled much of the Boer civilian population in the consequences of that singular style of warfare. The methods adopted by the British for dealing with the Commandos during this phase of the War have been widely viewed as draconian, and the British military and civilian administration during the War has been castigated by some historians as the instigators, in particular, of concentration camps. In fact the measures implemented by Roberts and Kitchener – lines of blockhouses and barbed wire, the eviction of the civilian population from their homes and the establishment of concentration camps – were not original; they had all been used by the Spanish Captain General Valeriano Weyler during the Cuban insurrection of 1895–98. It has even been asserted that the tactics adopted by Kitchener during the guerrilla phase of the War – concentration camps, scorched earth, and drives by mobile columns – were in fact suggested to the British by the Kaiser in an attempt to regain credibility after his earlier diplomatic indiscretions. There was thus little that was original in the tactics adopted by Roberts and Kitchener, but they were adopted with too little thought as to the outcome

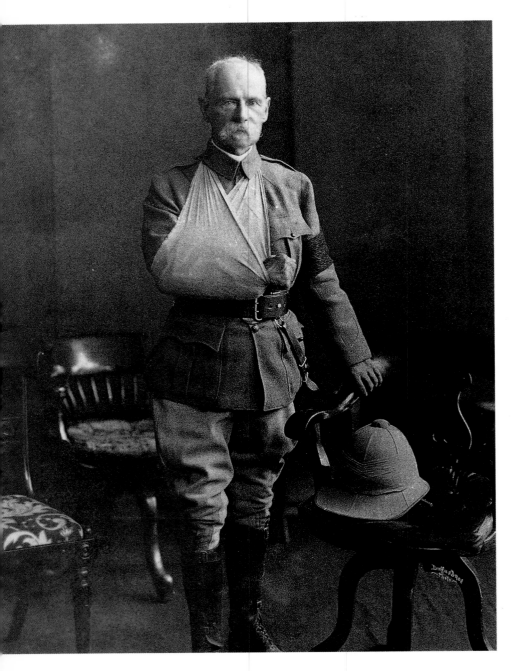

◄
Lord Roberts had the courage to take risks against the Boers and he was rewarded with a successful advance into the enemy's heartland.

►
An armoured train complete with additional protection. Roberts' strategy was heavily dependent upon the effective use of the railway network in South Africa.

for interned civilians. There was accordingly much unnecessary suffering, particularly among young internees, but it was not deliberate. When the full extent of the problem was realised, too late for many, conditions in the camps improved markedly. By early 1902 the death rate among the Boer refugees was less than that among the population of Glasgow. Black Africans too suffered in camps where the death rate was horrific, but they were also intensely vulnerable in their villages and on the veld. 50,000 black Africans served with the British forces either as scouts and trackers or wagon drivers, and the Boers often showed those who were unfortunate enough to be captured little mercy; in the words

of one eyewitness the Boers shot 'Africans like dogs'. In one instance a black African village was wiped out by Boer Commandos merely for having had a force of British troops there for some days.

The conditions of warfare experienced in South Africa were not to re-emerge until the Western Desert campaign in Egypt and Libya in 1940-1942. By then it was not horses' stamina which provided mobility across great distances but the mechanical facility of the petrol engine. South Africa between 1899-1902 thus bore little relation to armed conflict in Europe. But it starkly demonstrated the effectiveness of modern weapons and the colossal power of the entrenched defence.

"HAIRY MARY" ARMOURED TRAIN

A Boer family in the concentration camp at Port Elizabeth.
►

Thursday, August 1

CAPTAIN J ROY, DERBYSHIRE REGIMENT ON SPECIAL SERVICE WITH THE MOUNTED INFANTRY:

'Marched at 8 am. We had a Military Census last night the 7th M. L. were 260 with us here. Just jogged along today & got to Camp about 2.30. 10 miles W. of Springfontein I had a chance of going in command of escort to the Convoy, but as they go in tomorrow, & come out next day, I thought a day in Camp & a bath better. I went to the Refugee Camp at Bethulie to see what it was like, as there has been such a lot in the papers about the way they are treated. It was very clean & well-kept. The people seemed contented & everything is done for them that can be done. A lot of the tents are boarded, those that are not, have carpets down & beds for all – very different from what Tommy Atkins has to put up with. But they (the Boers) are most awful liars. I don't think they know what it is to tell the truth. We give boots & shoes to those that have none & they tell me that the women take the boots off their children & hide them & then say they have none, to get them out of us free. They all of course say they have no money to pay for things, but I did hear that if that Camp was thoroughly searched, the amount of money found would run into thousands – one man is said to be a millionaire & yet is content to appear a pauper & let us feed him free. It is hard on really poor deserving people if there are any such but what can you do? If this Millionaire was turned out of Camp & told to go & live at Cape Town or some such place & pay for himself, he would be quoted at home as a terrible case of cruelty. We stay here 2 days at least & I shall have a washing day tomorrow. A lot of Columns are wandering about here, we saw 2 today & know of about 5 more.'

The school and its pupils at Barberton Burgher camp.
►

The vast velds of South Africa on which the War was fought had a great influence on the pattern of the War. The mobility of the mounted Boers gave them a well-needed advantage as they were often out-numbered by the British troops.
▼

The fighting men

In the first and also in the last analysis war is a trial of strength between competing forces on the battlefield. In the Boer War the rival forces could hardly have been more disparate. On the Boer side young boys, women and grandfathers, long imbued with the personal skills of war, fought for their cause along with a sprinkling of military adventurers and eccentrics from around the globe. The British deployed some 250,000 Regular soldiers, many of them veterans of wars against savage enemies, supported by citizen soldiers, volunteers and the embryonic stirrings of national forces from across the Empire. On the battlefields of South Africa they shared a common experience. It was compounded of boredom, fear, frustration and astonishment at some of the tasks they were expected to fulfil and at the tactics that were being employed to supposedly assist them. Many never really understood why the War had started or what they were fighting for. How their own role fitted into the scheme of things was an even greater puzzle. Their view of events was fragmented and myopic as if they were fighting in a vacuum unconnected to the outside world. But there was mutual respect and a shared concern for the dying and wounded of both sides. They also shared the loss of optimism and sense of adventure that had characterised their early days in the field, and both Briton and Boer succumbed to the numbing tedium of military duty.

1899-02

◀
General Smuts in contemplative pose.

▶
Baden-Powell in heroic pose.

The lessons

Had their exertions and suffering been worth it? Even though they had withstood the might of the British Empire for nearly three years, the Boers had still lost their independence. The British had won a military victory and imposed their suzerainty on the Transvaal and the Orange Free State, but the cost in lives and resources had been out of all proportion. They had not crushed Boer nationalism and they had failed to improve the political and social prospects of the African and Coloured communities. The British had the considerable consolation prize of hard lessons learnt on the battlefield that would stand them in good stead as the Expeditionary Force took the field in France in 1914. The War also propelled the British into the consideration of how they as a Nation could prepare for the challenges of the new century. It was clear to many Army officers, for example, that they needed healthier recruits in order to produce soldiers who could cope with the physical demands of modern war. Soldiers must also be taught to think for themselves and to be prepared to use their initiative if the chain of command broke down in battle. Baden-Powell sought to encourage youngsters to emulate the skills of the Boers on the veld through the establishment of the Boy Scout movement. There was a general feeling as a result of the Boer War that the Nation needed to be more efficient in how it went about things in general. As the

Historical Section of the German Army's Great General Staff commented in its report on the Boer War: 'Fortunate is the Army whose ranks, released from the burden of dead forms, are controlled by natural, untrammelled, quickening common sense.'

For the Boers the tactics and means of waging war that had proved splendidly suitable for campaigns against native enemies on the veld had, in the end, proved too negative in the face of a determined opponent with vastly superior numbers. As the German General Staff crushingly noted: 'That their leaders, even in the hey-day of their success, never aspired to so much as even to contemplate the annihilation of their adversary, is in itself, an avowal of their military incompetence. The out-come was that they limited themselves to negative efforts, which can never result in positive gains. To hold on as long as they could to the position they had selected was the sole object of their fighting, which consequently exhibited none of the elementary characteristics of a serious life or death struggle.'

The Boers, of course, with the size of their population and its position in a hostile environment full of potential and actual enemies, could not afford to allow their war effort to become 'a serious life or death struggle'. To have done so might well have ended in the complete destruction of their Nation; a challenge which the British, of course, did not have to face.

Thursday, May 2

CAPTAIN J ROY, DERBYSHIRE REGIMENT ON SPECIAL SERVICE WITH THE MOUNTED INFANTRY:

'The more I see of the country, the more I wonder at the stupidity of sending Infantry to do the work out here, especially saying to Australia that Infantry were wanted. Fancy a hill a couple of thousand feet high with a great plain rolling up to it & Infantry attacking, without a scrap of cover except a few Ant heaps. With mounted men a party can dismount out of range work up closer, and another party go round & turn the flank. The Boers won't get cut off from their horses and always clear as soon as they have seen you going round the flank.'

▶

Lieutenant-General Lord Robert Baden-Powell at a Boy Scout rally in Chatham. Baden-Powell founded the movement in 1908 in order to promote physical, mental and spiritual development in boys.

GENERAL BEN VILJOEN:

'The British soldier, or "Tommy", who draws a very poor daily pay, for which he has to perform a tremendous lot of work, is, if not the most capable fighter, the most willing in all circumstances to offer himself as a sacrifice at the altar of duty, or of what he considers his duty, to his country. But if "Tommy" by any accident be asked to deviate from the usual routine in which he has been trained, he is a thoroughly helpless creature. This helplessness, in my opinion, is caused by exaggerated discipline, and by the system under which "Tommy" is not allowed to think for himself or to take care of himself, and this individual helplessness has undoubtedly been one of the shortcomings of the British soldier during the War. As regards the forti- tude of the ordinary British soldier, I must repeat what I have already said – that he is a courageous, willing and faithful warrior, and that it is to his fidelity and patriotism that the British Army may attribute its success.'

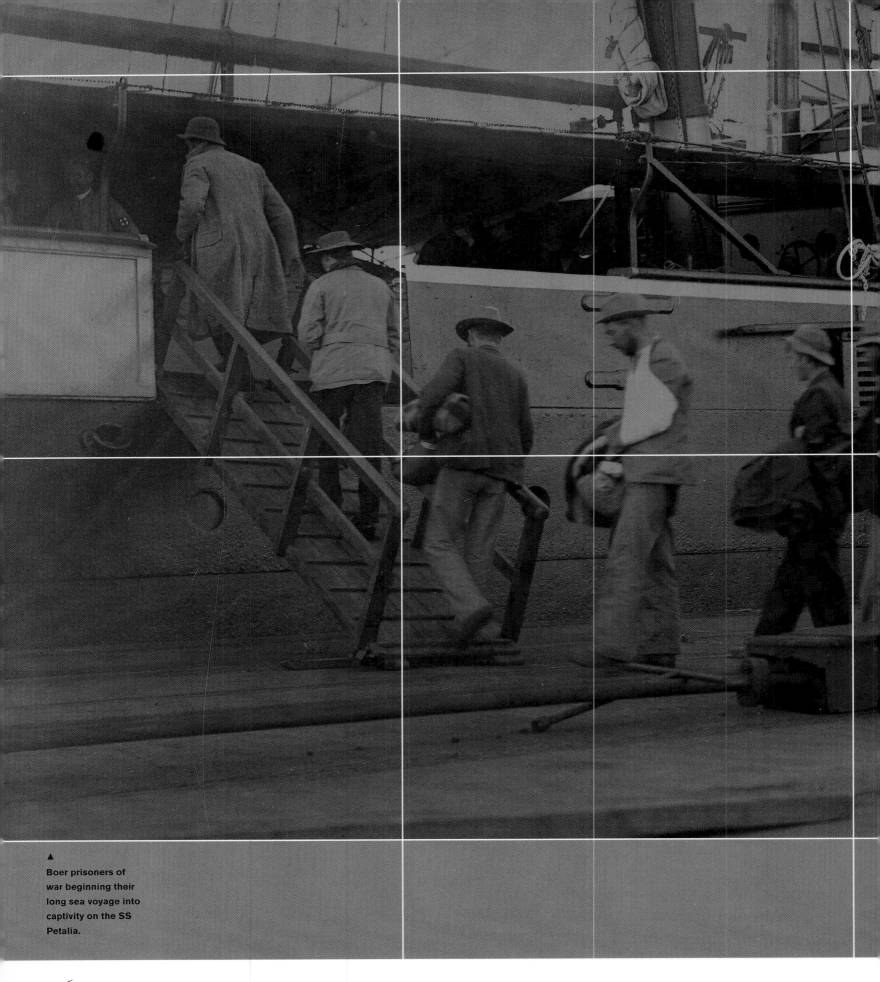

▲

Boer prisoners of
war beginning their
long sea voyage into
captivity on the SS
Petalia.

1899–02

BOMBARDIER **R J WAUGH**, G BATTERY ROYAL HORSE ARTILLERY:

'Men speak in glowing terms of "the joys of war" and what a splendid free life is to be led with the sky for one's roof and the veldt for one's bed, but I imagine there are very few soldiers who, after a few years of such a life, are not more than glad to return to civilisation and ease in preference to the nomadic life of a campaigner. Nevertheless, it is a fact that, if required, one and all are ready to take up arms again in the defence of our country and her rights. Such is the Britisher.

One reads in Olive Schreiner and other African authors' books of the "never-to-be-forgotten pleasure of sleeping out on the great South African veldt, the pale calm moon overhead, and only the shade of the wagon for covering". This is very pleasant no doubt but suppose the wagon was non-existent and the rain came down like it often does in South Africa? The pleasure would not be so pronounced then.

How composing it is to the soldier recently returned from a long campaign, to lie in bed about 5 a.m. and listen to the rain pattering on the roof, and think of the many mornings at the same time, or earlier (perhaps in the darkness before dawn) spent on the line of march with the rain coming down mercilessly on our practically unprotected bodies, and with no prospect of getting dry until such time as "Old Sol" saw fit to pity us and shine for our benefit.'

The following list of contemporary witnesses quoted in the text of this book indicates whether, as far as is known, the source has been published and if not where it can be found. The sources for the majority of the military witnesses can be located in the Archives of the National Army Museum in London. The remaining un-published sources are from the collections of museums in South Africa.

Lieutenant Eustace Abadie
The 9th Lancers

Henrietta Armstrong
a field nurse with the Boers:
Camp Diary of Henrietta E C Armstrong.
Pretoria 1980

Baden-Powell
Commanding Officer Mafeking:
National Army Museum 1968-10-42

Lieutenant C.E. Balfour
The King's Royal Rifle Corps:
National Army Museum 1996-03-36-6-1

Captain. G T. Brierley
Royal Artillery:
National Army Museum 1994-05-365-1

Winston Churchill
War Correspondent, the Morning Post:
Churchill, W My early Life. A Roving Commission.
London 1930

Lieutenant Frederic Creswell
Imperial Light Horse:
National Army Museum 1985-07-71

Howard Dent
Civil Surgeon with Robert's Field Force:
National Army Museum 1986-06-78

L. Hamilton Fox
3rd Cavalry Brigade:
National Army Museum 1992-02-47-1

Colonel J W Hughes Hallett
The Seaforth Highlanders:
National Army Museum 1985-11-13.4

Trooper Joe Hayward
South Notts. Hussars Yeomanry:
National Army Museum 1990-07-132

Lieutenant-Colonel Robert Kekewich
Commanding officer Kimberley:
National Army Museum 1990-07-117

John Lane
a British Uitlander commandeered for service with a Boer Commando: Unpublished diary, War Museum of the Boer Republic, Bloemfontein

Sophie Leviseur
a Boer woman in Bloemfontein: Schoeman, Karel (Ed.) Sophie Leviseur Memories. 1982

Private James McGowan
The King's Own (Royal Lancaster Regiment):
National Army Museum 1990-12-66

H V MacLennan
water engineer Kimberley:
National Army Museum 1995-06-42-8

Lieutenant R J K Mott
The Queen's (Royal West Surrey Regiment):
National Army Museum 1991-01-97

Sapper Walter Pells
Royal Engineers:
National Army Museum 1993-08-364-4

Sol. T Plaatje
a black African interpreter and writer in Mafeking:
Comaroff, John
The Boer War Diary of Sol T Plaatje. London 1973

Gustav Preller
a Boer artilleryman:
National Army Museum 1982-07-63-1

Private W A Pye
West Yorkshire Regiment:
National Army Museum 1985-09-7

Brevet-Lieutenant Colonel S H Rawlinson
(later General Lord Rawlinson of Trent):
National Army Museum 1952-01-33-7

S V Robinson
Civil Surgeon:
National Army Museum 1991-01-20

Captain J Roy
Derbyshire Regiment on special service with the Mounted Infantry:
National Army Museum 1991-01-83

Roland Schikkerling
a member of a Boer Commando:
Schikkerling, Roland
Commando Courageous. (A Boer's Diary).
Johannesburg 1964

Trooper Charles Snow
59th Coy. XV Battalion, Imperial Yeomanry:
National Army Museum 1990-07-96-9

Alfred Stafford
South African Light Horse:
National Army Museum 1996-05-121

Captain William Stewart
Mounted Infantry:
National Army Museum 1987-07-33-74

Arthur Tomey
National Army Museum 1980-09-8-7

Matthys Uys
Boer prisoner of war, St. Helena:
Unpublished diary

General Ben Viljoen
a Boer commander:
Viljoen, Ben
My Reminiscences of the Anglo-Boer War.
London 1902

Bombardier R Waugh
Royal Horse Artillery:
National Army Museum 1987-07-24

Henry Werwe,
Boer prisoner of war, Ceylon:
Unpublished diary,
War Museum of the Boer Republic,
Bloemfontein

1 | Arthur Conan Doyle (third from right) and party en route to South Africa.

2 | The Court of Summary Jurisdiction sentences an African spy to death. Beneath the No. 2 is Magistrate Bell and to his right, leaning against the wall, is the diarist Sol T Plaatje.

3 | General French (bottom row, second from the left) and his staff.

4 | War correspondent Edgar Wallace.

Amery, L S
The Times History of the War in South Africa 1899–1902.
7 volumes, London 1900-1909

Barclay, Glen
The Empire is Marching. A Study of the Military Effort of the British Empire 1800–1945.
London 1976

Benbow, C
Boer Prisoners of War in Bermuda.
Bermuda Historical Society Occasional Publications No. 3. 1962

Colvin, F F & Gordon E R
Diary of the 9th (Q.R.) Lancers during the South African Campaign, 1899 to 1902.
London 1904

Davidson, A & Filatova, I
The Russians and the Anglo-Boer War 1899–1902.
Cape Town 1998

De Wet, C R
Three Years War (October 1899–June 1902).
London 1902

Du Cane, Hubert (translator)
**The War in South Africa...
Prepared in the Historical Section of the Great General Staff, Berlin.**
London 1906

Ensor, R C K
England 1870–1914.
Oxford 1936

Firkins, Peter
The Australians in Nine Wars.
Adelaide 1971

Fisher, J
That Miss Hobhouse.
London 1971

Fuller, J F C
The Conduct of War 1789–1961.
London 1961

Hamer, W S
The British Army. Civil-Military Relations 1885-1905.
Oxford 1970

Hannah, W H
Bobs: Kipling's General. The Life of Field-Marshal Earl Roberts of Kandahar, V.C.
London 1972

Jones, Archer
The Art of War in the Western World.
Oxford 1989

Kruger, Rayne
**Good-bye Dolly Gray.
The Story of the Boer War.**
London 1959

Lee, Emanoel
To the Bitter End. A Photographic History of the Boer War 1899-1902.
Harmondsworth 1985

Le May, G H L
British Supremacy in South Africa, 1899–1907.
Oxford 1965

Luvaas, Jay
**The Education of an Army.
British Military Thought, 1815–1940.**
London

Magnus, Philip
Kitchener. Portrait of an Imperialist.
London 1958

Maurice, F & Grant M H
**History of the War in South Africa 1899–1902.
Compiled by the Direction of His Majesty's Government.**
4 volumes, London 1906–1910

Meintjes, Johannes
President Paul Kruger. A Biography.
London 1974

Pakenham, Thomas
The Boer War.
London 1979

Schikkerling, Roland
Commando Courageous. (A Boer's Diary).
Johannesburg 1964

Sibbald, Raymond
The War Correspondents. The Boer War.
Stroud 1993

Smith, I R
The Origins of the South African War 1899–1902.
London 1996

Spiers, E M
The army and society 1815–1914.
London 1980

Spies, S B
**Methods of Barbarism?
Roberts and Kitchener and Civilians in the Boer Republics January 1900–May 1902.**
Cape Town 1977

Stanley, George
**Canada's Soldiers 1604–1954.
The Military History of an Unmilitary People.**
Toronto 1954

Surridge, Keith
**Managing the South African War, 1899-1902.
Politicians V. Generals.**
London 1998

Symons, J
Buller's Campaign.
London 1963

Viljoen, Ben
My Reminiscences of the Anglo-Boer War.
London 1902

Warwick, Peter (ed.)
The South African War. The Anglo-Boer War 1899–1902.
Harlow 1980

◄

Transports in Table Bay.

GENL. C. NIEUWOUDT'S COMMANDO.

LAST TO SURRENDER IN THE O.R.C. JUNE 16. 1902.

Photographic Acknowledgements

British Film Institute Stills, Posters & Designs, London 129 Top, 132 left, 132 right, 134 left, /Joseph Rosenthal 46-47 Bottom, 63, 81, 107, 115 Bottom, 135 Top, 144 Bottom Right

War Museum of the Boer Republics, Bloemfontein 2-3, 5 Centre, 30 Bottom, 56 right, 58, 59 Top, 67 right, 70, 126, 127, 139 Top Left, 139 Top Right, 139 Bottom, 148 Top Right, 149 Centre Right, 149 Bottom Left, 149 Bottom Right, 151 Bottom Left, 151 Bottom Right, 158, 160 Bottom Left, 161 Centre Left, 164 Bottom Right, 179, 190

Black Watch Regimental Museum, Perth 49

E.T. Archive, London 10 Top Right, 12 Bottom, 14 left, 15 Bottom, 16 left, 33 Bottom, 34 left, 37, 50, 64, 71, 72 left, 72 right, 77 Top Right, 79 right, 121 Top Left, 128 Bottom Right, 152, 171, 198 Top Right, 198 Bottom Left /Consolidated Goldfields 24 right, */London Museum* 184 right */MuseumAfrica* 36 right, */National Army Museum* 17 Bottom */Private Collection* 170 Top Left, */Rhodes House Library* 23 */University of Witwatersrand* 10 Bottom Left

Hulton Getty Picture Collection, London 4 left, 8, 18 Top, 19 Top, 22 Top, 24 left, 25 Top, 36 left, 44, 45, 56 left, 57, 102, 131 Top, 164 Bottom Centre, 178 Bottom, 183 right, 184 left, 192, 193, 194-195, 198 Bottom Right */Reinhold Thiele* 10 Bottom Right, 43 right, 90 Top, 93, 198 Top Left

MuseumAfrica, Johannesburg 5 right, 20, 38 left, 41 left, 41 right, 47 Top, 53, 55, 61, 66 left, 66 right, 67 left, 68 Bottom Left, 68 Bottom Right, 74 Top Right, 74 Bottom Left, 74 Bottom Right, 76, 77, 77 Top Left, 85, 87, 88, 95 left, 97 Top, 98, 100 Centre Right, 109 Top, 110 Bottom Left, 110 Bottom Centre, 110 Bottom Right, 111, 112 Top Left, 113 Top, 113 Centre Left, 116 Centre Right, 118, 119 Top, 119 Centre Left, 119 Centre, 120, 121 Centre Left, 131 Centre Left, 134 Centre Right, 137 Top, 138 Bottom Left, 140, 141 Bottom Right, 142, 143, 148, 149 Top Left, 150, 153 Top Centre Left, 154 Top, 154 Centre Right, 167, 168, 189, 191 Top, 191 Bottom */Frank Neave* 40 left

National Cultural Institute and Museum Pretoria 16-17 Top, 52, 80, 83, 86, 106, 140 Bottom Left, 159, 160 Bottom Right

National Army Museum, London arlin, endpapers, 4 Centre, 5 left, 12 Top, 30 Top, 33 Top, 35, 38 Top Right, 54, 60, 62, 74 Top Left, 84, 91 Top, 92 Bottom, 94, 96 Top, 96 Centre Right, 100 Top, 101 Top, 108 Top, 112 Top Right, 114, 115 Top, 116 Top, 117 Top, 123, 124 Top, 134 right, 136, 138 Bottom Right, 144 Bottom Left, 147, 153 Top, 155, 164 Bottom Left, 165 Top, 170 Bottom Left, 173 Top, 173 Bottom Left, 173 Bottom Right, 174, 180, 181 left, 181 right, 181 Centre, 182, 183 left, 188, 202

National Archives Pretoria 4 right, 14-15 Top, 28, 43 left, 59 Bottom, 146, 156, 162, 177
Private Collection 27, 175 Top Left, 175 Top Right

Public Record Office, London 34 Bottom Right, 40 right, 79 left, 92 Top Left, 117 Centre Left, 121 Top Right, 124 Centre Right, 128 Bottom Left, 161 Top, 178 Top, 185

Royal Photographic Society, Bath 10 Top Left, 65 */Horace Nicholls* 26 Main Picture, 32 left, 42, 48, 68 Top, 95 right, 130 left, 130 right, 163, 186, 196-197, 200
Tate Gallery Publications, London 38 Bottom Right

jacket

National Army Museum: front cover top left; top spine. **E.T. Archive:** bottom left; */University of Witwatersrand* centre left. **Hulton Getty Picture Collection:** front cover centre. **War Museum of the Boer Republics:** front cover & front flap bottom right; bottom spine. **Museum of Africa:** back cover & back flap